NAVIGATING
the STORM

Resources of HOPE for Church Leaders

Hope Network Ministries

CONTENTS

CHURCH HEALTH

Acknowledgements

Compiling a book with many contributors and preparing it for publication is a daunting task. We are thankful for the many people who used their gifts to make this work available and helpful to others.

To all our partners and associates, your heart for God, the church, ministry, and the growth of the kingdom blesses people around the world.

To Brad Cox and Carson Reed for writing the foreword and afterword, respectively. Your partnership in the gospel and kingdom collaboration is a blessing to all.

To Dr. Tim Hadley, thank you for your help with editing and proofreading. Your willingness to be a part of this project added an extra layer of professionalism to this printed work.

To Beth Hadley, thank you for the time you spent coordinating this project—the countless emails, meeting deadlines, organizing, and putting all the pieces together. You bless others and are the glue that holds us together daily.

To Bridget Price, thank you for your creativity in the design of the cover and your ongoing assistance in the ministry of Hope Network.

To our spouses, thank you for the many years that you have stood by our side and supported us in ministry. Your love, wisdom, prayers, and encouragement have helped us survive the world of ministry, and you have handled each aspect with tremendous grace.

To our God, we are humbled to participate in your kingdom life. May our work be a blessing and honor you always.

FOREWORD

I was asked to write the foreword for *Navigating the Storm: Resources of HOPE for Church Leaders* for one simple reason. I believe in the work of Hope Network. I have tremendous respect for the partners who serve in this ministry, and I have been personally challenged and encouraged by these men and women of faith.

The High Pointe Church of Christ, where I preach, has also been blessed by the coaching we received that helped our ministers, shepherds, and ministry leaders work together as a team. Hope Network Ministries helped to move our church from an unhealthy place to one of strength and vitality. We could not have made this transition without the help of the entire team at Hope Network Ministries.

As a preacher and leader of a church, I'm often called in to help couples and families embroiled in relational turmoil. As I listen to them go back and forth, I'm amazed at how much strife, anger, and conflict this couple has endured, and for so long! The same few questions go through my mind:

- How did I miss what was going on with this couple? They seem like the perfect family.
- Why am I being brought in at the crisis stage when this relationship is hanging by a thread? It would have been so much easier had I been brought in sooner.
- Why wasn't this couple more proactive in building and maintaining their marriage? Why didn't they go through our twelve-week marriage builder class in the Spring, or the weekend marriage seminar the year before? There were people and materials available to them if only they

would have taken advantage of these resources before the conflict started.

I would imagine church consultants ask similar questions when they are brought in for the first time to work with a church in crisis:

- How did I miss what was going on within this church? It has such a great reputation within the brotherhood.
- Why wasn't I called in sooner? A lot of damaging things have taken place. Now there is so much more for this group to unravel.
- Have the leaders around this table spent any time on their own to proactively prepare themselves to be a healthy member of this team? There are all kinds of people and materials available to them if only they had taken advantage of these resources before the conflict started.

That's why this second book from Hope Network, *Navigating the Storm: Resources of HOPE for Church Leaders*, is such a vital resource for church leaders. These pages contain the wise counsel of trained consultants you will wish you had received long before you picked up the phone to bring them in.

Often as a leader in a local body, even though Solomon has told us nothing is new under the sun, we buy into the myth that, "No one knows our church like we do!" As you read through the examples in this book, you will see that the men and women writing these chapters know you, your church, and your ministries inside and out. Unlike bringing in one partner to help, in *Navigating the Storm: Resources of HOPE for Church Leaders*, you have the entire complement of the Hope Network team sharing from their individual strengths and varied experiences to bring health to you as a leader and to your church.

If you are looking for a quick-fix resource, or an external bandage for a temporary wound, those are not the purposes of this book. *Navigating the Storm: Resources of HOPE for Church Leaders,* as the title suggests, is designed to provide you with a roadmap for holistic health from the inside out—practices that will equip you and your team to work effectively to advance the Kingdom of God. May the Lord bless you as you pursue the work to which you have been called.

In His service,
Brad Cox
Senior Minister
High Pointe Church of Christ

Thank you for serving as a church leader. Your presence among God's people matters.

We are blessed to co-lead a network of gifted people who love God, the church, and God's mission in the world. The network continues to flourish and we are grateful to our founders, Lynn and Carolyn Anderson. Their hearts and home have always been open. Lynn's work, *They Smell Like Sheep* has characterized the Andersons' way of life for countless church leaders. We stand on their shoulders in this ministry.

This book is all about being helpful and healthy as congregational leaders. Our goal was to provide a collection of practical tools for leaders and churches that can be readily used without us being present or to provide minimal coaching through a phone call or video conference.

Are we helpful and healthy? This question is paramount in all our work—mentoring, guiding, consulting, and interim ministry. Each person in the network is committed to the local congregation and God's kingdom purposes. We are committed to helpful processes, solid biblical and theological reflection, and kingdom collaboration. We enjoy what we do and coming alongside of you in being God's people matters to us.

Thank you for your ministry with God's people. We live in challenging, yet exciting times for kingdom ministry and growth.

We look forward to coming alongside you to the glory of God.

Grady D. King & Jon Mullican

GROUP LEADERSHIP

VISION

A Peek into the Future

Tim Woodroof and Jon Mullican

Imagine two churches.

Same age, same size, same talented membership, same level of commitment, even the same general community. Similar ministry staff with similar competencies. Each church blessed with sincere, earnest shepherds. Can you see these churches in your mind's eye?

Now fast-forward ten years. One of these churches has flourished. The other . . . not so much.

Christ's Church has grown numerically, though that's not the most important part of its story. CC has enjoyed a prolonged period of peace and impact. Oh, there have been moments along the way, certainly: a few disgruntled members, a ministry or two that never got off the ground. But for the most part, the church is

1

actively sharing faith and changing lives. Members of CC are aware of their spiritual gifts and engaged in various ministries of the church. The tone of worship is grateful and joyful. It is a church looking to the future. The leaders of CC decided long ago they wouldn't try to be a church for everyone . . . a church that did everything. It was enough for them to concentrate on a few things, a few ministries, and keep in touch with the surrounding community.

As a result, Christ's Church and its members have managed to keep their eye on the kingdom, recognize God at work through them in the world, and experience a unity that comes from working together in ministries that matter and make a difference.

Jesus's Church, on the other hand, has been in steady decline. The last ten years have been a struggle. Oh, there were some achievements along the way: the occasional baptism, a life touched here and there. But increasingly, the church emphasized doing *more* rather than doing *well*. Projects and programs multiplied. There was an ever-expanding list of ministries with an ever-expanding budget. No one paused to ask, "How effective are the ministries of our church?" No one wondered how effectiveness might be measured. No ministries were ever cut or allowed to die of natural causes.

Gradually, members of JC began to question what the church was about and why their involvement mattered. They were active in a wide range of church events. They seemed to stay busy all the time. But everyone was going in so many different directions, JC members lost confidence they were making a *meaningful* impact. Spinning so many ministry plates became exhausting. And as the exhaustion grew, a critical and nostalgic tone grew with it.

The answer, of course, was to do even more. The leaders of JC renewed their commitment to be a church for every ministry and pay attention to every opportunity. "Why limit what God is trying to do?" they asked each other, though the question became more disheartening as they seemed to have less time and fewer resources available for each new request.

Two churches. Different futures. Why the divergence?

Were the struggles of the second church the result of moral failings or less-than-committed members? No. Were those struggles the consequence of unfaithfulness, some doctrinal impurity? Not at all. Did God ordain a different future for the first church than the second. I don't think so.

Of all the reasons churches decline or thrive, one reason stands out consistently. Churches rise with vision . . . or fall in the absence of it. Vision is a reminder of where a church is going. Vision keeps the "main thing the main thing." Vision shapes the present and, thus, creates the future. Vision feeds the yearning of members to belong to something of significance. Vision provides focus and prevents distraction. Vision saves a church from merely "good" things by directing it to "best" things.

> *Of all the reasons churches decline or thrive, one reason stands out consistently. Churches rise with vision ... or fall in the absence of it.*

Vision. Does your church have it?

Pursuing God's Vision for Your Church

As important as it is for your church to have a clear vision, having the *right* vision is even more critical. And the right vision does not happen accidentally. It begins with asking a few basic questions and following an effective process.

Here are some questions church leaders should consider as they peer into God's preferred future for their churches:

1. Are we willing to accept that a vision for our church is necessary?

> *Where there is no vision, the people perish . . .*
> *(Prov. 29:18)*

Think of Abraham without God's challenge to travel to "a land I will show you." Can you conceive of the Exodus story without Moses and the burning bush . . . without Israel's hope of the Promised Land? What would have become of David's reign without his dream of a united kingdom? What if there had been no Damascus Road experience for Saul, no burning aspiration to become the "Apostle to the Gentiles"? Imagine the Antioch church without a vision strong enough to free them from the patterns of Jerusalem so Gentiles could be reached.

Everywhere you turn in Scripture, God gives vision to his people. He sets goals. He commissions and directs. He paints his preferred future for those he loves.

When God's people hear God's vision and respond faithfully, they thrive. When they embrace God's vision, they find purpose and meaning. When they partner with God and his vision, their lives have significance and impact and "the nation prospers."

Without godly vision, two things occur to God's people (neither of them good):

- People wander and drift, without direction and goals, without any real basis for unified action, without common cause (a definition of ineffectiveness).
- Or other people's agendas and ambitions replace God's agenda and ambitions. Someone else's goals drive the plans of God's people (a definition of unfaithfulness).

In the absence of godly vision, the same two consequences occur in churches today. Members either wander and wonder (and are doomed to ineffectual church lives) or they embrace other agendas and goals (and waste themselves chasing unworthy ends).

Is vision necessary? Only if you take Scripture and an effective future for your church seriously.

2. Are we willing to believe God already has a vision for our congregation?

> *"For I know the plans I have for you," declares the Lord...*
> *(Jer. 29:11)*

Developing a vision for your church is not the same as "originating" a vision or "inventing" a vision or stitching a vision together out of whole-cloth. You don't establish vision with coin-flips or Ouija-boards. Godly vision has nothing to do with membership polls and personal preferences.

God has already crafted a unique vision for your church. He knows what he wants you to accomplish, which needs to meet, where your ministry-focus should be, who he intends you to reach, and what kind of kingdom-

The question is not "Does God have plans for your church?" but "Have you been listening?"

5

impact you are meant to make. The question is not "Does God have plans for your church?" but "Have you been listening?"

God has (for instance) determined the make-up of your congregation: the people he has gathered there as members . . . the experiences they bring with them . . . the gifts with which he has equipped them . . . the interests and sensibilities they possess. Surely a godly vision for your church will take such matters into consideration. He has provided a history for your congregation: ministries you have done well (or poorly!) . . . proven strengths and weaknesses . . . leadership models that have worked (or floundered) . . . a track-record of follow-through (or ball-dropping). Surely a godly vision will build on and account for that history. He has placed you in particular times and circumstances: the community the church is a part of . . . the needs of your neighbors . . . seasons of plenty or want . . . open doors and burnt bridges. Surely a godly vision will address this wider context of the church.

By listening to Scripture, to God's Spirit, to your congregation, and to your community, you can hear God's vision for your church. Discovering how God has equipped your church, you learn what God expects you to accomplish together. Paying attention to the needs of your neighbors, to the opportunities in your community, helps you recognize the work God is calling you to do.

As a result, establishing a vision for your church isn't an act of *invention*. It is, rather, an act of *submission* to the will of God revealed through his word, his people, and his world.

3. Are we willing to *see* God's vision for our church?

*I will pour out my Spirit on all people. Your sons and daughters
will prophesy, your young men will see visions, your old men
will dream dreams. (Acts 2:17)*

A vision is . . . *visual*. The basic idea of "visioning" implies an
ability to *see* something. So close your eyes. Throw yourself into
the future of your church. What do you see?

Yes, eventually a vision must be painted with words. It must be
described in nouns and verbs and adjectives. But vision begins
with a picture: a clear, full-color, richly textured image of tomorrow's church. It is something viewed with the mind's eye. It is
imagined (i.e., "an image is formed") by someone (or some
group) in such a way that a portrait of what the church's future
could or should be is captured.

So, can you *see* God's tomorrow for your congregation?

- What does an *effective, vibrant, loving, transformative*
  church look like (to you and to God)?
- If someone were to photograph your church ten or twenty years down the road, what images, what activities,
  what faces, would you hope they capture?
- Are you seeing vignettes of ministry, relationships, worship, transformation, holiness, and faith-sharing unfold-
  ing like a movie on a screen? (Such stories are closely
  connected to images. After all, stories are "word pictures.") Does your vision for the church allow you to tell
  stories about what the future of your church looks like?

Bringing vision into clear focus requires imagination. Imagining
something *godly* requires inspiration. Invite your church to *see* a

7

godly vision (through prayer, fasting, and discernment) and then trust God to encourage that vision according to his preferred future for you.

If you take your time at this, if you do it well, you will be able to *show* others the future of your church, not just *tell* them. The resulting portrayal will enthrall people. Painting that future will cause spines to tingle. Telling those stories will encourage partnership with God. A godly vision — when seen and shared — motivates God's people to action! And that's something we need more of...much, much more!

4. Are we willing for vision to be specific?

"Do not go among the Gentiles or enter any town of the Samaritans. Go rather to the lost sheep of Israel." (Matt. 10:5-6)

Funny thing about pictures...they are very specific. Certain faces and events are portrayed. A particular moment is captured. Pictures aren't meant to be generic. And neither are visions.

Jesus sent his disciples out (Matt. 10:5-42) with a very specific vision of the ministry he wanted them to do: go to the lost sheep of Israel . . . preach that the kingdom of heaven has come . . . heal the sick . . . no gold or silver...find worthy people, bless them with peace . . . if people won't listen, leave . . .expect opposition. The list goes on. Thirty-eight verses of very specific, detailed instruction.

> *...the key to vision is not how much ground is covered by a church's vision, but how specific and contextual that vision can be.*

Do you think God has anything less specific in mind for your congregation? You can't just throw a Bible at the church and say, "There! There's the vision for our church!"

Yes, the church exists to glorify God, feed the hungry, make disciples, fulfill the Great Commission, heal the sick, care for the needy, preach the gospel, love each other, serve the world...the list goes on! And a godly vision must take all these matters into consideration.

But the key to vision is not how much ground is covered by a church's vision, but how specific and contextual that vision can be.

Who is God calling you to "go" to? Who does he want you to reach? What is he asking you to preach? Are there any "sick" people in your church's future and what kinds of diseases has God equipped you to heal? Who are the "worthy ones" in the community your church is meant to bless? Who is likely to ignore and oppose you? How are you to handle that as a congregation of God's people? What priorities would God set for you? What difference does he want your particular family of believers to make in the world? Are there a few things you ought to be doing really well as a church?

> *A lack of vision does not condemn a church to do nothing. It (more likely) condemns a church to do everything.*

The more *specific* your vision for the church can be, the more guidance that vision can give you for the future. The more *contextual* the vision is (taking general principles like "make disciples," for instance, and filling in the "who/what/where/when/why/how" blanks), the more effective your church will be at its kingdom business.

5. Are we willing for our vision to provide focus?

It would not be right for us to neglect the ministry of the word of God in order to wait on tables. (Acts 6:2)

A lack of vision does not condemn a church to do *nothing*. It (more likely) condemns a church to do *everything*. In the absence of vision, a church suffers ministry ADD, says "yes" to too many things, is unable to focus, and (as a result) greatly limits its impact. Churches without clear vision have ministries a mile wide and a millimeter deep. They are doing many things, but nothing well and transformatively. The sheer pace of work to keep all those ministry plates spinning ensures there is little time or energy left to evaluate ministry effectiveness, deepen ministry impact, or kill off ministries whose time has passed.

A vision does little good if it can't help a church say "No." You can be convinced your church should have a vision, that God has given you a vision, that the vision is specific and unique…but if a church does not exercise the discipline to say "No" to *good* things so it can say "Yes" to *best* things (those related directly to the church's vision), vision remains just a wish and a dream.

As churches age, as they grow, as budgets expand, they tend to accumulate ministry pounds. They keep packing on the good works, adding line items, setting directions that have more to do with individual interests than congregational effectiveness and impact. (One of the authors of this chapter once worked with a church that boasted of 168 budgeted ministries! When it was suggested they trim that list down to ten, they almost choked.)

But how can you keep so many ministry-balls in the air? How do you recruit and train leaders for so many different works? How do you evaluate the kingdom effectiveness of all those ministries? You don't. You decide (of necessity) that more is better, that quantity of ministry trumps quality of ministry, that the church is not in the business of *evaluating* ministries so much as *supporting* them, no matter the fruit.

Until your people grow tired and discouraged, that is. Until membership and giving begin to decline. Until those you go to church with start wondering whether the ministries of the church are making any real difference, any significant difference. Until someone asks you, "If this church vanished suddenly, would anyone around us notice?"

A Process for Visioning

Discovering or uncovering a church's vision requires prayer, time, effort, committed people . . . and a good, godly *process*. Common steps that help churches discover vision are listed below. Typically, the decisions required, the pace set, and the steps taken are determined by church leaders (i.e., elders and often the ministers).

Consider Using a Guide
Since a Vision Process will be accomplished by a church infrequently (every 10 years or so), it can be extremely helpful to employ a guide: a third-party expert who can help the church work through the visioning process. Such an expert will have experience aiding other churches with their visioning, understand the need to customize a church's process to its culture, and recognize a church's idiosyncrasies, tendencies, strengths, and limitations.

Choose a Time Horizon
How far into the future will you choose to look? To be clear, this process emphasizes *vision* (or God's dream for your specific

church), not planning or implementation. One can dream further into the future than one can plan. We'll discuss planning below.

Typically, visions look at least 10 years ahead. If your needs are more immediate, it may be that your church should address urgent issues (like conflict management or debt burden) before moving into a visioning process. Be aware, however, that near-term issues can frequently prevent looking forward effectively. The urgent "now" tends to take precedence over the important "tomorrow."

Yet "tomorrow" is not so far away. Consider that looking back ten years (to 2006) seems like only yesterday. The iPhone would soon be launched. Google bought YouTube for $1.65 billion. Samuel Alito became a Supreme Court justice. The Pittsburgh Steelers beat the Seattle Seahawks to win the Super Bowl. Looking 10 years ahead may seem daunting or intimidating, but the future is not that far away.

Determine Participants in the Vision Process
Selecting, directing, and supporting the people who will guide the vision process for your congregation involves several sub-steps:

1. **Vision Team** — It is strongly recommended that a team of 7 to 15 individuals be formed to steward the vision process. Who makes up this team should be determined by the culture of your church. For some churches, the vision team will consist of elders and ministers only. At other churches, a cross-section of the church will be chosen — young and old, men & women, single & married. Those chosen should exhibit the following characteristics:

- Commitment to the local church body (participation on the Vision Team should not be used to enfranchise marginal members or as a sop to those considering leaving)
- Mature, thoughtful Christ-followers (but do not equate maturity with age!)
- Team orientation (lone rangers need not apply)

2. **Commission** — Church Leadership should provide the Vision Team with a written commission (usually no more than one typewritten page) providing parameters for and a description of the expected outcome of the team's work, and when that work is due. (Vision processes should not be rushed – five to nine months is typical.) This "commission" should identify a chosen core process (see below) and include specific expectations to ensure that:

- the leadership is clear on what it is asking the group to accomplish, and
- the group is clear about their responsibility to the leadership.

3. **Support People** — As the Vision Team does its work, the team should feel free to access gifted people and needed skill sets found within the church to help with the vision effort. Demographers, economists, and futurists can be of great value. Alternatively, these people could be placed directly and intentionally on the team from the beginning.

4. **Focus Groups/Large Group Conversations** — The Vision Team, following their leadership commission, may choose to engage the entire church (or significant portions of the church) through large-group conversations or

Focus Groups. Seeking expertise in such methods is highly recommended. By engaging the members of the church in a conversation about the church's future, the eventual vision can be more fully owned by those who participate, lessening the need to "sell" the vision once it is formed.

5. **Surveys and Assessments** — The Vision Team may also choose to engage the church through a survey or assessment instrument. [The Siburt Institute for Church Ministry has recently launched a statistically validated and reliable Church Health Assessment (CHA) that can provide information about a church's health in nine areas of church life. This can aid the Vision Team in understanding where the church stands with respect to leadership trust, facility satisfaction/fit, value of education programs, etc.] Surveys can be used to learn useful information about the church's well-being, habits, gifts, etc.; however, surveys can also generate frustration and confusion. If surveys or assessments are used, it is highly recommended that the questions be reviewed by a professional and the results be shared (at minimum) with those who participated in the surveys. People deserve to know what was learned from the survey. To not do so is to poison the well for future surveys.

Choose a Core Process

Once a time horizon and participants are chosen, a core process is needed. Exactly how will the team proceed? Again, choosing the core process is a decision to be made by church leadership. While the details of the processes are beyond the scope of this chapter, listed below are some resources that can aid in choosing a process. (Remember, even when accessing these resources, making use of a guide—someone who has been there and done that—can be extremely helpful as the Vision Team moves through its work.)

- *God Dreams* and *Church Unique,* both by Will Mancini
- *Visioneering* by Andy Stanley
- *The Power of Vision* by George Barna
- A series of posts found on the Interim Ministry Partners website can be very helpful for thinking through process: http://interimministrypartners.com/resources/developing-a-mission-statement/

Work the Plan

Once a core process is identified, the Vision Team can move forward with its task. The team knows how far to look into the future, how participative the leadership wants the process to be, what process to use, and when to complete the task. So get to work. Read the suggested materials. Conduct the assessments. Start talking to each other and to the church. Start dreaming. Start painting that picture of what your church will look like years from now.

> *Start dreaming. Start painting that picture of what your church will look like years from now.*

Communicate the Work (Process)

As the process unfolds and the vision takes shape, good communication is critical:

- The Vision Team should touch base with leadership from time to time to confirm things are headed in an acceptable direction. It would be a shame if the team worked for

months on a vision only to realize the result was not acceptable to the church's leaders.
- Frequently updating the congregation on the team's progress is also recommended, since many will be participating in some level of the process and all will be interested in the final product. A well-informed group is more easily led!

Communicate the Vision (Result)

Once a vision is formed, pictured, and described, the Vision Team should first communicate the vision to the leadership. This will serve several purposes:

- It allows the leadership to hear/see/understand the vision
- It allows leaders to push, prod, poke, and probe the vision (a necessary part of adopting the vision and making it their own)
- It allows the Vision Team and leadership to learn valuable lessons on how best to communicate the vision to the congregation

When both the Vision Team and the church's leaders are unified in their support of the vision, it should be communicated to the entire church by the Vision Team and immediately ratified by the leadership. This communication can be accomplished via small home-groups, verbal announcements and slide presentations in class or during worship services, or (preferably) all of the above. Obviously, if different venues are chosen and multiple presentation are made, the same message must be communicated or the church will become confused about what is next, what is most important, and where things are headed.

Be aware that new (or renewed) vision will be disruptive for some in the congregation. A certain percentage of members will hear "My ministry is less important than the ministries specifically mentioned in our vision" or "We're throwing out our traditions!" or "Nothing will change that I want to see changed." Verbal explanations of a church's vision can only go so far. That's why, once the vision has been well and clearly articulated, *action* becomes necessary.

Implement the Vision

Vision is the "WHAT" of church. WHAT will we become? WHAT is our purpose? WHAT does God have in store for us?

Implementation is the "HOW" of church—how the vision is accomplished. Every core process should have, at its end, the question of "How will we move toward the vision?" Notice the key word *toward*. Once a vision is discovered and articulated, it cannot be realized in a year or even three, but it can be approached . . . moved *toward*.

> *Vision is the "WHAT" of church... Implementation is the "HOW"...*

The final task of the Vision Team is to create a basic year-one, year-two, year-three implementation framework or plan. Executing that plan is NOT the team's responsibility. Rather, the Vision Team completes its work with this plan and can hand the results to leadership for implementation.

"HOW?" is now the question leaders must ask and are responsible to accomplish. Often, leaders choose to form yet-another team: an implementation team (comprised of a few Vision Team members and existing leaders), charged with the responsibility to execute the vision.

Once this team is formed, implementation of the vision should start immediately. John Kotter (*Leading Change*) recommends that some "early wins" be initiated — i.e., finding and focusing on things in the vision that most everyone wants to see happen and that can occur quickly and relatively easily. Such early accomplishments provide momentum and allow church members to realize church leaders "mean what we say."

A Model for the Vision Process

Process is important for conversations so critical to the health and future of your congregation. Done poorly, a visioning process can waste lots of time, frustrate members, and result in few "actionable" plans. Done well, however, a visioning process can reinvigorate your people, refocus your efforts, and shape a healthier and more effective future for your church.

Here is a graphical representation of the model we have proposed for consideration as you define a visioning process for your congregation

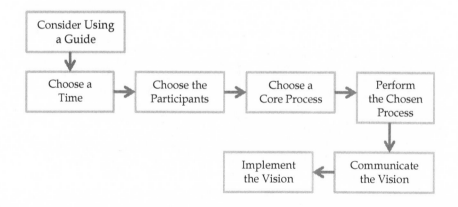

Conclusion

Who you will be ten years from this moment will be determined by what you choose to do in this moment. Today is the seedbed of tomorrow. And tomorrow is closer than you think.

Imagine two leaders from different churches reading this chapter at the same time. Both love their churches and want them to thrive. Both are sincere, committed, thoughtful followers of Jesus. Can you see these leaders in your mind's eye?

This chapter resonates with one of these leaders. He "gets" the importance of vision. He realizes how critical a clear vision will be for the future of his church. He is convinced his congregation has a call from God, should be on a mission from God, and how critical it is for the church to hear and pursue God's calling. He wants his church to do a few things well, to focus on key and primary ministries, to value depth of impact over breadth of impact. And he knows only a clear vision and a disciplined commitment to that vision can keep a congregation on track for the long run.

> ...*a visioning process can reinvigorate your people, refocus your efforts, and shape a healthier and more effective future for your church.*

So, two days after reading this chapter himself, he shares the chapter with his fellow leaders and invites them to read as well—read and prepare to discuss. He requests that next week's elder/minister meeting be dedicated to a discussion of the church's vision. In that meeting, he asks some difficult questions:

- Where are we going as a church?
- Are we pursuing God's vision for our church?
- Can we *see* the church God wants us to be?

19

- If we could support only three ministries, which would we choose?
- Are we willing to focus our efforts and attentions for greater impact?
- Are our members unified in their understanding of where God wants us to go as a church?

The discussion following these questions proves to be difficult, enlightening, convicting. It is evident to everyone around the table that—as a group—they have not valued vision as they should, they have not cast a compelling vision to the church, and—while the church is involved in many good things—they have not led their members to focus on *best* things. They recognize in their members the beginning symptoms of fatigue and stagnation caused by a lack of vision and focus. They are honest with each other about declining levels of involvement in and excitement about the church's ministries. They confess concern to each other about the long-term impact of this decline.

> *Who you will be ten years from this moment will be determined by what you choose to do in this moment.*

Years later, this meeting will be remembered as a turning point for the church. As a result of this come-to-Jesus discussion about vision, more time is dedicated to prayer, study, and conversation on the subject. The leadership group reads through some challenging resources. They broaden the discussion by including church members. They make a few phone calls and find someone experienced and skilled in leading churches through the visioning process. They set aside an initial weekend . . . then another . . . and another.

What emerges from this attention to vision is a common sense of clarity about who this church is, how it is equipped, where it is going, and what God expects it to accomplish. The church learns to focus. Members see how their ministry matters. A renewed involvement, a refreshed enthusiasm results. The trajectory for the next decade is set by a courageous act of visioning. It makes all the difference for the church's future.

On the other hand, this chapter resonates with the second leader as well. He also "gets" the importance of vision. But as he sets the chapter aside, his cell phone chirps, and a church member shares her frustrations with the children's program. Next Wednesday night, he has committee meetings before and after class time (a class he teaches!). The church is presently involved in a capital campaign (the building needs a new roof) and that effort seems to dominate everyone's time and energy. Besides, his business is particularly demanding just now—he doesn't have much bandwidth left for pushing a vision discussion.

He sets aside this chapter, fully intending to take it up again and begin the vision discussion when things calm down. Days become weeks. Weeks become months. The urgent keeps crowding out the important. The meeting remembered as a turning point for the church never happens. The dialogue so vital for establishing vision doesn't occur.

Vision. Does your church have it? Will you, having read this chapter, do something with what you've read? Or will you set the chapter aside...just for now...just until things calm down?

Who you will be ten years from this moment will be determined by what you choose to do in this moment. Today is the seedbed of tomorrow. And tomorrow is closer than you think.

Sailing Toward Maturity
Proactively Exploring Islands of Conversation

Jon Mullican

The Dire Need: Where do we go from here?

Today's church is in serious trouble. Societal changes are rocking the world of church. Supreme court rulings and social mores and technology and drug legalization and…you know the list. Amidst the whipsaws of change, church leaders are expected to "manage" these situations, comfort their flocks, and hold the church together. Attempting to meet these expectations is a Sisyphean task, wearing down the best of our leaders and lessening our will to continue. What is to be done? How can we make it through tomorrow, much less next year or the next decade? Who will help the church navigate these troubled, confusing, and challenging times? And where is the church headed? Where is it going?

The Journey: Let's get moving

Some of our most memorable stories come in the form of "journey." From Abraham's faith walk to the Israelites' desert wandering to Paul's missionary journeys, people of faith understand that our life with God is a journey, a time of travel and movement and experience. We were not created to sit, but to stand and to walk and to move.

What if we put the church on the water—into a sailing ship—and considered her current situation and what might be done to change it. What if we embarked on a journey, following the Holy Spirit as Paul did, listening and adjusting our proverbial sails as the spirit called us forward? I realize this is a huge assumption: that we would actually brave listening to the call of God and move in a bold direction guided only by the spirit of God. Some would say that if the church were on the water, it is "dead in the water," adrift with no "way" on, ignoring the wind or using it to point away from God's direction.

> *We were not created to sit, but to stand and to walk and to move.*

For the purposes of this chapter, I'm going to assume a willingness to follow God's direction. We'll explore a way of thinking about how to lead the church—how to sail this ship toward things that will mature the ship's crew, the body of Christ. Rather than waiting for our ship to drift into these situations or, God forbid, be blown onto the rocks of these issues, what if we proactively explored these matters thoughtfully? To further the analogy, let's consider thinking of the items below as islands to explore on the way to doing God's will. This could include but is not limited to exploring things like:

- How to interpret scripture (How to read the Bible)
- Whether to use musical instruments in worship
- How to address enfranchising women into church leadership or greater participation
- How to minister to those who experience same-sex attraction
- How to address major differences within the body regarding politics, treatment of the poor, worship, receiving immigrants, etc.

If these items above are scary territory to move toward purposefully, then doing so at the whim of the world should frighten you beyond comprehension!

Traveling on water gives us tremendous degrees of freedom. We can choose which island to explore dependent on current conditions, our need to travel specifically to one island without having to travel first to another, and how difficult it might be to explore one island over another.

So let's consider what traveling to these islands of conversation would entail. Let's first consider who will lead us there.

A Designated Leader

In the Churches of Christ, a plurality of male leaders are chosen from those gathered. These men are called Elders or Shepherds. These shepherds are inescapably responsible for the spiritual well-being of the congregation, the church. Usually, these leaders (sometimes in concert with the congregation) call a trained minister to preach and provide further spiritual leadership for the church. Larger churches add ministers as needed to aid the church in its mission to reach young people or the community, etc. Deacons or ministry leaders can also be assigned to perform specific tasks within the church. The shepherds and ministers and deacons/ministry leaders together are usually considered the leadership team of the church (some churches would consider only the shepherds as the leadership team, others the shepherds and ministers as the leadership team).

This model of being led by a group is foreign to most of our experience. Likely we are led by one person at work or even at play. We are used to seeing a Head Coach or the Superintendent or an Executive Director. Multiple leaders mean long conversations about what to do, what to say, how to say it, in order to gain agreement. While foreign, we

> *... having a point person for a season or for a specific purpose can be extremely helpful.*

believe this method of leadership to be biblical and appropriate. This should remain. AND, as we discuss exploring new places and new waters, designating a leader for one portion of the journey can make sense. To be clear, having a point person for a season or for a specific purpose can be extremely helpful. Where the ship goes generally remains in the hands of the group. How to proceed there, at what pace, and what approach—these matters can be delegated to a "chief among equals" so that a specific portion of the journey goes well.

For example, let's assume the shepherds of a church collectively agree to mature their church by a journey toward inclusion. This journey could have them explore the island of enfranchising women. Once the choice is made to explore this island, A LEADER could be assigned to ensure this part of the journey is cohesive, well explored, and completed. By assigning one leader, accountability and duty are more easily performed.

Our experience shows that designating a specific person to lead a portion of the journey provides for a better experience and outcome when compared to expecting the entire group to work through the details of approaching the island, exploring it, and declaring the exploration complete and then incorporating that experience into the life of the church.

A Dedicated Leadership Team

Accepting the plurality of leaders means that those leaders can be counted on to stay the course as the ship is steered toward islands for exploration. After a decision has been made to explore an island is no time to have even one person on the leadership team personally abandon ship!

The team should discuss and confirm explicit expectations of behavior and commitment BEFORE embarking on the journey toward and onto any island of conversation. Certainly circumstances of sickness, death, and loss would be reasons for stepping off a team. However, great damage is done if a team member leaves because the waters get rough or the exploration becomes more difficult than expected. Keep your nerve! If you aren't sure you can manage the trip, do everyone a favor and step clear.

If a team member does choose to step down, LET THEM! I realize you might prefer they stay, but if they aren't up to the journey, begging and persuading them to continue generates confusion and uncertainty in the individual and the team, and rarely does it help. Asking "Are you sure, Bob?" is worthwhile. Asking twice or three times or four begs for trouble. Let others make decisions for themselves.

Adding to the team willy-nilly is not recommended either, especially in the middle of an approach to or the exploration of a conversation island. Leadership groups take time to build trust and camaraderie. Take care in adding to the team and do so at a time when things are settled in the church or do it at intervals of 4 or 5 years. It takes time to add solid team players and adding one here or one there harms team chemistry and can be less than helpful.

A Willing Crew—or at Least a Strong Minority

True leaders do not wait for all, or even most, of those being led to agree with their decisions before moving ahead. True leaders make the best decisions possible with the information available after having consulted God and their trusted advisors. True leaders do not wait for perfect conditions or perfect information or perfect agreement. True leaders decide and act on what matters to the betterment of their followers. During the United States Civil War, Lincoln's chosen military leader, General McClellan, waited and waited

> *True leaders do not wait for perfect conditions or perfect information or perfect agreement. True leaders decide and act on what matters to the betterment of their followers.*

and waited to attack General Lee's forces in southern Virginia. He was waiting for perfect conditions, perfect resources, and full agreement from his junior officers. His reticence to act, some believe, lengthened the war and eventually found him dismissed.

All that being said, one must have at least some willing to go where the leaders point. A willing crew, or a strong minority of them who say "yes" to the leadership is essential to sailing toward the islands for exploration. Consider the difference between those following Moses at the time they reach the promised land and those following Joshua as they prepare to enter the promised land. Moses had too many grumblers and complainers and whiners. They rebelled against God and were sentenced to die in the desert. With that generation eliminated, Joshua had people at the ready, pledging themselves to his leadership.

To go blindly onto the water without understanding where your people stand regarding the coming journey is folly. If leaders probe and find significant lack in attitude or preparation or commitment, remedial work is necessary. Maturing must come through smaller trials.

If we are going to venture into open water toward islands of conversation, we'll need a sturdy ship to get us there. That sturdy ship is called governance.

A Strong and Sturdy Ship

I submit that the ship a church sails on to explore the islands of conversation is its governance structure.

For our churches, governance is simply how the leaders exercise control over the church. How will we organize ourselves as leaders? How will decisions be made? To whom shall we delegate? What will we never delegate? Typically, in Churches of Christ, governance is understood as "how we've always led." This can work quite well for a very long time, even in difficult circumstances. However, with the environment in North America changing drastically, our backgrounds being more varied, and our adherents expecting to participate in decision-making, it is worthwhile to complete the following before embarking on the journey:

1. Chronicle or codify the governance structure of the church.
2. Ensure each leader signs off on this structure and commits to it.
3. Adhere to what is written and ensure it is upheld.
4. Communicate this governance structure to the church body.
5. Expect some challenges to any changes in how things are typically done and respond thoughtfully.

Few things challenge the leadership more than choosing to hold a proactive conversation about a possibly controversial subject. The governance structure — the vessel that carries you safely to the islands — must be sturdy, supported, and understood. And the challenge of traveling to and successfully exploring these islands will strengthen the ship, the governance structure, by exposing weaknesses in it and fixing those weaknesses.

> *Few things challenge the leadership more than choosing to hold a proactive conversation about a possibly controversial subject.*

The minister of Central Church of Christ chose to allow another faith group to use their building for worship. This meant the use of musical instruments in the building on Sunday afternoons. Building-use decisions were delegated to the minister. Central were acappella worshipers When some in leadership learned of this other faith group using the building and worshiping with instruments, they protested — they challenged the very structure they had agreed to — building use decisions having been delegated to the minister. The governance structure came under challenge. This conversation was not planned but the conversation was necessary. The content was the use of the building by another faith group. The issue — the island of conversation was — have we delegated well and do we trust the person we've delegated to. This church chose to hold to its written commitment and allow the minister to make the decision. The other faith group used the building for over three years, outgrew the space they were provided, and moved into their own facility. The experience taught both the minister and the leaders about trust, about having a thoughtful conversation when disagreements arise. This strengthened the ship—the governance structure—and all remained in leadership going forward.

Without the sturdiness of the governance structure—the commitment to governing in a particular way—the church leadership would have spent an inordinate amount of time and energy on something that was, in the end, a simple decision by a trusted teammate.

How's the Weather?

With a designated leader, a dedicated leadership, a willing crew and a sturdy ship (governance structure), we are ready to consider what island to visit. And yet it makes sense to consider the "weather," that is, the general conditions surrounding the congregation—both internal and external—before we head toward any particular subject. What is going on in and around the church? Has the church been calm for several months or even years, or has it suffered tragedy or turmoil? Embarking toward an island of conversation while the church is still recovering from the shutdown of an area factory affecting many in the congregation would be foolish. Moving out while the church mourns the death of a patriarch of the congregation is equally silly. Ask the question: "If this were my personal family, should I begin this conversation with them or should I wait a while?" Of course, the smallest disruption can be an excuse for delaying embarkation until Jesus returns. A good leader will know if the weather, the milieu within and nearby the church, is conducive for "ship's movement."

Approaching Land and Welcoming Help

Assuming a decision has been made to approach and explore an island of conversation, what is the best way to go about it? If no maps existed of these different islands, if no intelligence has been gained or is available, then one would have to survey the entire island to know the best approach to it. Fortunately, some have already explored most of the islands of conversation associated with churches. Some would call them experts. To keep our nautical analogy alive, I'd like to call them conversational pilots.

In tricky or unfamiliar waters, ship captains hire a pilot, normally an ex-ship captain and a highly experienced ship handler who possesses detailed knowledge of local waterways, e.g., actual depth, direction, and strength of the wind, current, and tide at any time of the day. By boarding a pilot, the captain retains responsibility for the ship but utilizes the knowledge and experience of the pilot to help ensure the ship safe passage through a strait or into and out of a harbor.

Churches can bring in conversational pilots, experts who have navigated a specific conversation dozens of times, aiding churches as they move toward the islands of conversations as well as help them explore it. Using a pilot can keep a church off the conversational rocks and aid the church in exploring the nuances of these important conversations. The conversation approached will dictate what conversational pilot to use. A list of known pilots for specific conversations is below:

Conversation	Conversational Pilots [1]
How to Interpret Scripture	Grady King, Carson Reed, Tim Woodroof
Women's Use of Gifts	Ken Cukrowski
Same-Sex Attraction	Sally Gary
Use of Instrumental Music	Bret Testerman, Greg Anderson
Addressing Major Differences	Carlus Gupton, Jon Mullican Greg Anderson
Church Vision/Mission	Jay Jarboe, Jon Mullican

Using a conversational pilot early in the approach to the conversational island increases the opportunity that the conversation will go well. If the congregation is anxious about the topic at hand, just an announcement that the conversation is to be taken up could send some in the congregation reeling. While no one can control the response of others, how the topic is broached or approached matters to the overall process of exploring the island, and a conversation pilot's experience can improve the likelihood of a good outcome. Retaining a pilot for the exploration of the conversational island can further improve the direction the process travels.

> *Using a conversational pilot early in the approach to the conversational island increases the opportunity that the conversation will go well.*

A word about who to involve in the approach and exploration: If you are a Star Trek fan, you'll remember that when the Enterprise orbited a planet, Captain Kirk and Spock and McCoy and Scotty were usually the ones who did the planetary exploring, leaving the Enterprise's crew on the ship to watch from afar or be invaded by aliens or whatever. While some pre-work by

---

[1] This is by no means an exhaustive list. Others are available and competent help should always be seriously considered before approaching these conversations.

leadership is often necessary before the approach and exploration of these important conversations, "leaving the crew behind" can often create issues of its own. I've seen elder groups study a topic by themselves for years, sometimes in secret. From the solitary (or secret) study, several things can go poorly. First, the elder group may come to a conclusion, and then they have some choices to make: do they announce their conclusion or do they announce that they want the church to study the subject with them? Inclusion of others once your mind is made up is not really inclusion. Lengthy studies by the elders leave the congregation on the sideline and risks distancing one from the other. Once a decision to approach and explore has been made, get the congregation onto the island with you and explore together. By including them in the process, they learn as you learn and trust is strengthened.

Some might consider both the use of a pilot and congregational inclusion as a loss of control. In both cases the elders retain responsibility and authority over what happens: when the church approaches, when it explores the island of conversation, when to leave, and the eventual conclusions reached about the conversation, all the while maturing the church by showing them that you believe they can handle the journey.

This chapter provides a strategic look at approaching and exploring important conversations within the church. The actual details of the conversation itself are beyond the scope of this chapter.

Conclusion

The church can be viewed as shipboard workers, ready and able to approach and explore islands of conversation, the activity of which will mature them and ready them for future challenges. A designated leader and a dedicated leadership group along with a strong governance structure (ship), considering the current milieu (internal and external) and using a pilot greatly improve the likelihood of a successful approach and exploration of the subject island chosen. Yes, significant pitfalls remain and no guarantees can be made. However, purposefully moving toward an island proactively can improve the experience compared to allowing the winds of the world forcing you onto these islands by circumstance and situation.

Useful Understandings for a Leadership Team

Doug Peters

"Leadership in a non-profit, largely volunteer, faith-based organization is the toughest kind of leadership!"

That sentiment was clear as I was privileged to gather with several great Christ-following leaders. They are the captains of industry and directors of business. And they are also leaders in their churches. They are CEOs, CFOs, Presidents, Entrepreneurs, and Owners. They each have demanding positions of power and influence. Yet, they readily acknowledge that leading their churches brings some of their most unique and difficult challenges.

These leaders know how things operate in the office and the boardroom. Effectiveness can be fairly easily seen, measured, and rewarded. The bottom line is evident. There are clear channels of organization and communication. If someone or a segment is not on board with the organization's mission and vision, there are set policies to move personnel out or into different areas of responsibility. Attendance of all key players within the organizations they lead is mandatory and full participation is not optional or subject to other competing priorities. Tasks are assigned and expectations are almost always met with a high standard of quality and excellence. But in the church, the group they often give the next largest amount of their lives to, things are not always so clear.

While these "Level-Five Leaders" (see *Good to Great*, by Jim Collins) often give 50, 60, or more hours a week to their occupations, they also dedicate considerable time to leading their churches. They are elders, shepherds, and overseers. And they find it to be tough! If you listen carefully, you will hear them use terms like frustrating, trying, and discouraging. I hear phrases like "herding cats" and "nailing Jell-O to the wall" as they describe life on a church-leadership team. Do not get me wrong. Most of these leaders desire to sacrificially serve Christ's church and can also relate many great blessings from that experience. It is not all doom and gloom. But it nearly always could be better!

I have found that these same leadership concerns are almost universally consistent and vexing no matter the church or leader. White collar or blue . . . Rural or urban . . . Tie or jeans . . . Mega or mini . . . Every congregation's leaders would do well to ask some basic questions and come to some *Useful Understandings* related to their ministry of leadership in the body of Christ.

While most of the leadership groups I consult with are in autonomous churches and contextually unique, I find that they all can benefit from asking intentional and proactive questions related to how they will work together. Clearly thinking through and defining their roles, functions, relationships, and "ground rules" can set them up for greater kingdom effectiveness into God's future. They may not all be led to do things the same way, but they can all benefit from at least asking some basic questions and coming to agreement about how they will serve together.

Several years ago, my friend, mentor, and former elder Wilson C. "Dub" Orr shared with me the value of leader teams coming to some *Useful Understandings* about how they would operate. Through the intervening years I have found myself frequently reflecting on his wisdom and noting a variety of key decision

> *Church leadership teams, such as elder/minister groups, greatly benefit from the discipline of asking good questions about how they will serve together.*

points that would be better settled in advance. Blessed is the leadership team that takes the time to prayerfully ask some important questions and develop some *Useful Understandings* to maximize their kingdom leadership capacity.

How will our church leadership lead?

Will your ministry of leadership be *Proactive* or *Reactive*? *Intentional* or *Indiscriminate*? *Consistent* or *Chaotic*? And what can you do to increase the likelihood of preferred outcomes?

Church leadership teams, such as elder/minister groups, greatly benefit from the discipline of asking good questions about how they will serve together. These *Useful Understandings* bring several practical, systemic, and spiritual benefits:

Efficiency — Leaders with predetermined understandings of their working relationship will be able to invest more of their time together in spiritually and relationally substantive matters.

Mutually agreed upon leadership "ground rules" enable leaders to focus on pursuing the God-given mission of the church instead of reactively sorting out how they will function each time a new "hot issue" stands before them.

Objectivity—The best time to establish group norms and procedures is not when a significant decision is looming and anxiety is elevated. Objectively sorting out how leader teams will make various types of decisions during a season of intentional discernment (such as the interim season) is ideal.

Accountability—The process of asking good questions and adopting *Useful Understandings* enables leadership team members to hold each other responsible to sound principles. Healthy accountability within a group is possible only if there are previously agreed-upon goals and standards. Ambiguity does not lead to accountability.

> *Ambiguity does not lead to accountability.*

Harmony—While diversity of thought and giftedness is often a leadership-team strength, conflicts tend to arise whenever there are competing core values and different basic understandings within the group. Leaders that know how diversity and dissent are to be handled are more likely to be able to maintain the unity of the Spirit in the midst of the storm. An ounce of prevention is worth a pound of cure!

Expectancy—By investing themselves in casting a vision for how their group will function, effective leaders also prepare their leadership team and church for the future. Prospective elders who are trying to discern if God is calling them to serve will benefit from a clear knowledge of how the group intends to function. Minister candidates will appreciate having an accurate awareness of the leadership culture they are considering. New leaders can covenant with other leaders for the sake of the church.

The Interim Season — that occasion when a church is in a spiritual discernment process to identify a minister — is an ideal time for church leader groups to step back and prayerfully contemplate how God is calling them to most effectively serve God's people into God's future. Wisdom suggests that until a church answers the *"Who are we?"* question, they are not ready to answer the *"Who are we looking for?"* question. In the same way, wise leaders will do well to discern and clarify some *Useful Understandings* about how God is calling them to lead before they invite new leaders into their team.

Useful Understandings Among Elders

All ministry is contextual and all churches are different. A church of 100 members with two elders and a single paid minister will obviously function differently than a church of 1,500 members with twenty elders and a staff of several ministers. Regardless of contextual diversity, there are some important and basic categories for all leader groups to consider. First, consider *Useful Understandings* among elders.

> *All ministry is contextual and all churches are different.*

Accountability
What level of accountability will exist among elders?
- Will each single elder be in spiritual submission to all the others? If so, how?
- Commitment to confidentiality? Confidentiality and spouses?
- Group self-regulation?

- Commitment to spiritual disciplines?
- Elder covenant/written agreement?
- Commitment to hold each other accountable to spiritual standards of interpersonal interaction and communication? (Serving by the fruit of the Spirit instead of the works of the flesh [Gal. 5:19-26]; Wisdom from above instead of wisdom from below [James 5:13-18]; Maintaining unity [Eph. 4:1-3]; Wholesome talk and interaction [Eph. 4:29-32]).
- Commitment to peaceably resign if requested by a majority of elders?

Selection
How will elders be selected and what determines their periods of service?

- Directive selection process controlled primarily by current elders?
- Participatory selection process involving administrative team of members?
- Level of congregational participation in selection?
- Congregational spiritual discernment/spiritual practices in selection process?
- Selection regularly scheduled or as needed?
- Set terms of service?
- Rotation?
- Once an elder, always an elder?
- Will elders be periodically reaffirmed?
- Provision for sabbatical or leave of absence?

Leadership Style

What basic style(s) of leadership will we value and commit to practice?

- Single, united style?
- Multiple styles encouraged? (Directive for some situations, participatory for others)
- Basically authoritarian/ autocratic/ directive?
- Basically participative?
- Ministers viewed as part of the leadership team? How so?
- Congregational participation?
- People-centered?
- Institution-centered?
- Emphasize elder, overseer, and shepherd equally or according to availability/life stage/giftedness?
- Elder teams? (Oversight/Administrative team, Shepherding team, etc.)

Organization

How will we organize ourselves to serve faithfully and effectively?

Decision-making

- Majority?
- Unanimous?
- Consensus (if so, how defined)?
- Dissent in and following decision-making?
- Agreed upon post-decision unanimity?
- Silent dissent?
- Open but majority-supporting dissent?
- Procedure for when a leader(s) cannot support the group decision?
- Commitment to spiritual discernment processes?
- Minister involvement in decision-making?

Delegation of decision-making?
- All involved in each decision?
- Decision made by those present only?
- Individual elders or elder teams to make decisions in defined areas?

Quorum requirement for meetings?
- Any present make decisions?
- Definition of quorum, if required?

Meeting Procedure
- Chair?
- Chair Tenure/Rotation?
- Agenda?
- Minutes/Notes?
- Open meetings?
- Pre-scheduled?
- Topic Control?
- Meeting Times / Frequency?
- Time discipline in meetings?
- Meeting dismissal discipline?
- Spiritual disciplines and prayer during meetings?

Meeting Attendance
- Leadership team meetings to include all or some staff ministers?
- Except when? (salary or personnel discussions?)
- Elders only?
- Separate elder team meetings? (Oversight Team, Shepherding Team, etc.)
- Invited participants?
- Always open to all?

- Except for when?
- Different types of meetings? (Ministry/Administration/ Mission-Vision, Prayer only, etc.)

Prayerful consideration of the above categories and questions will result in *Useful Understandings* that will enable leaders to serve together more effectively into the future.

Useful Understandings Between Elders, Ministers and Others

The New Testament uses a variety of terms to describe those who carry out roles and functions of leadership and ministry in the earliest church. Many read the various texts with an eye toward an "Organizational Chart" often found in business, government, or the military. This perspective emphasizes authority and position. Viewed purely through these lenses, elder/overseer/ shepherd groups become standing boards at the top of the pyramid, where the proverbi-

> *After Jesus, it is less a "pecking order" and more of a "purposeful order" of spiritually gifted leaders that are intended to serve together in unity for the benefit of the body of Christ.*

al "buck stops" and paid preachers/evangelists/ministers become the hired hands to carry out necessary functions as prescribed by the board. In this model, congregational serv-ants/deacons (*diakonos*)/ ministry leaders, directors, coordina-tors, secretaries/assistants and "regular members" fill out the base of the pyramid.

However, the New Testament picture is much more fluid. Yes, there is a "head" of the church, and his name is King Jesus the Christ! And yes, there are other leaders that serve by giftedness and calling. But the New Testament picture is more like an organism than an organization. It is less like a board and more like a body (1 Cor. 12, Eph. 4).

In Eph. 4:1-16 Paul describes Jesus as calling and gifting apostles, prophets, evangelists, and shepherds/teachers. While they may function in a diversity of complementary roles, they all are working toward the same purpose and goal—to equip God's people for ministry so that the body is built up in unified maturity to increasingly look like the head—Jesus Christ! The head of the organism is King Jesus and he calls and gifts a diversity of people to serve in a variety of related ways for his purposes. After Jesus, it is less a "pecking order" and more of a "purposeful order" of spiritually gifted leaders that are intended to serve together in unity for the benefit of the body of Christ.

With that perspective in mind, it is vital that church leaders consider how elder groups relate with preachers, congregational servants, (deacons) and others in the congregation.

Elder Group Relationship with Preachers/Ministers

- Will Preachers/Ministers have a signed Employment Agreement or Letter of Agreement for Clear Understanding? Agreements generally cover such matters as: Ministry Role/Title, Job Description/Responsibilities, Intended Philosophy of Leadership Team Relationships, Desired Philosophy of Ministry, Supervisory Responsibilities, Evaluation Practices, Ministry Resources/"Tools" Provided, Days Off, Vacation Policy, Annual Office Holidays, Notice Policy, Termination Clause, Expense Account/Reimbursement Plan, Continuing Education, Seminars/Lectureships/Conferences, Speaking Opportunity Policy, Sundays-Away Policy, Base Salary, Housing Allowance Acknowledgement, and Benefits

(Insurance Options: Health, Disability, Life, etc.; Retirement, Reimbursements, etc.).

- Will there be an agreed-upon and signed Job/Role Description?
- Will the agreement be mutually evaluated on an annual basis?
- Will all elders be in liaison with all staff?
- Or, will individual elders or elder teams be in liaison with certain staff ministers?
- Will there be a designated ministry staff member serving as staff team leader, coordinator, or chief of staff?
- What are attendance expectations for leadership team meetings?
- How will regular ministry staff evaluations/reviews be conducted?
- How will ministry staff relate to deacons/ministry leaders

Congregational Servants/Deacons/Ministry Leaders

- Will you recognize deacons, congregational servants, or ministry leaders?
- How will they be selected?
- Will they be selected to serve "at large and in general"?
- Or, will they be selected by giftedness and serve in specific ministries?
- Will only deacons staff ministries or may any gifted/qualified person be equipped to lead ministries?
- Will you select only a pre-agreed-upon number of deacons?
- Or, will you select all considered qualified/gifted regardless of number?
- To what degree will elders and preachers delegate ministries to other congregational servants?

- How will ministry staff and staff-led ministries relate with deacons?
- Will you encourage deacons to establish ministry teams?
- Will individual deacons or deacon teams with a chair lead and oversee ministry areas?
- How will deacon accountability and feedback take place?
- How will you equip women servants/ministry leaders (Rom. 16:1)?
- Will women lead only ministries to women?
- Or, will you equip women to lead any ministry where they have appropriate giftedness?
- How will women serve on mixed-gender teams or ministry initiatives?
- How will women serve in group decision-making? Teaching/Team Teaching?
- To what degree will you recognize a gifts-based approach to ministry regardless of gender?

The Congregation as a Whole
- Will you have regular, open congregational spiritual business meetings?
- If so, what decision-making limitations will spiritual business meetings have?
- What will be your primary channels of communication with the congregation?
- How will your congregation be able to supply regular input to leadership?

These *Useful Understandings* are not intended to lead to the same conclusions in every church. In fact, I am convinced that all ministry is contextual and all leaders must prayerfully discern God's leading for the flock they have been entrusted the obligation to equip for ministry. Every church can benefit from asking intentional and proactive questions related to how they will work together. They may not all be led to do things the same way, but they can all benefit from at least asking some basic questions and coming to agreement about how they will serve together. May God bless you as you seek God's will!

Non-Anxious
Leadership

Tim Woodroof

Late on a Friday night, John H. was arrested for drunk driving. He blew twice the legal limit. By Saturday morning, the arrest was reported on local news outlets and immediately went to Facebook and email and text messages.

And then the Center Hill Church began to implode. For seven years, John H. had preached for CHC. He was charismatic, well-spoken, and highly-respected. Everybody in the congregation—from teens to singles to young parents to golden-agers—loved John. The church had doubled in size under his leadership.

And now this.

By Saturday afternoon, the elders were bombarded by phone calls from anxious church members. Some were angry, demanding John be fired (if not drawn and quartered during Sunday's worship!). Others were worried sick about the dire impact of John's arrest on the church — "We'll lose half our members!" Still others called to report conversations with heart-broken teens or deeply-disappointed friends.

Saturday night, the elders held an emergency meeting. John H. was asked to attend, but, still reeling from events and the reactions of his wife and children, declined. As one of the elders closed the conference-room door, he quipped, "It happened Friday, but Sunday's comin'." None of his peers thought the comment was very funny. Tomorrow morning — by any measure — would be awful.

Cast all your anxiety on him because he cares for you. (1 Peter 5:7)

Crises and the Anxieties They Provoke

Every church teeters on the brink of anxiety-inducing events that can tear it apart.

- A church leader is caught in an affair.
- A deacon embezzles funds.
- Theological tensions within the congregation erupt into open discord.
- A financial crisis finally forces a congregation to face the reality that, without radical transformation, its days are numbered.
- A popular preacher resigns or is fired.
- Two teens in the youth group are killed in a car wreck.

Church leaders delude themselves if they believe their churches are immune to such forces. Stability in the past is no guarantee of stability in the future. The future is ripe with looming crises. A traumatic and church-threatening event may not occur in your congregation tomorrow or next week. But it will occur eventually . . . in every church . . . and it can happen at any time.

However, it is not this *potential* for crisis that most threatens the health of churches. It is, rather, how crisis is *handled*. Certainly, handling the crisis itself — circumstances and consequences and communication — is a primary leadership task when churches are threatened. But it is also critical (and equally important) for leaders to handle *anxious members*.

Inevitably, some church members will react anxiously to threatening events. They will allow their anxieties to determine the shape and strength of their reactions. And they will attempt — consciously or not — to infect others with their anxiety.

- "We've got to make a decision right now!"
- "This is black and white . . . clear as the nose on your face . . . why can't you see that?"
- "I've talked to several people who are thinking of leaving!"
- "This is awful . . . how could you let it happen?"
- "We don't have any choice in the matter!"
- "Stop debating and DO something!"

Anxious members say all manner of things to each other and to church leaders in times of crisis. We cannot regulate how they react or what words they use or the tone of their voices. We cannot prevent their anger or confusion or desperation or lack of faith. We cannot script their lines to ensure less reactionary, more reasoned conversations.

What we can do, as leaders, is regulate *ourselves*, control our own reactions, and refuse to allow anxious members to contaminate us with their anxiety.

Anxiety is the mother of all manner of sin. It gives people permission to:

- Speak immoderately, make demands, announce ultimatums
- Over-simplify complicated situations to clarify a course of action
- Eliminate legitimate options, narrow the range of choices, cut off discussion
- Sink into paralysis (or, alternatively, feel justified in behaving rashly)
- Place pragmatics above principles, practicalities over ideals
- Feel out of control (or justify ever-greater levels of control)
- Avoid and evade conflict . . . placate rather than resolve.

When church members act in these ways, it is lamentable (for it is not Christ-like). But when anxious members persuade *church leaders* to act in these ways, it is tragic.

Peter Steinke (in his pivotal book *Congregational Leadership in Anxious Times: Being Calm and Courageous No Matter What*) champions the virtues of non-anxious leadership. This little book is a "must read" for anyone called to be a church leader in these present, anxiety-prone days.

Because leaders love their congregations, they are vulnerable to the same anxieties that can overwhelm church members . . . perhaps more so, because they care so much. But because church leaders care about their churches, Steinke says they must choose to be less anxious than the people they serve . . . or, at least, less controlled by their anxiety. It is precisely in anxious times that church leaders must avoid anxious behavior, if they are to lead their churches to healthier and more productive futures.

> *It is precisely in anxious times that church leaders must avoid anxious behavior, if they are to lead their churches to healthier and more productive futures.*

How can we do that . . .practically speaking? By making two leadership commitments during troubled times: to be *present* and to be *differentiated*. And by incorporating related disciplines that permit leaders to rise "above themselves" when their church faces hardships.

The Present Leader

When it comes to congregational leadership — especially in anxious times — *showing up* is half the battle.

Leaders should never underestimate the power of *presence*. In difficult times, church members don't need their leaders to be charismatic, eloquent, brilliant, and wise. They do need them to be *present*, to be accessible and approachable, to be visible whatever the circumstances.

But *presence* can be difficult when the sky starts to fall. Just *showing up* can be a challenge for church leaders.

In anxious times:

- Leaders can be nervous about being around anxious church members, fearful of awkwardness or uncomfortable with expressions of raw emotion.
- Some leaders are so conflict-averse, they won't risk interactions where confrontation is a possibility.
- Leaders may lack a sense of *permission* to step into tensions because they don't want to intrude or don't have a pre-existing and profound personal relationship or haven't embraced their God-given spiritual authority.
- Leaders assume members want answers and solutions. Lacking those, leaders can avoid members and—thus—deprive them of the one thing they need most: assurance, touch, engagement.
- Leaders often go into *crisis mode*, meeting behind closed doors and engaging in secret discussions with other leaders . . . effectively absenting themselves at the very time the church most needs to see their faces and feel their touch.

And so, for many leaders, simple *presence* in anxious times must be *intentional*. Here are some "presence rules" for you to consider:

- *It is always better for a leader to show up than to stay away.* If you're going to make a mistake, make it in the direction of presence rather than absence.
- *Come early and stay late.* During difficult days for the church as a whole, determine to be at every assembly of the church, positioned where people can "get at you" — the foyer, the back of the auditorium, and/or the door of the classroom.

- *Don't schedule leader meetings around church gathering times.* Yes, it's more convenient for leaders to meet during class time on Sunday mornings or Wednesday nights. And, yes, traumatic times call for more frequent meetings—there are only so many nights in a week! But leaders need to be available to members, not hidden away in an office or meeting room.

- *Run towards the tension.* Whenever you find yourself (as a leader) reaching for reasons to stay away or evade or escape, recognize those reasons are probably rooted in your personal anxieties rather than your leadership instincts. Fight the temptation to avoid the difficult.

- *Set and protect boundaries.* Working with anxious members does not mean offering yourself as a sacrificial lamb to a member's irascibility. There are boundaries to behaviors you can and should insist upon. Anxious members might require extra patience. But they do not need *carte blanche* to behave in ungodly and hurtful ways.

> *Without presence, there is no leadership—especially when times are tough.*

Presence is necessary. Presence is foundational. Presence is powerful. Without presence, there is no leadership—especially when times are tough.

The Differentiated Leader

First, leaders throw themselves into stormy waters (with a commitment to *presence*). But then they must find a way to keep their heads above the waves.

When you are surrounded by anxious members and the temperature of the room keeps rising, when demands and ultimatums come thick and fast, when people all around you are using immoderate words and strident tones, what is a good leader to do?

Many things, no doubt. But they all begin with a commitment to practice *differentiation.*

"Differentiation" is the ability to:

- Balance the tension between being an individual ("I can do what I want without reference to others") and being a member of a group ("I must do what the group wants without reference to me").
- Value both the "self" and the "group" by serving others without becoming lost in them.
- Embrace our God-given role as *leaders* and recognize that role must inform the way we see ourselves and the group ...how we respond personally and interact with the group.
- Manage our emotional lives by a core *within* ourselves (character, principles, core values) rather than surrender our emotional lives to outside forces.
- Take responsibility for regulating ourselves for the greater good of the group.

It is one thing to belong to a group (like a church) . . . to be committed to a group . . . to feel responsibility for a group. It is another thing entirely to be *consumed* by the group . . . *meld* with the group . . .

> *Godly leaders don't allow themselves to identify so closely with the church and its anxieties that, in the end, the church and its anxieties identify them.*

act *co-dependently* with the group. Faithful leadership of a church doesn't mean you drink the Kool-Aid, surrendering your "self" in order to adopt a "herd mentality." In fact, *faithful* leadership requires you *not* imbibe, actively resist "groupthink," refuse to surrender your values and principles to the group, and remain true to yourself even as you try to interact with and lead others. Godly leaders don't allow themselves to identify so closely with the church and its anxieties that, in the end, the church and its anxieties identify them.

There is a fine balance between maintaining your sense of membership and your sense of self. Too much *separation* from church members and you will cease to be trusted and followed by them. (Remember the power of presence.) But too much *fusion* with the group and you will cease to listen to your own inner voice and better angels. Keeping a balance between presence and co-dependency defines *differentiation*.

Here are some "differentiation guidelines" for you to consider:

- *Remember who you are.* Differentiated leaders know themselves, what they believe and value. These *identity convictions* do not change with time or circumstances or the anxieties of others. Being "true to yourself" is a hallmark of non-anxious leaders.
- *Remember whose you are.* Differentiated church leaders are even more committed to Christ than to the churches they serve. Especially in times of crisis, church members can lose their way and advocate the most graceless solutions. Keeping and modeling "the mind of Christ" is the essence of godly, non-anxious leadership.
- *Monitor your personal anxieties.* Keep a finger on your emotional pulse. Recognize that even the best leaders grow weary and angry and frustrated and impatient. Anxious leadership springs from such emotions. It may not be possible to avoid such feelings. But it is possible not to give in to them.

- *Monitor the anxieties of others.* Keep a finger on the pulse of members — especially as they interact with you. Behind the words members speak and the actions they take is a mix of emotions and motives and back-stories. Listen for the anxiety, not just the words — and then be willing to rise above it.

- *Don't take things so personally.* Effective leaders do not allow themselves to be defined by the problems they face...or the accusations and blame of the people they lead. When leaders identify too closely with the difficulties they are navigating, anxious leadership is only a heartbeat away.

> *Never make decisions for the short-term that jeopardize the long-term health and mission of the church.*

- *Memorize Rudyard Kipling's poem IF.* "If you can keep your head when all about you are losing theirs and blaming it on you . . . " (I wonder if Kipling ever led a church?)

- *Always keep the end in mind.* As a church leader, you are the guardian of your church's character and future. Remember where you and the church are going. Remember the kind of church Jesus calls you to build. Never sacrifice the goal for the sake of expediency. Never make decisions for the short-term that jeopardize the long-term health and mission of the church. Keep in mind the question, "What kind of church will we be tomorrow if we act this way today?"

The Rest of the Story

Sunday morning proved to be as difficult as expected . . . but not as disastrous.

The elders met early that morning to pray and promise solidarity with each other. Clearly they weren't ready to make a decision to resolve the situation (though the temptation of a quick and clean solution was strong, considering how uncertainty can affect many members). They were determined not to abandon John H. (they hoped there might be a way to redeem the situation), even though they knew this hope would upset some members and appear as "dithering." Most of all, they longed to transform a situation that threatened the church and shamed the cause of Christ into an opportunity for greater unity in the congregation and stronger witness to the community.

But reaching for such a solution would require time . . . and unity among church leaders. There could be no panic among this group, no haste. There could be no breaking ranks. As the assembly hour approached, these tired, burdened men looked around at each other, asking "Are we together in this?" with their eyes, each elder nodding his commitment to the others.

One of them handed out copies of a written statement to be read during the worship hour. In it were bullet points to guide their individual conversations with members that morning and in the days ahead:

> Friday night, John H. — our Pastor — was arrested for drunk driving. Most of us have heard the news. All of us are affected by it. In the days ahead, there will be discussions and decisions that will impact the future of our congregation — for better or worse. May God shape those discussions and guide our decisions.

> We love John H., his family, and the Center Hill Church. The events of this weekend are heartbreaking. But it is for times like these that God has called his church to be godly. As your shepherds, we are committed to navigating these stormy waters in a Christ-like manner.

We ask four things of the members of our church family:

1. *Please be praying. Beg for God's guidance, forgiveness, and healing. Pray for John H. and his family. Pray for our church. Pray for us.*
2. *Give us time. We will not make a hasty decision about something so important to this church and to the life and ministry of our brother John. We have listening to do . . . talking . . . discernment. All this takes time.*
3. *Talk to us. We want to know how you are feeling, what you are thinking, and which course of action you believe we should take. We will be calling on you in the days ahead to hear what you have to say.*
4. *Guard your tongues. Guard your hearts. What happened Friday night was sinful. But what happens now, as we react or respond, can be just as sinful. We encourage you to conduct yourselves by Paul's command to the Ephesians: "Do not let any unwholesome talk come out of your mouths, but only what is helpful for building others up according to their needs, that it may benefit those who listen."*

May God bless and guide us in the days ahead.

Again, they looked around at each other, taking a silent poll. Looking at his watch, one of their number announced, "We need to be in the foyer." Pause for a deep breath . . . pause for silent prayer. And then the group walked out of the conference room together, ready to meet their people—with all their questions and worries and messy emotions—in a united, non-anxious way.

MISSIONAL GOVERNANCE PHILOSOPHY FOR LEADERSHIP TEAMS

Carlus Gupton

Two scenarios

Scenario 1: A thriving congregation seems effective by most metrics. There is strong missional momentum. The leaders know they are at least partially responsible for this, and are grateful to be a part of it. On the other hand, they often feel more like observers and permission-givers than catalysts. They do not want more control, but want to challenge themselves and the congregation beyond busyness, to faithful and keen attunement to God's work in their missional environment. Their pressing concern is not what the congregation as a whole is doing, but on their functioning as leaders. These are high-functioning leaders who want their meetings, their interactions with each other and with the church, their deliberations and decisions, and their use of time and talent to be better aimed at what matters most.

Scenario 2: The second scenario is less positive. The congregation is not thriving, and the leaders do not work well together. Discussions on important issues, which are often controversial, quickly become polarized. In addition, the relationship between elders and ministers is strained. There is gridlock, stalemate, and stagnation. Sub-groups of leaders form coalitions and either act covertly on separate agendas or openly manipulate the system toward their perspective. Individual team members are tempted to go rogue in the name of progress. These are low-functioning leaders who want to move beyond their differences, learn better ways to work together, and have a system of accountability to guard against the polar extremes of dominance and acquiescence, over-function and under-performance.

These two situations are complex and multi-faceted, but one strategy that may improve the focus of high-functioning leaders and partially alleviate the frustration of low-functioning teams is to agree on a philosophy of missional governance. There are many aspects to a governance model. This chapter will focus on three.[1]

- Missional alignment
- Gift affirmation
- Empowering philosophy

---

[1] The six dynamics of leadership team effectiveness include spiritual formation, mission alignment, gift affirmation, respectful relationships, empowering belief systems, and functional structures. This chapter focus only on the second, third, and fifth of these.

Missional Alignment

Mission, as used in this discussion, means how well leaders are focused on a biblical and Christ-centered understanding of congregational purpose. Alignment is achieved when every aspect of leadership facilitates this purpose.

While a certain level of mission focus is encouraged by scripture and common sense, it is punctuated differently by pragmatic evangelicals and missionals.[2]

Pragmatics frequently adopt a corporate model expressed in well-crafted statements of mission, values, and vision, often as part of a strategic plan. Usually, the criteria for effectiveness are the number of those reached by a church's proclamation of the gospel and the variety of faith-based services offered. A corollary is how existing members as well as new converts reflect commitment to the mission through ministry involvement. Leaders try to construct systems of "ministry mobilization" that help members identify their spiritual gifts and empower them to use these gifts in as many ministries as the congregational infrastructure can support.

For missionals, the emphasis in not on mission clarification, but mission participation. The concept of missio Dei (mission of God) is variously defined, but universal to most constructions is that God is sovereignly at work to bring about his eternal purpose, and the church's task is to prayerfully discern the movement of God in their time and place and faithfully join him in spreading his kingdom on earth. In contrast to the pragmatic

---

[2] These terms reflect an older but still useful classification by Robert Webber in *Younger Evangelicals* (Baker, 2001) that distinguished between traditional evangelicals characterized by program-based established churches, pragmatic evangelicals characterized by the attractional church growth movement, and younger evangelicals characterized by missional communities.

perspective, the criteria for judging effectiveness is not the number of people attracted, but the church's engagement of their communities and the world through incarnational service. Since this will look different in each faith community, the criteria are more general, sometimes referred to as "patterns of faithfulness."[3] Statements of corporate core content are still used, but are "reverse engineered, drawn from what a congregation has actually been doing and the meaning of those practices for the people who do them. Formalized theological affirmations should move from what a church actually does back to articulation of it. They are symbols of the journey."[4]

Churches of Christ fall into both streams. This discussion does not prescribe which stream a church should flow into, and does not suggest a particular definition of mission, but focuses on the function of leaders to *embed* mission into the congregational culture. It reflects the concern shared by pragmatics and missionals alike that their congregations embody a culture that frees members to follow God's leading into Christ-honoring ministry. On that level, the dynamics of how leaders create mission-engaged congregational cultures are the same, whether pragmatic or missional.

This leads to our concern of how leaders may keep mission at the forefront. We are helped by MIT professor and organizational theorist Edgar Schein, in one of the most influential management books of our time, *Organizational Culture and Leadership*.[5]

---

[3] See Lois Y. Barrett (ed.), *Treasure in Clay Jars: Patterns in Missional Faithfulness* (Eerdmans, 2004).

[4] George R. Hunsberger, "Reflections for a Conversation on Theology in Congregational Life," *Gospel and Our Culture Network*, http://www.gocn.org/resources/articles/reflections-conversation-theology-congregational-life

[5] Edgar H. Schein, *Organizational Culture and Leadership*, 4th Edition (Jossey-Bass, 2010). The discussion on culture-embedding is in chapter 14.

Schein discusses *culture embedding*, i.e., disseminating the mission so that it shapes every person and function in an organization. In other literature, this is called *mission alignment.* He draws a distinction between *primary* embedding mechanisms and *secondary* articulation and reinforcement mechanisms. Primary factors are fundamentally necessary for mission alignment, and secondary factors that articulate and reinforce but are not sufficient to propel the mission forward. Note the list of *secondary* mechanisms.

- Organization design and structure
- Organizational systems and procedures
- Organizational rites and rituals
- Design of physical space, facades, and buildings
- Stories, legends, and myths about people and events
- Formal statements or organizational philosophy, values, and creed [6]

Well-meaning church leaders often over-emphasize these formal expressions of congregational culture. They attend a conference or read a book, and with great excitement issue statements, teach classes, and provide new structures for an improved ministry system. This may be accompanied by complicated audits and elaborate plans. Schein suggests these strategic efforts may result in little real return. Not long after the herculean effort, the plans and flow charts may collect dust except with a small group of frustrated strategically-oriented leaders. The only outcomes

> *The point is not to disparage good planning strategies, but to warn against relying on them too heavily. . . . They support mission, but cannot carry mission effectively throughout the congregation.*

---

[6] Ibid., 236.

besides a few bookmarks and unused boxes of watermarked stationery may be a couple of ministries that could also have resulted from something far less elaborate.

The point is not to disparage good planning strategies, but to warn against relying on them too heavily. They are secondary ways of expressing and reinforcing mission. They support mission, but cannot carry mission effectively throughout the congregation. They are the external expressions of a deeper internalization of mission.

Schein's list of *primary* embedding mechanisms, on the other hand, have to do with the essential character of the leaders and how they, and eventually those who follow them, act in ways that are congruent with mission.

- What leaders pay attention to, measure, and control on a regular basis
- How leaders react to critical incidents and organizational crises
- Observed criteria leaders use to allocate scarce resources
- Deliberate role modeling, teaching, and coaching
- Observed criteria leaders use to allocate rewards and status
- Observed criteria leaders use to recruit, select, promote, retire, and excommunicate organizational members [7]

This is the hard work of congregational mission alignment. Whatever happens on this primary level is what "takes" in the congregation. Even if leaders construct excellent statements and plans, the people will follow what they see on the primary level. This is the "real" congregational culture, the "actual" expression

---

[7] Ibid.

of mission. If at this primary level leaders act incongruently with their mission statements and plans, the members will disrespect the leaders and disparage the statements. On the other hand, if there are no statements, but the leaders are great exemplars of consistently focusing on what really matters, they are more likely to get good results from the congregation than they

> *... mission-aligned leaders move away from fixing complaints and make decisions based on a strong sense of kingdom values.*

would with statements and plans alone. The secondary mechanisms could help in such a situation, allowing members to have more clarity on how to follow their leaders.[8]

Schein's primary mechanisms underscore the importance of keeping missional concerns at the forefront in decision-making. This requires abandoning the "illusion of congregational happiness" that is preoccupied with quelling complaints and keeping them from occurring. This results in churches shaped more by consensus theology and falsely empathetic accommodation to people's sensitivities than by the challenge of mission. By contrast, mission-aligned leaders move away from fixing complaints and make decisions based on a strong sense of kingdom values. The chart on the next page illustrates this principle.[9]

---

[8] Two popular level integrations of both the primary and secondary mechanisms, though expressed in different terms, are by Andy Stanley, *Making Vision Stick* (Zondervan, 2007) and *Visioneering: God's Blueprint for Developing and Maintaining Vision* (Multnomah, 2005).

[9] From my chapter, "Breathing New Life Into Established Churches," in *Doing God's Work: A Primer for Church Leaders* (Dallas, TX: Hope Network Ministries, 2013), 15, which adapts material from Gilbert Rendle, "The Illusion of Congregational Happiness, in *Conflict Management in Congregations* (Alban Institute, 2001), 83-94.

Focus Less on *Pleasing the Preferences* of Your Members	Focus More on *Pursuing the Purpose* of the Kingdom
• Who wants what? • How do we satisfy… [a person or a group]? • What should we do about…[a problem or a complaint]?	• What does scripture call us to be and do? • What are we called to do in this chapter of our history as a congregation? • What are the goals that we set out to accomplish? • What are the appropriate strategies for our ministry, and how will we measure their attainment?

In summary, a chief consideration of missional church governance is that it be *missional* indeed, always aligning the practice of the leaders and the ministries of the church toward the advancement of God's mission. This requires intentional effort, especially in those areas that are most crucial to embedding a shared sense of purpose into the congregational culture.

Gift Affirmation

The second aspect of missional governance highlighted in this discussion builds on the first, and further suggests that effective leadership teams must understand, empower, and activate leadership gifts that are central to mission effectiveness. They strive to unbind the spiritual gifts and natural strengths of each member toward the fulfillment of mission. Team-building exercises that allow the discovery of each person's orientations, alongside intentional efforts to align team functions with those orientations, combine to create missionally-flourishing team cultures.

There are several ways to understand and capitalize on team gifts. I will mention five.

- *Spiritual-gifts inventories* — I have catalogued many resources for gift discovery on my website.[10] Most of them are not scientifically validated, and require interpretive interaction among the people who actually experience each other's service. Some of the free web-based inventories are as useful as any of the paid versions. These include the *Team Ministry Spiritual Gifts Inventory* (available in multiple languages), the *Spiritual Gifts Assessment Tool*, and *SpiritualGiftsTest.com* adult and youth versions.[11] These inventories attempt to profile each person in light of the gifts described in the five New Testament lists.[12]

- *Natural-strengths assessments* — The most widely-used tool to discover strengths is produced by Gallup, the *StrengthsFinder 2.0*. It is based on extensive research, including hour-and-a-half interviews with over 80,000 managers, resulting in 120,000 hours of recordings and 5 million pages of transcript. The essential revelation was that people function best when they are able to capitalize on their strengths, not improve upon weaknesses. The research continued into the discovery of thirty-four domi-

---

[10] See the page on Spiritual Gifts http://www.lifeandleadership.com/ministry-resources/spiritual-gifts.html, and the larger contextual resource guide on Involvement and Spiritual Gifts in Ministry,
http://www.lifeandleadership.com/ministry-resources/involvement-spiritual-gifts-in-christian-ministry.html.
[11] See the *Team Ministry Gifts Inventory* at https://gifts.churchgrowth.org/cgi-cg/gifts.cgi?intro=1, the Spiritual Gifts Assessment Tool at https://www.elca.org/Our-Work/Congregations-and-Synods/Faith-Practices/Spiritual-Renewal/Assessment-Tools, the SpiritualGiftsTest.com at http://www.spiritualgiftstest.com/tests
[12] Romans 12:6-8; 1 Corinthians 12:8-10, 28; Ephesians 4:11;1 Peter 4:11.

nant talents/themes/strengths[13] that were arranged into a profile, *StrengthsFinder 2.0*. The profile has been validated on over two million participants as a way of revealing each person's unique strengths sequence.[14] A special application, *Strengths-Based Leadership*, helps participants understand the distribution of their strengths along four domains of leadership — executing, influencing, relationship building, and strategic thinking.

- *DISC Personality Test* — DISC is one of the most popular tools for understanding self and others, used by over 40 million people worldwide. It is a *behavioral styles* profile that helps people understand themselves, enhance good relationships, improve strained relationships, build teams, increase work effectiveness, and refine leadership skills. It is simple, understandable, and non-technical, yet as accurate as many of the more complex learning instruments. The extensive research on DISC Profile highlights four behavioral preferences and describes how these shape what we contribute to and need from our relationships. The four DISC personality styles are:

  D — Dominant, determined, decisive doers
  I — Influencing, inspiring, interactive initiators
  S — Steady, stable, submissive servants
  C — Conscientious, cautious, competent coordinators

  DISC consists of 24 questions that measure where a person appears on the high-average-low scale for each of these styles. DISC does not peg or fix one into a particular type. It simply describes one's current pattern, ex-

---

[13] See the full list and description at http://www.strengthstest.com/strengths-finder-themes.
[14] See http://strengths.gallup.com.

plains the most common behaviors associated with that pattern, increases understanding of those with different orientations, and provides a basis for adjustments and changes that may improve relationships. See the extensive resources at DISCPersonalitySource.com.

- *Grip-Birkman* is a comprehensive behavioral *and* spiritual gifts assessment looking at three primary questions: *Where am I strong? Where am I weak?* and *Who do I need?* This in-depth tool provides insight into how one's natural behavior interacts with the supernatural empowerment of God. The focus of this assessment is how one can powerfully play their God-designed role in the Body of Christ most effectively. Grip-Birkman gives the opportunity to separate the natural behaviors (the Birkman Method®) from the supernatural or Spiritual Gifts (Your Leadership Grip). It also helps people hone in on their primary three or four spiritual gifts. Trained Grip-Birkman coaches enable people to go deeper in understanding who they are naturally from birth and how they are powerfully gifted. They also help participants move from "I to We," going from individualized priorities into meaningful community, or body life.[15]

It is tempting to regard Grip-Birkman as a combination profile that replaces the need for spiritual gifts inventories, natural strengths profiles, and behavioral styles assessments. A healthier perspective is that it helps one to understand the relationship between each of these dimensions, but does not replace the importance of focused attention on each component, which can at times be achieved more effectively by unique, targeted tools such

---

[15] This description comes directly from the Grip-Birkman website, http://www.gripbirkman.com/grip-birkman-introduction.

as StrengthsFinder 2.0 and DISC. Yet, its comprehensiveness is partially why Grip-Birkman is the preferred model of HOPE Network Ministries.

- *APEST*—Alan Hirsch has developed a team-building model based on the description in Ephesians 4:11-16—Apostles, Prophets, Evangelists, Shepherds, and Teachers. This model is detailed in a section of Alan Hirsch's *The Forgotten Ways,* and on the APEST website, which also includes a helpful profile.[16] Hirsch's model assumes each function is a kind of missional orientation, not necessarily an office of leadership, and that each person uses their gifts in the direction of one or more of these orientations. There are other ways APEST is understood, which are described below. Regardless of how one understands APEST, the idea is that since Paul describes these functions as the *very* mechanism for achieving ministry effectiveness and Christian maturity, we should strive to understand and benefit from each function.

Each of these is helpful in highlighting different aspects of individual and team capabilities—spiritual gifts, natural strengths, behavioral styles, and missional orientation.

Among Churches of Christ, of the five methods mentioned above, the one that has least familiarity is APEST. The current discussions usually refer to Alan Hirsch's description of the APEST functions.

---

[16] For a more complete description, see Alan Hirsch's website, http://www.theforgottenways.org/apest, and the booklet, http://www.theforgottenways.org/uploads/what-is-apest-sidebar_7_0_1.pdf. See also J. R. Woodward, *Creating a Missional Culture: Equipping the Church for the Sake of the World.* IVP Books, 2012; and J. R. Briggs and Bob Hyatt, *Eldership and the Mission of God: Equipping Teams for Faithful Church Leadership.* IVP Books, 2015.

- **Apostles** extend the gospel — As the "sent ones," they ensure that the faith is transmitted from one context to another and from one generation to the next. They are always thinking about the future, bridging barriers, establishing the church in new contexts, developing leaders, networking trans-locally.
- **Prophets** know God's will — They are particularly attuned to God and his truth for today. They bring correction and challenge the dominant assumptions we inherit from the culture. They insist that the community obey what God has commanded. They question the status quo.
- **Evangelists** recruit — These infectious communicators of the gospel message recruit others to the cause. They call for a personal response to God's redemption in Christ, and also draw believers to engage the wider mission, growing the church.
- **Shepherds** nurture and protect — Caregivers of the community, they focus on the protection and spiritual maturity of God's flock, cultivating a loving and spiritually mature network of relationships, making and developing disciples.
- **Teachers** understand and explain — Communicators of God's truth and wisdom, they help others remain biblically grounded to better discern God's will, guiding others toward wisdom, helping the community remain faithful to Christ's word, and constructing a transferable doctrine.[17]

As one might expect, there is debate about whether scripture intended for these functions to operate beyond the era of the early church. There are also questions about whether the roles as

---

[17] From Alan Hirsch, http://www.theforgottenways.org/apest.

reconceived by Hirsch and other current authors are congruent with the biblical record. Others side-step the controversy by insisting that the "five equippers" may not be gifts primarily, but ministry orientations that guide the exercise of gifts, that the body of Christ as a whole should use their collective gifts in ways that fulfill the apostolic, prophetic, evangelistic, shepherdly, and teaching functions of the church.

Each of these interpretations has merit, but a careful reading of text and history suggests caution.[18] For example, the few textual references to apostles point primarily to the Twelve, with minimal application to others (Acts 14:14, Rom. 16:7, Gal. 1:19). Also, neither Scripture nor early Christian history suggest the recognized presence of apostles beyond the initial founding of Christianity. Regarding evangelists, there are only two references (Acts 21:28; 2 Tim. 4:5). The shepherding function is interchangeably linked to the elders/bishops (cf. Acts 20:28; 1 Peter 5:1-4). Also, the most thorough discussion of congregational leadership in scripture, the Pastoral Letters, speaks most clearly about the role of the evangelist (namely Timothy and Titus), then bishops/elders and deacons. Of all the five functions of Ephesians 4:11, only one, evangelist, has anything that approximates role clarity from the Pastorals. There is relative silence on how to define apostles, prophets, and teachers.

The common thread in the New Testament regarding all of these designations, however, is that each has something to do with the ministry of the Word. This seems to be Paul's main concern in Ephesians 4:11, that the work of each APEST role is that the church not be "tossed to and fro by the waves and carried about

---

[18] Gleaned considerably from Ty Grigg, "APEST: Not So Fast!: A Pushback on APEST as a Model for Church Leadership," in *Missio Alliance*, http://www.missioalliance.org/apest-not-so-fast-a-pushback-on-apest-as-a-model-for-church-leadership-by-ty-grigg.

by every wind of doctrine" (4:14). This could explain why the terms are interchangeable in the New Testament. Paul was an *apostle* (as in all 13 epistles), *prophet* (Acts 13:1-2; 1 Cor. 13:2), and *teacher* (1 Tim. 2:7), and there is no question that he both *evangelized* the lost and *shepherded* the saved. Timothy is told to *teach* sound doctrine in his work as an *evangelist* (2 Tim. 4:1-5).

Perhaps this suggests that leaders must fulfill, or at least respectfully uphold, all functions — apostle, prophet, evangelist, shepherd-teacher. Together they are part of the Word-oriented authoritative leadership of the church.

> Each role listed in Ephesians 4:11 implies the exercise of leadership and spiritual authority recognized by the community of believers. For example, the metaphor of **shepherd** was applied to kings in the Ancient Near East. A first-century reader would likely hear the term "shepherd" as a reference to a community leader, not just as a caring orientation. The role of **apostle** implies a commissioning (a sending) by Jesus or a community of Jesus. A **teacher** implies authority in relationship to students . . . The most natural reading of the text points to these people as ones recognized as having spiritual leadership and authority in the church — not as intrinsic *orientations* that each believer develops.[19]

Understood this way, each of the five functions is an important nuance of the leadership of the church, which when combined with the others, leads the church into missional maturity. It is hard to escape the importance Paul placed on each. Perhaps the loss, even active suppression, of these crucial dimensions of New Testament leadership partially explains the church's immaturity

---

[19] Ibid

and ineffectiveness (i.e., "tossed about . . . immature . . . infantile," Eph. 4). The function of evangelism has been marginalized and made itinerant rather than localized, while the function of prophecy and apostleship are ignored altogether. It is rare to find these currencies in local church leadership. Instead, they are found more commonly in roles such as consulting or parachurch ministry.

Generally, our churches have migrated toward the shepherd-teachers, which forces them to bear the entire burden of leadership without the benefit of the others. Also, given their orientation, shepherd-teacher types develop churches where care and instruction are abundant, but apostolic expansion, prophetic clarity, and evangelistic fruit are scarce. The result is churches that value empathy and consensus above the challenge of mission.

Briggs and Hyatt describe in more detail what happens when one function is emphasized at the expense of others:

- Churches led by strong *teachers* tend to be intellectual, knowledge-based communities where doctrine is of utmost importance. In these communities, spirituality can easily be equated with Scripture study and knowledge.
- Churches led by strong *pastoral/shepherding* types tend to do well at loving each other and caring for the needs of the body. In these communities, spirituality is equated with love and the "one-anothers" of the New Testament.
- Churches with strong *prophetic* voices tend to speak truth to power and do well at justice-oriented ministry. In these churches, spirituality is equated with care for the poor, the marginalized, and the outsider.
- Churches led by *evangelists* tend to be characterized by a heart for those who don't know Jesus and a strong em-

phasis on evangelism. In these churches, spirituality is equated with a heart for the lost and telling others about Jesus.

- Churches with a strong *apostolic* ethos tend to break new ground, constantly pushing the bounds of creativity in ministry and forging ahead into new territory as a church. In these communities, spirituality tends to be experienced as something new every other month.[20]

A better way to envision church leadership is to "make room for all of these foundational gifts on elder and leadership teams. In this way we provide a well-rounded team that is set free to equip an increasingly well-rounded church." [21] The church benefits from a leadership team where "all the concerns brought by a balanced, mutually submissive group of apostles, evangelists, prophets, shepherds and teachers are considered and factored into the life of the community."[22]

Hirsh encourages faith communities to use tools such as the APEST profile and the mPULSE assessment to discover and affirm each team member's contribution to missional movement in their settings. Even if a church does not have representation of each APEST currency in their local contexts, they should glean from outside resources to achieve a more full-dimensional ministry.

> *One of the most common reasons leadership teams falter is that they do not capture the capacity God gives people through spiritual gifts, natural strengths, behavioral styles, and APEST missional leadership functions.*

---

[20] Briggs and Hyatt, *Eldership and the Mission of God*, Kindle Locations 1407-1416.
[21] Ibid., Kindle Locations 1401-1406.
[22] Ibid., Kindle Locations 1417-1419.

To summarize this section, one of the most common reasons leadership teams falter is that they do not capture the capacity God gives people through spiritual gifts, natural strengths, behavioral styles, and APEST missional leadership functions. Leaders may not appreciate the distribution of abilities on their team and simply alternate assignments, forcing leaders into roles they are not suited for and disallowing those with strong inclinations to emerge. Many leaders have never known the thrill of being used by God for what they were created to do. An empowering team culture helps people discern their gifts and then, insofar as possible, arranges team efforts to capitalize on the distribution of those gifts.

Empowering Philosophy

A third dimension of missional church governance is to adopt an empowering perspective. Difficulties on leadership teams often stem from members operating from different paradigms. Among most Churches of Christ, it is often the difference between the hierarchical/controlling and empowering approaches.

> *Many leaders have never known the thrill of being used by God for what they were created to do.*

The Power of Leadership Belief Systems
All leadership teams operate from a philosophy, or belief system, whether consciously or unconsciously. This is not the same as the "core beliefs" of a congregation that may appear in a faith statement. Instead, leadership belief systems are the widely shared understandings of how the leaders interact with each other and with others in the congregation. These are the deeply held, often unconscious assumptions that powerfully motivate leadership behavior. These may not be obvious, and are seldom

written. Even if written, there could still be a powerful under-current of informal, tacit rules.

For example, when considering working for a university, I sat with the dean of the faculty and asked "What is your philosophy of leading faculty?" Without hesitation, he said, "I hire faculty who do not need supervision, and I get out of their way to let them do their jobs effectively. I am their chief advocate on the administrative cabinet, and I do all I can to say 'yes' to provide the resources they need. There are clear standards, and I lay them out on at the beginning. Every class you teach will be evaluated both by both students and peers, and there is an extensive assessment report at the end of each academic year. I involve the faculty at every level of decision-making regarding the curriculum and instructive policies of the school." He articulated a belief system of *accountable, empowering partnership*.

By contrast, consider a church worship ministry that has planned several changes for the assemblies. They met with the elders extensively over a long period and gained complete approval. One of the elders seemed half-hearted in his support, but he never raised questions and gave an approving vote in the meetings. He was not able to attend the last pre-launch meeting the Wednesday before the Sunday the changes were to begin, but he was the only elder in attendance on the commencement Sunday. The deacon in charge came to this elder a few minutes before services to explain a slight change that was congruent with what had been approved, but differed in a few minor details. The changes were largely out of his control, and were actually an adjustment due to media issues. The elder saw this as an opportunity to voice his pent-up opposition. He quickly shut down the commencement of the new worship initiatives by saying, "You are not to make these changes today, and if you do, I will see to it that you are removed as a deacon for insubordination." The deacon implored, "I don't understand. You have been in these meetings all along where we gained approval, and you even cast a supportive vote. The changes are completely in line with what we proposed, but I just did not want you to be surprised." The elder shook his finger in the deacon's face and said, "Young man, I am an elder in this church, and when an elder tells you do something or to stop doing something, you do it, no questions asked. Do you understand me?" The elder's reaction is an example of a *controlling, authoritarian* belief system.

Another example is an elder who is a high-ranking executive in a local firm, and is the "go-to" elder for the new youth minister. Before this elder was appointed, the previous elders, the ministry staff, and the deacons/ministry coordinators had been through an extensive development plan to shift into a more empowering model of ministry. The newer youth elder was not a part of that effort, and carried into his new role a more hierarchical understanding of the relationship between the elders and the ministers. In one instance, the elder and youth minister disagreed on a policy issue. The youth minister preferred a course of action based on his experience with youth and parents, while the elder had his own preference. To break the impasse, the elder said, "I really don't see why we're having this conversation. You are younger than my son, and I have over twenty-five years of executive experience with hundreds of employees under me. This is the way it's going to be, end of discussion." While there were indeed problems in the youth minister's behavior which may have required clear lines of authority, the elder followed a path toward submission that while efficient, was largely ineffective. He also conveyed a *paternalistic* belief system about his role in relation to the youth minister.

Leadership belief systems are the default mental models behind all decisions. They are usually deeply ingrained, and are more

influential than any ministry structure. Changing these philosophies, even with very intentional effort, takes at least seven years
before they are fully integrated into the congregational culture.

Contrast Between Two Leadership Belief Systems

Many Churches of Christ operate from a hierarchical/controlling
belief system, and there is usually a healthy desire, especially
among members, to shift to a more empowering model. Below is
a comparison of the two systems.

	Hierarchical/ Controlling Belief System	Empowering Belief System
Prime Directive	"Lead first" through the exercise of structural authority. Heb. 13:17; 1 Tim. 3:4-5	"Serve first" through sacrificial devotion to the growth of others. Matt. 20:24-28; 1 Peter 5:1-4; Eph. 4:11-16
Primary Metaphor	Monarchy, elders as official executors of the law of Christ[23]	Under-shepherd, servant leader, spiritual director

---

[23] An extensive study of literature in the Churches of Christ revealed "the
model for church polity most often invoked is that of the monarchy. It can be
outlined in these terms: The king (God) has communicated those laws (N.T.) to
the king's subjects (Christians). Duly appointed officers (elders) within each
community, have now been assigned the responsibility of governing their
community according to the laws of the king. They wield authority, because
they represent the king as the executors of his laws; yet they cannot be
authoritarian, because they are also his subjects." - Timothy Willis, "'Obey
Your Leaders': Hebrews 13 and Leadership in the Church," Restoration
Quarterly, 36 no 4 (1994): 317. Willis references writings by numerous authors
in the Church of Christ dating from 1950-1978 in publications such as Gospel
Advocate, Firm Foundation, and other separately titled volumes. This belief is
sometimes echoed when members encourage each other to agree with an
unpopular elder decision by saying, "Well, you know the church is not a
democracy!" While they rarely articulate what the church actually is over
against a democracy, what they mean is that the church is Christ's monarchy,
and elders, as executors of the laws of the king, have authority to make
decisions and expect full compliance.

Type of Authority	Positional, legal-rational, autocratic	Relational, moral, wisdom figure, sage
Use of Power	Leaders possess power over others to control and limit their capacity to act apart from permission.	Power belongs to God and leaders share power with and for others to liberate and expand others' opportunities to use themselves in service of a shared sense of purpose.
Scope of Authority	All-encompassing; autocratic; absolute except when in violation of scripture; a tendency to frequent micro-managing directives from elders	Situational; shared, decision-making entrusted to the ones doing the ministry; infrequent, maturational directives from elders
Method of Organization	Bureaucracy, layers of delegated authority diminishing from top down, slow, controlling	Partnership, each one a minister covenanting with others on ministry teams; lean, quick, permission-giving
Philosophy of Management	Paternalism, "The elders always know what is best and will take care of us," members answer to the elders, there are many things only the elders should know.	Stewardship, entrusting leadership to those who show capability of self-direction, trust-building, and accountability.
Method of Decision-Making	Leaders make decisions *for* others so as to keep them from having to deal with the tough issues and to ensure safe outcomes.	Leaders involve others in making macro-decisions about shared beliefs, purpose, and vision and then mentor and equip others to increasingly make their own choices in the micro-operation of ministry efforts.

Philosophy of Ministry	Members dutifully fulfill assigned responsibilities for the ongoing of the church's functions according to well-defined roles within safe parameters.	Ministry partners are liberated and equipped to confidently employ gifts in unity with others to fulfill a shared vision, taking risks in order to make the most meaningful differ-ence.
View of People	Caution and guardedness – people will get things done only with careful monitoring, tasks are assigned to those who have proven loyal to the elders and will govern themselves to bring safe results.	Trust and hopefulness – people are responsible, trustworthy, creative, resourceful, valuable, gifts from God who are endowed by the Holy Spirit.
Provision of Ministry Training	People learn as they go. Trial and error based on participants' intuition and current exposure to ministry models. Budget only for the local completion of ministry tasks.	Leaders budget for and provide exposure to new ideas and resources to increase the church's competence, confidence and creativity.
Role of Elders	Make decisions, manage the affairs of the church, maintain order and harmony, take care of subordinates, protect the flock	Mentor, teach, equip, nurture, be an example, seek Christ's vision for the church
Role of Members	Submit to positional authority of elders, obey, operate only within boundaries of specific approval	Priesthood, called into incarnational ministry according to gifts and calling, compelled by the church's kingdom vision, guided by elders' teaching and example.

		Model servants with spiritual qualities to guide ministries, governed by the church's vision, guided by elders/ministers teaching and example, and held accountable by empowering ministry structures.
Role of Deacons	Administrate areas of church work to lighten the load for elder-management, minimal delegated authority	
Role of Paid Ministry Staff	Employees of the church, internally focused chaplain/administrators, supervised by the elders, no clear place in the hierarchical system	Trusted, accountable co-laborers of the elders, deacons, and each other; empowered to lead members into externally focused ministry that fulfills the church's vision

Dr. Carlus Gupton, 2016

An In-Depth Critique of the Hierarchical Model

1. The hierarchical belief system is often well-intended, but self-defeating.

This is illustrated by an elder I worked with for several years who was a retired military captain and insurance executive. He was an honorable man and sacrificially devoted to the welfare of the church. He had excellent administrative skills, but had a controlling philosophy and practice. He was committed to Christ from the depth of his soul, and was among the few I had witnessed shedding genuine tears over "the wayward." Because I was his preacher, he loved me like a son, and was very generous and supportive. Given the strength of both of our personalities, there were occasional clashes, enough that his wife often chastised him for being too hard on me. Of course, I was not alone in my struggles with his autocratic style. In one conversation, I asked him respectfully, "Can you help me understand why you exercise such tight control over church affairs?" Tears welled up as he said, "I worry every day that the lackadaisical faith of so many in the church will mean they are lost eternally. And I will have to give an account for that. I am determined no one under my watch will lose their soul." While one might argue that he needed a healthier theology of discipleship and of his role, it is easy to see how if one believes like him, the stakes are high for elders and those under them. His autocratic style was well-motivated. He was fulfilling his duty to God and his brothers and sisters in Christ, and he would never shirk his duty. He guarded their souls with every ounce of his being.

2. The hierarchical belief system inevitably results in the misuse of power.

There are at least three definitions of power:

1. The ability to limit others' capacity to act apart from us.
2. The ability to influence outcomes through one's *positional* authority.
3. The ability to set others free to use their gifts.

There are subtle temptations associated with the first two, and it is rare for persons who possess power to resist it. This is why Jesus and the apostles warned against any understanding of spiritual leadership that depends fundamentally on the exercise of positional authority (Matt. 20:24-28; 1 Peter 5:1-4).

Jeffrey Jones interacts with Parker Palmer's reflections on Jesus' wilderness temptations (Lk. 4:1-15) regarding the subtle temptations of power.

The power leaders hold in congregations is God's power, to be used for God's purposes. "Power and glory are not the devil's (or anyone else's) to give. They belong to God alone, and only through God can we share in them."

We must guard against the illusion that power does not corrupt—that it is a neutral force that can be used for good or ill depending on the moral fiber of the user: "Power . . . has a life of its own. Once we have seized it, it seizes us, and wrestling ourselves from its grip requires superhuman effort. If power over things seems at first like a tool, those who hold it may soon become tools wrapped in power's own strong hand."

> "Power... has a life of its own. Once we have seized it, it seizes us..."
> – Parker Palmer

Recognizing the inherent corrupting nature of all power, our aim as leaders is always to share power as broadly as possible—to give it away as much as possible and sometimes simply refuse to use it. WE DO NOT EMPOWER OTHERS. ONLY GOD EMPOWERS. For us, empowering others involves creating the setting in which they can draw upon God's power to accomplish God's purposes.[24]

3. *The hierarchical belief system is biblically and theologically unhealthy (overemphasizes positional authority).*

In Heb. 13:17, the designation of "leaders" is not limited to elders, and contextually includes those who "spoke the word"

---

[24] Adaptation of Parker Palmer, *The Active Life: A Spirituality of Work, Creativity and Caring* (Jossey-Bass, 1990): 109-111, from Jeffrey Jones, *Heart, Mind and Strength: Theory and Practice for Congregational Leadership* (Rowman and Littlefield Publishers, 2008), 118.

(13:7).[25] Also, the verb translated "obey" is from a root (Gk. *peitho*) meaning to be persuaded or convinced, to take the advice of, to trust. Some argue convincingly that *peitho* in this instance connotes a response to verbal argumentation to sway opinion, pointing to such use of the word in over 40 occurrences in the N.T. This would have the emphasis on being persuaded by leaders, with the rationale for "yielding" to the leaders being their responsibility toward God, not their position of authority. Others challenge this interpretation, pointing out that when this word appears in the grammatical construction such as we find in Heb. 13:17, it is always translated "obey or follow."[26] The ambiguity partially explains the variance in translations. The older version of the NIV (1984) says, "obey your leaders and submit to their authority," whereas the new NIV (2011) says, "have confidence in your leaders and submit to them."

The argument over translation is actually moot with regard to the function of leaders when one understands the type of leadership and influence that is underscored in this passage. The attitude the members should have toward their leaders is compared to their attitude toward past leaders mentioned in 13: 7. The readers are reminded of their earlier leaders' "way of life and their faith." It is the person — not the office — of those leaders that is emphasized. Moreover, the primary focus is what those leaders taught. They are identified as "those who spoke the word of God to you"; the "outcome" of their lives and their "faith" was a reflection of what they taught. Willis observes that

---

[25] See the excellent word study of the various terms regarding leadership in the New Testament by Lynn Anderson, *They Smell Like Sheep* (Howard Publishing, 2002), 187-204.

[26] When *peitho* is followed by a noun referring to a person or a thing in the dative case it is translated "obey or follow" (Bauer, Arndt and Gingrich, *A Greek-English Lexicon of the New Testament*, p. 639; cf. Abbott-Smith, *Manual Greek Lexicon of the New Testament*.). Along with Heb. 13:17, this construction occurs in Rom. 2:8, Gal. 5:7, James 3:3, where it is difficult to understand the term in any sense other than obey.

the main concern of the writer is the possibility of apostasy; and the primary means for the leaders to combat the apostate teachers is not by appealing to any structural authority they derive from their offices, but by their power of persuasion.[27] Lynn Anderson refers to this as "moral suasion."[28]

Neither this passage nor any other would uphold an anarchic fellowship where persons go against their leaders and do whatever they wish, claiming they "have failed to convince us" (i.e., have not been persuasive). For members to demand "moral suasion" as an excuse for remaining stubborn until convinced is not the point of this passage. But neither is blind submission to positional authority. The idea is for leaders to live and teach in such a way that the church can follow without obstacles regarding their integrity, and for followers to maintain a cooperative spirit. It is a misuse of the text to uphold either a hierarchical dominance among leaders or chronic resistance (whether active or passive) among members.

Also, "the words expressive of such authority are absent from all New Testament texts about elders. They do not have controlling authority (Gk. *exousia*), power (Gk., *dunamis*); their position is not that of master (Gk., *despotes*) or ruling official (Gk., *archon*)."[29] If the writers were wanting to emphasize positional authority, they had several clearer terms at their disposal.

There is also a clear NT witness against spiritual leadership that depends upon the exercise of positional authority in Matt. 20:24-28 and 1 Peter 5:1-4. This is not to suggest that the scriptures do

---

[27] Willis, "Obey Your Leaders," 322-323.
[28] Anderson, *They Smell Like Sheep*, 207ff.
[29] See the discussion of N.T. texts such as Heb. 13:17; 1 Thess. 5:12; 1 Tim. 5:17; and 3:4-5, 12 in Jack Lewis, *Leadership Questions Confronting the Church* (Gospel Advocate, 1985), 9-12. See also Everett Ferguson, "Authority and Tenure of Elders," *Restoration Quarterly*, 145-147.

not grant elders positional authority, but that it denounces this as the foundation for understanding and practicing the role.

4. The hierarchical belief system is developmentally restrictive.

This is one of the most obvious weaknesses with the hierarchical model of leadership. It keeps the congregation in a perpetual state of immaturity. Leadership styles must be situational, being only as directive as is necessary in early stages of development, but increasingly more trusting as the maturity and capability of those being led increases.

5. The hierarchical belief system may seem more efficient, but is much less effective.

It may seem more efficient to simply make board-like decisions and gain compliance, but leaders must engage the hard tasks of helping others learn and develop by finding their own way through the opportunities and challenges of life and ministry. This may even mean allowing people to experiment and make mistakes. It may be that as people struggle with the issues inherent in ministry leadership, they come up with much better solutions than elders who are less directly involved.

The controlling model is often tidier, and the empowering model is "messier." Empowering requires more patience and suffering love. Elders who are highly results-oriented, or have low frustration tolerance, or who are accustomed to handling corporate issues in environments that are time- and profit-constrained, or who prefer their "reports" be very compliant and submissive, etc., may struggle with this. They may simply make decisions for others because they seem to need or want it, or because they do not trust others to operate on their own, or because it is easier and less cumbersome to just tell others what to do. They may even push their fellow elders into "getting on with it," when more time is needed to help others along.

Facilitating growth in ministry maturity usually requires an environment that allows all involved to feel three types of satisfaction:

- Personal — they feel valued as capable human beings. They feel others have heard them and taken their feelings and needs into account.
- Process — they see that the processes followed are responsible, productive, and fair, involving all who have a stake in the outcomes.
- Product — they see an end result that forwards the mission and is good for everyone impacted.

Hierarchical/controlling types tend to jump to "product" satisfaction and short-change the other two.

6. The hierarchical belief system creates a we-they dichotomy.

Ian Fair discusses another aspect of ineffectiveness for the controlling model:

> [Controlling] leadership has the tendency to create a love-hate dichotomy among followers. Some, with a definite need for structure and control in their lives, join a congregation because of its strong directive leadership. Others, with a strong self-image and resentment to external structure and intrusion, leave because of the frustration that can be created by what they perceive to be the excessive control of directive leadership.

Excessive use of a directive or authoritarian leadership style can result in organizational frustration, resentment, lethargy, and a "we-they" mindset that deprives the congregation of much of the vitality and giftedness of its workers. This should not be interpreted to mean that there is never a place for directive leadership style. It simply means that leaders should be extremely circumspect in their decision to employ it.[30]

7. The hierarchical belief system is culturally obsolete.

Leadership *style* is affected by: 1) political, philosophical, and socio-economic concerns; and 2) the circumstances and maturity of the congregation; i.e., it must be determined by the shifting conditions where leadership is taking place.[31] In that respect, two cultural conditions mark the obsolescence of the controlling model.[32]

- *Distrust of those in power* — Americans no longer believe they can trust their leaders, and are demanding greater accountability on the part of all leaders, from presidents to pastors. The research of Robert Webber among younger evangelicals is also instructive. The teens-twenties-thirties of our churches have a very strong aversion to boomer-style corporate leadership models or anything

---

[30] Fair, *Leadership in the Kingdom,* 186-187. There are indeed times when servant leaders must wield strong directive authority. A similar concept is Speed Leas' *compelling* or *forcing* style of conflict management. Leas offers insight on when this style is helpful and how to use it effectively in *Discover Your Conflict Management Style, revised edition* (Alban Institute, 1997), pp. 12-17.
[31] Ibid., 183, reflecting upon the research of organizational psychologist, Edgar Schein.
[32] Shawchuck and Heuser, *Managing the Congregation: Building Effective Systems to Serve the People* (Abingdon Press, 1985), 167-168.

that smacks of *top-down mentality.*[33]

• *Rapid change and increasing complexity* have created conditions that bureaucracy simply cannot control. In an environment of rapid change, churches must structure themselves to become lean, flexible, courageous, and quick.

Challenges in Aiming Toward Empowerment

While empowerment is preferred over hierarchical control, the shift to empowerment is usually fraught with difficulties. Below are some of the more common struggles.

1. The desire for empowerment may be an overreaction to control that "swings the pendulum from one extreme to another, continuing the dichotomy between servant and directive leadership. They are not opposites." [34]

2. The campaign for empowerment may be a manipulative effort to shift the balance of power, where some insist that the elders have less power in order to give someone else more power.

3. Empowerment may be part of a "spiritualistic" overcorrection to cumbersome structures, disparaging models and structures in the interest of "just trusting God and being led by the Spirit." A popular perspective in some churches is the idea that order and structure stifle the Spirit (as if the Spirit does not himself bring order out of chaos). It may be that "empowerment" is set forth out of disdain for order and accountability in the interest of just letting everyone do as they please. Neither extreme is

---

[33] See "Pastors: From Power to Servanthood," in Webber, *The Younger Evangelicals*, 147-153.

[34] Alan Roxburgh, *The Missionary Congregation, Leadership, and Liminality* (Trinity Press, 1997), 63.

healthy, but the spiritualistic not only violates the stewardship dimension of empowerment, but also misunderstands the role of the Spirit.

4. Empowerment may over-shift into the extreme of disengagement. Not uncommonly, leaders who attempt this shift may swing to varying levels of administrative neglect or overly-permissive, laissez-faire extremes that are disengaged from the responsibilities of oversight.

5. Participants may lack the responsibility to steward their roles as partners. The freedom of empowerment includes the accountability of each person for the success or failure of the congregation's efforts. If members lack a commitment to discipleship, or fall back on the elders when things become too difficult, or act in ways that violate trust, it is hard for empowerment to gain traction.

6. Facilitating a shift of this magnitude is long-term and complex. This is not merely an adjustment to the status-quo, it is a major redevelopment of the entire congregation. While a congregation may experience some positive benefits soon into the change, the complete embedding of empowerment into a congregational system take years, not months. The research of John P. Kotter reveals that anchoring deep and lasting change into an organizational culture is rarely accomplished in less than seven years. It simply takes that long for an organization of any kind to fully let go of old attitudes and patterns of behavior, and have the new ones permeate the system and anchor themselves. There is no short-cut. Change takes time. You know when you are there when the day comes that

the minister and key appointed leaders can be replaced without the system reverting to what it was.[35]

7. Shifting to empowerment may be plagued by self-sabotage. Both those who want the change and those who do not may derail partnership/stewardship. Leaders should never underestimate the power of homeostasis, i.e., the tendency of organizations to revert to a stable status quo when challenged, even if that status quo is less preferable than the new order implied by the change. Without a well-designed change process, progress will stall and the homeostatic forces will pull the congregation back into old patterns. There are various ways this can happen. Elders may become frustrated with the messiness of helping others grow. Members who are accustomed to elders running the church pressure the elders to "step up and lead." Members may find zones of resistance to the congregational direction within the eldership and try to manipulate an elder(s) into pushing for a certain agenda. Newer elders who have not been a part of a change to an empowerment model bring in the traditional hierarchical understanding and damage the effectiveness of the team.

Among Churches of Christ, there are two special concerns in the transition to an empowering belief system.

Structures that Facilitate Empowerment
In the empowering belief system, governance and order are secured primarily through the shared sense of congregational purpose — the identity, mission, values, and vision. The elders bring the congregation into a process to define and embed a

---

[35] Mary K. Sellon, Daniel P. Smith, and Gail Grossman, *Redeveloping the Congregation: A How To For Lasting Change* (Alban Institute, 2002), xiv.

strong sense of purpose into the congregational culture. This purpose forms the basis for how all aspects of congregational life will operate and be evaluated. This raises the question, however, of how leaders structure their relationships to steward the church's mission.

One form of empowering structure that is quite popular among non-profits is "policy governance," developed by John and Miriam Carver. [36] When policy governance is practiced in churches, the elders devise a written statement of organizational purpose or *policy* (the "ENDS") that guides all of the mission-related decisions and activities of the congregation (the "MEANS"). They devote their energies to devising and continually refining policy/purpose, not necessarily to all the micro-decisions at the various levels of the congregation that may express that policy/purpose, but to the policy/purpose itself. This also tightens the boundary of elder-meeting agendas, as they delegate all decisions that are not policy-related. They work to make sure everything in the congregation expresses the purpose.

Another feature of non-profit policy governance is the relationship between the board and the CEO or staff. In churches, this requires designating one of the staff (usually the preacher) as the "Lead Minister," who oversees the work of the rest of the ministry staff. For this reason, strict plural-elder congregational polities where all elders are equal in authority, such as those by Strauch and Swartley, reject Carver. [37] Carver alone, without modifications, is probably more compatible with plural-elder understandings that welcome a minister who is the primary

---

[36] See a full description and suggested resources on the Carver website, http://www.carvergovernance.com/index.html.
[37] Alexander Strauch, *Biblical Eldership: An Urgent Call to Restore Biblical Church Leadership, Revised and Expanded Edition.* Lewis and Roth Publishers, 1995, 77-78.

leader, such as Gene Getz *Elders and Leaders*,[38] Aubrey Malphurs *Leading Leaders*,[39] and Heuser and Shawchuck *Leading the Congregation*.[40] But with some adaptations, it is probably useful for a variety of congregational-leadership structures.

Les Stahlke has developed a church-friendly adaptation of policy governance, the Relationship Model.[41] Stahlke inserts a more relational feel and broadens the level of involvement and decision-making. The essential difference is that in the Carver Model, the governing board makes policy decisions somewhat unilaterally and then works toward compliance. Stahlke places greater emphasis on affirmation of persons at all levels of the congregation, shared decision-making, and mutual accountability. Stahlke's website lays out the "Ten Principles of Governance, Leadership, and Management in the Relationship Model" [42] which reveal a few differences with the Carver Model. For example:

- Principle #3: Decision-making proceeds from shared values, vision, and mission, not unilaterally from the Board or the Senior Pastor. Decisions are made as close as possible to where they are implemented.
- Principle #4: Circles of authority and responsibility are defined clearly and are maintained equal in size by plac-

---

[38] Gene Getz, *Elders and Leaders: God's Plan for Leading the Church, A Biblical, Historical, and Cultural Perspective*. Moody Publishers, 2003.

[39] Aubrey Malphurs, *Leading Leaders: Empowering Church Boards for Ministry Excellence*. Baker, 2005.

[40] Roger Heuser and Norman Shawchuck, *Leading the Congregation: Caring for Yourself While Serving the People, Revised Edition*. Abingdon Press, 2010, 182-189.

[41] Les Stahlke with Jennifer Loughlin, *Governance Matters: Balancing Client and Staff Fulfillment in Faith-based Not-for-Profit Organizations*. GovernanceMatters.com, 2003. Stalkhe has also written a church-based version, *Church Governance Matters: Relationship Model of Governance*. Governance Matters, 2010.

[42] See http://governancematters.com/ch/relmod/10princ.aspx

ing limits on authority or by negotiating expectations of responsibility.[43]

These features are not inherently negated in Carver's formal expressions, but Carver may play out practically in ways that unintentionally minimize shared decision-making, distributed authority, and mutual accountability. To the extent this is true, Stahlke may be a helpful corrective. According to his website, Stahlke specializes in guarding against the "Seven Deadly Sins" of organizations: sloppy leadership and management, abusive leadership and management, vague strategic direction, unclear roles and responsibilities, unclear expectations, square pegs in round holes, and forgiveness confused with accountability.

Many faith-based non-profits and churches have adopted Stahlke's model. It is recommended by the National Association of Church Business Administration.[44]

To the extent that either Carver or Stahlke are applicable to churches, they focus almost exclusively on congregational oversight, or the *episcopal* function, but not so much on the relational, mentoring, or *shepherding* function. As such, it does not adequately express the full wealth of the elder role, but may help with corporate oversight. Elderships may use either model to streamline the congregational infrastructure and administrative dimensions, giving them more time for relational and spiritual needs of the flock. When used in this way, it may be compatible with the philosophy of shepherding in Lynn Anderson, *They Smell Like Sheep.*

---

[43] See http://www.carvergovernance.com/model.htm
[44] Recently renamed as the Church Network, www.nacba.net.

Empowering Relationships Between Elders and Ministers

When considering empowerment in Churches of Christ, a special consideration is the relationship between elders and ministers, which often suffers from a lack of cooperation. Most ministers, if given a safe environment where they can express their deepest source of frustration, will inevitably come around to their relationship with elders. Elders do not always punctuate the problem to the same degree, and in fact are often surprised to discover that ministers are so dissatisfied. What seems like a "team" relationship to a minister may mean inclusion in all of the meetings and decision-making. But the elders may define team as the elders deliberating by themselves and the minister(s) cooperatively carrying out their wishes, because after all, "We're all on the same team." This is even more difficult when there is a significant age gap between the elders and ministers. Ministers most often want a strong voice in the leadership of the church, but the elders see them much like their own sons or daughters, and have difficulty allowing someone who lacks the wisdom of experience to sit at their table and strongly influence church matters. Elder-minister teams often begin in the honeymoon phase of a new minister's tenure with good intentions, but stall after a few years. They may increasingly separate to where there is no meaningful communication between them.

> *Elders ... are often surprised to discover that ministers are so dissatisfied.*

The problem must be owned by both groups. Since ministers are most often the ones who bring up the issue, the discussions usually center around how elders should change. This is not the whole picture, however. All relational problems are co-causal to some extent. Both ministers and elders must assess their healthy and unhealthy tendencies toward achieving a lasting and productive relationship.

We must also be careful in assuming there is only one way of structuring a healthy relationship between elders and ministers in each setting. There are, however, universal principles:

- The elders and ministers must respect each other's roles, and work intentionally to understand and value each other's perspectives on all matters affecting the church.
- The elders and ministers must find a good stride in the "inhale-exhale" of meeting separately and meeting together in the way that best suits their respective gifts and the needs of the congregation.
- The elders and ministers must behave toward each other in ways that increase mutual respect, and refrain from anything that weakens trust and cooperation.
- The elders and ministers must institute checkpoints where each can express openly to the other, without fear of recrimination, how the relationship can be improved.
- The elders and ministers must refrain from concepts such as rank and superiority on either end, but strive to regard each other as fellow-servants.

There are a number of legitimate ways of securing these larger interests. Some leadership teams operate with little distinction between the groups. While there is the realization that a difference exists, they see their work as more alike than different, and thus lead together. Others want the minister to lead, adopting the academic model of *primus inter pares,* or the "first among equals" for the lead minister, allowing him to define the vision and lead congregational matters under the elders' advisement.

Conclusion and Exercise

As leadership teams seek to activate the principles of mission alignment, affirming of roles and gifts, and empowering belief systems, the key is for all members of the leadership team to communicate well and frequently to arrive at shared understanding. An exercise that helps is to construct a philosophy of missional church governance. Begin by gathering a discussion of the entire leadership team, including elders, ministers, deacons, and others. Ask each member of the group to either pre-read this chapter in preparation for the event, or have someone make a presentation of the material in the chapter. Using the principles of the chapter as a basis for discussion, engage the group in candid conversations, using questions like the ones below.

- When I consider the information from this reading/presentation, it has brought to mind these positive and productive behaviors among members of our leadership team . . .
- When I consider the information from this reading/presentation, it has brought to mind these negative or unproductive behaviors among members of our leadership team . . .
- The things that enhance our working relationship the most, and which I want to always characterize our work are...
- The things that weaken our working relationship the most, and which I would rather not characterize our work are...

In these exercises, the more specific all participants can be, the better. After the discussions, synthesize the composite perspectives into an expression of church governance similar to the examples that were presented at a recent conference.[45] It may

[45] This is listed with other tools at http://www.acu.edu/siburt-institute-for-church-ministry/resources/ministry-tools.html, and the direct link to the document is
http://www.acu.edu/content/dam/acu/website/Siburt%20Institute/Documents/Resources/Church%20Governance.pdf.

help to appoint a sub-committee or task force to construct a draft statement and then bring it back to the larger group for refinement and ratification.

Of course, constructing such a statement is only the beginning. For it to be embedded into the congregational culture, refer back to the discussion of Edgar Schein's primary culture embedding mechanisms. With consistent practice, the congregation can be blessed exponentially with missional efforts that allow the church to be a sign, foretaste, and instrument of the kingdom of God.

LEADING BY CONSENSUS

Evertt W. Huffard

*Love is patient; love is kind; love is not envious or boastful or arrogant
or rude. It does not insist on its own way; it is not irritable or resentful,
it does not rejoice in wrongdoing, but rejoices in the truth. It bears all
things, believes all things, hopes all things, endures all things.
Love never ends...Let all things be done for building up.
1 Cor. 13:4-8; 14:26 (ESV)*

*...making known to us the mystery of his will...which he set forth in
Christ as a plan for the fullness of time, to unite all things in him,
things in heaven and things on earth. Eph. 1:10 (ESV)*

Autonomous congregations in the USA enjoy the freedom of
choice—as in the choice of leaders, location, doctrine, ministries,
purpose, finances, staff, and worship styles. Church members
select leaders from among themselves who they expect to
manage the business of the church with integrity and wisdom.
They assume that the leaders will keep the peace and guard the

unity of the congregation (understood by some as pleasing everyone). These leaders often lack any training or orientation to equip them to lead. Their appointment process focuses on the qualifications to be an elder rather than on developing competencies for mentoring, communication, conflict management, delegation, or teaching.

When the speed of change outstrips the adaptability of the leaders to respond well, the size and complexity of the church exceeds the resources of the elders, and multiple generations stretch the unity of the church, leaders get locked into a crisis-management style of leadership. The ideal of unity gets lost in the reality that strongly expressed opinions leave little room for dialog, for learning from each other, for reasoning together — for consensus. Definitions of consensus include terms like unity, harmony, solidarity, and agreement — the very thing we all want in our church and among the leaders. Human history and church history illustrate the reasons many will give up hope on consensus before they ever get started. It will not develop without an intentional commitment to unity and a lot of hard work.

If I were to list the priorities of the role of shepherds in the church, my list would look something like this:

1. To care for the spiritual condition of every disciple of Christ;
2. To empower, equip, and mentor disciples to fulfill God's mission;
3. To discern God's mission (purpose, direction, goals) for the church — then empower leaders (deacons, preachers, ministry team) and allocate resources to fulfill that mission.

The first two priorities are more relational/spiritual—the third one is a bit more task/spiritual.[1] The popular notion that elders primarily make decisions for the church has always frustrated me. So, for me to write a chapter in this book on how elders make decisions (#3) rather than on shepherding (#1 and #2) challenges my own preferences. However, because I have been burdened by the painful consequences of the failed execution of change in churches and I seem to have some gifts of administration, I am willing to let the Spirit lead me to give more thought to this and take me where I may not want to go.

Actually, the three priorities involve a lot of decisions. The first one involves discernment of the individual needs of a diverse group of believers and the best way to nurture their faith. The second priority involves decisions on how to match the spiritual gifts of a believer to specific roles or ministry opportunities. These first two focus on the individual in contrast to the focus on the corporate, collective, organizational aspects of the church. As I reflect on my experiences as an elder for ten years in a large church, it disturbed me that the *third priority consumed so much energy that I never felt I was doing what shepherds should be doing.* I knew I was not alone when other elders expressed the same frustration about spending most of their time "putting out fires" and never getting to the heart of what they thought they should be doing as shepherds.

The natural response to this problem would be to streamline the elders meetings to get through the "business stuff" as quickly as possible. Time pressures force short-cuts to be made in business decisions, which suppress dissenting voices, minimize implica-

---

[1] I use "relational/spiritual" and "task/spiritual" to reflect my philosophy of ministry that spiritual gifts cover the whole spectrum of relational or task priorities. One is not spiritual and the other secular.

tions, and polarize leaders and the church by voting (majority rule). All this does is create even more shepherding challenges.

+   +   +   +   +   +

Here are two common scenarios to consider as I make the case for the value of leading by consensus to maintain unity in the church.

Scenario 1 (S1) — Seeking Consensus among the Elders[2]

George drove home from a really long elders meeting questioning how long he should continue as an elder. Last month, the chairman of the elders proposed that it was time to find another preacher, and he seemed to have the support of the group. Because George had been especially close to the preacher and his family, he did not feel good about this process nor think it would be best for the church. When he presented the strengths of the preacher and reasons to give him more time to address some of the criticism, he did not feel like anyone heard what he said. At one point in the last meeting, the chairman even ignored his proposal to give the preacher an annual evaluation before letting him go. The other five elders sat there in silence each time he made a defense of the criticism of the preacher or expressed concerns that this decision would lead to polarization in the church. After all, more than 30% of the members have come to the church in the past seven years. He felt strongly that more than half the members really loved the preacher and his family. He also knew from his weekly meetings with the preacher that the real issue involved tension between the

---

[2] I have created two scenarios that are a mix of details from real situations but morphed enough to hide the identity of any one place. If it fits a church you know it is purely coincidental.

preacher and the chairman of the elders. The preacher was in his seventh year and George suspected that his growing influence was a threat to the "lead" elder. Needless to say, George did not feel free to say anything else in the meeting tonight. The chairman called for a vote: four wanted to make the change while George and one other elder were against it. To make matters worse, George served as the elder over the ministry team, so he was asked to notify the preacher of the decision and work out an exit strategy.

Outcome: [This story typically has one of two endings.]

[A] The preacher suspected this could happen and agreed to leave peacefully as soon as school was out and his family could move. The announcement to the church by the chairman of the elders was vague, just "it was time for a change." It took the preacher six months to find another place to serve. He was able to "move on" but his wife remained angry and bitter for years. Some of the younger families lost confidence in the elders. During the long 18-month preacher search the church lost about ten families. The two elders who voted "no" resigned within a couple of years. –OR–

[B] The preacher challenged the decision and confronted the elders about the unfairness of the process. During the meeting, the two elders who supported him said nothing in the meeting (presumably to give the elders a united front). The meeting did not go well. As a result, George resigned the next week. Within two months the preacher started a new congregation across town, taking the two elders with him and about 20% of the congregation. The tension between these two churches lasted for decades.

What difference would consensus among the elders have made? What could they have done differently? Was there anything else George could have done?

+   +   +   +   +   +

Scenario 2 (S2) — Consensus between Elders and a Ministry Team

Tim leads a ministry team of four people: a worship leader, a youth minister, a children's minister, and a part-time involvement minister in a church of 400 members. He came from a small church where he preached for five years while in graduate school. Several elders of the church sought him out because they wanted to appeal to younger families and appreciated his energy and enthusiasm. Tim jumped at the opportunity to make a difference and felt empowered to serve. He was drawn to this church because it seemed open to change from his conversation with a couple of the elders and the worship leader. He attended elders meetings and in his second year began to feel more empowered to lead the church through changes that would help the church appeal to younger adults. Sharing the values of gender equality with a younger generation, the ministry team started making some changes involving women more in the worship services and ministry.

Last night, in an elders meeting, it became clear that some of the elders resisted the idea of the children's minister making announcements at the end of services Sunday morning to promote VBS. It seemed to be the best way for her to create more enthusiasm for volunteers and for children to participate. The objection seemed so silly and minor that it angered Tim enough to lash out at the elders. This came on the heels of reports of women praying in some of the small-group meetings, the appointment of a woman to chair the missions committee, and a woman on the praise team singing a solo the previous Sunday morning. The chair of the elders meeting asked for a straw vote to see how serious the issue might be. The vote was four to four. Some of the elders had received a lot of negative feedback from members. They decided to put everything on hold and to study the issue for three months. Tim provided them with some resources on the topic. The next Sunday, during the weekly shepherd's time at the end of the worship service, an elder mentioned the study the elders were involved in and asked the church to pray about this. This spooked some members and within three weeks ten families left — assuming they knew "where all this is going." The elders did not want any more fallout. In the end, the status quo prevailed, frustrating Tim and the whole ministry team. Tim quit meeting with the elders. Convinced that little change would take place, some of the ministry team started looking for another church to work with and some of the young families started to visit other churches.

Outcome: The church lost about 100 members within a year from "both ends." Those who were not open to any change and those who were convinced that nothing would ever change.

Tim had full consensus within the ministry team but did not have it with the elders. Would consensus have been possible? If so, how?

+   +   +   +   +   +

What's the Problem?

One might think the problem in these two examples of conflict would be that something happened in the church that caused people to leave. While that is regrettable, it is unavoidable in autonomous churches populated by autonomous members. The threat to leave to get what one wants cannot represent a spirit of Christ, faithfulness, fellowship, nor spiritual maturity. The historical phenomenon in America of desiring churches after our likeness has fueled religious division and splits that disregard Jesus's plea for unity. We have assumed it is not possible, so we don't even try. Unity does not appear to be a core value nor a spiritual priority in these scenarios. While a dissenting voice that constantly threatens to leave cannot be allowed to dictate policy in a church, it would not be right to disregard that person. Neither would it be right to hope they would leave and go to another church without any attempts to respectfully listen to them and learn from each other.

> *Behold, how good and pleasant it is when brothers dwell in unity!*
> *Ps. 133:1*

The problem is the absence of a love that allows for a process to learn from each other to maintain the unity of the spirit in the bond of peace. That process is called "consensus." Whatever the reasons were for the chairman of the elders (S1) to dismiss the preacher, they could not justify a disregard for incorporating all the voices within the eldership so wise steps could be taken to treat the preacher right, to respect those in the church who were being blessed by his ministry, and to improve the effectiveness of the preaching ministry. No matter how right Tim and the ministry team (S2) may feel about an issue, they are not free to disregard the opinions of other leaders and fellow believers.

> *There is neither Jew nor Greek, there is neither slave nor free, there is no male and female, for you are all one in Christ Jesus. Gal 3:28*

The problem is the absence of the joy and peace that reconciliation brings. These are dark moments in the life of these churches. Wounded spirits and broken trust become fertile opportunities for a ministry of reconciliation or for Satan to win a local battle. When we fail to find a process to avert these unhealthy behaviors among us or see little hope for reconciliation, we totally abort our greater mission to a lost world. We destroy our witness. We disappoint and dishonor God. We miss a fundamental foundation-al doctrine that has far more instruction in scripture than can be found to support the opinions, issues, or traditions that we encounter in church conflicts.

> *Wounded spirits and broken trust become fertile opportunities for a ministry of reconciliation or for Satan to win a local battle.*

Spiritual Alignment

I am not sure what to call this next section, but when I reflect on the following scriptures I have difficulty aligning them with the behaviors represented in S1 and S2. While conflict is unavoidable, efforts to apply these spiritual principles would surely change the tone of the discussion and possibly create a better outcome.

- **John 17:11,23** Jesus expected "complete unity" among his disciples as a witness to the unity of the Father, Son, and Spirit as well as evidence of his incarnation and his love. God's eternal mission involves the unity of all things under Christ.
- **Acts 1:14** The first disciples of Christ in Jerusalem, along with the mother and brothers of Jesus, honored him by being in "one accord" as they shared a devotion to prayer and service.
- **Acts 15:25** As divisive as the issue of circumcision was in the Jerusalem meeting, the leaders were able to listen to each other, to understand what God had been doing, and

to "come to one accord" in sending representatives to bless the uncircumcised Gentile believers.

- **Rom. 14:1-3** When dietary codes threatened the unity of the believers in Rome, Paul pleaded with them to welcome each other and not quarrel over opinions.
- **1 Cor. 13:4-8** Whatever the issue, we will openly express our thoughts (trusting that our brothers and sisters will not respond in an arrogant or rude way) and we will not insist on our own way or issue (because we love our brothers and sisters).
- **Eph. 4:3-6,13** Spiritual maturity will not be determined by the more noble issue or theological principle we might master, but by an eagerness to maintain the unity of the Spirit. Maturity will be assessed by our ability to attain the unity of faith and knowledge of Christ.
- **Phil. 1:27; 2:2** Possibly the most passionate appeal Paul makes for unity can be found in his plea for followers of Christ to stand "firm in one spirit, with one mind striving side by side for the faith of the gospel...being of the same mind, having the same love, being in full accord and of one mind."
- **Col. 3:14** It will not be possible to claim we love our brothers and sisters if we are not "all together in perfect unity."
- **1 Peter 3:8** A final appeal by Peter was for the followers of Christ to "have unity of mind, sympathy, brotherly love, a tender heart, and a humble mind."

When we brush these spiritual values across the canvas of our church they bring new light, healing, peace, and joy. Wherever these truths shape the behaviors of followers of Christ, they can honestly call themselves the church of Christ.

114

How can these spiritual ideals trans-form the reality of our divisive human nature? I would not claim to have the answer, but I could suggest a discipline or process that would at least help. Consider leading by consensus.

> *When we brush these spiritual values across the canvas of our church they bring new light, healing, peace, and joy.*

Consensus Values Community and Unity

These scenarios have several things in common. The clash of values may be the most obvious, especially the tension between the value of empowering individuals to lead the church how they think best and the value of making sure every voice counts. With the disruption of fellowship experienced in each scenario, the missing voice may have been the one for unity and harmony.

Tree Bressen describes the process of consensus as a shared desire to search together to find what is best for the group.

> The search for consensus relies on every person in the circle seeking unity. Group members don't need to think the same, have the same opinions, or support the same proposal in a unanimous vote. Rather, what is earnestly sought is *a sense of the meeting*. This is the essence of what the group agrees on, the common ground, the shared understanding or desire. The method is founded on life-affirming assumptions about human nature and is struc-tured to call forth those positive parts of ourselves, weav-ing into being the "co-intelligence" of the group to meet the needs of the whole.[3]

---

[3] Tree Bressen, "Consensus Decision Making," in *The Change Handbook: The Definitive Resource on Today's Best Methods for Engaging Whole Systems*, edited by Peggy Holman, Tom Devane, et. al. (Barrett-Koehler Pub., 2007), p. 213.

Every person involved in the two scenarios had much more in common than they had differences in opinion. When we focus on the problem or issue, or vote to save time, we ignore what unites us. Voting creates winners and losers. Consensus generates understanding and unity.

> Consensus decision-making is a process that seeks to arrive at decisions that everyone can live with, by seeking to resolve or mitigate the concerns of the minority. In contrast, voting simply overrides the concerns of that minority, without regard for the effect on the group's long-term unity.[4]

Consensus is NOT a compromise where two sides find a middle ground that neither one likes but agree to live with it since they cannot find time to consider the problem in depth.[5] I can think of many times in an elders meeting when an issue would come up that some of the elders had some knowledge of, but others were hearing it for the first time. Perhaps you are like me: the first time I encounter something I do not understand or I know that it has the potential to cause problems — I am inclined to be against it. If the issue is being forced on me, I will be even more resistant to it and not even want to talk about it. This explains some of the tension on both sides in S2.

> *Voting creates winners and losers. Consensus generates understanding and unity.*

Consensus is NOT unanimity. Diana Christian posted a good blog on the myth that consensus-with-unanimity is good for the

---

[4] Rachel Williams and Andrew McLeod, "Consensus Decision-Making," (June 2008) accessed on 12-14-16 at kohalacenter.org/wp/wp-content/uploads/2014/01/Intro_to_Consensus.pdf.
[5] Michael Avery, Barbara Streibel, et.al., *Building United Judgment: A Handbook for Consensus Decision Making* (The Fellowship for Intentional Community, 2014), p. 78.

community because one contentious person can block the process.

> Consensus-with-unanimity was created in the 1600s by the Quakers because of their deeply held values of equality, justice, and fairness, and thus was a reaction against autocratic rule and outright tyranny. They had the insight that anyone who saw problems in a proposal that the group couldn't see, even after much discussion, should be able to block the proposal in order to protect the group. Leftist activist groups and communitarians in the 1960s and '70s—also with deeply held values of equality, justice, and fairness—adopted consensus-with-unanimity partly because it seemed so fair and equitable—and thus partly as a reaction against not only autocracy, but also majority-rule voting, because in the latter a proposal can pass even if up to 49 percent of the group is dead-set against it.[6]

Prerequisites for Consensus

For consensus to work well, the following are necessary. So please don't skip this list (do your homework!) before you move to the next section that gives practical steps in the process of consensus. If you have identified with anything in the two scenarios and are eagerly reading this chapter for practical answers, there is an extremely high probability that you will need to address several of these prerequisites before you can even talk about consensus in your group—all of which could

---

[6] Diana Leafe Christian, "Busting the Myth that Consensus-with-Unanimity is Good for Communities," Intentional Communities blog, June 7, 2012; see http://www.ic.org/busting-the-myth-that-consensus-with-unanimity-is-good-for-communities/.

take time. This may be the reason some prefer to vote (and get it over with) and others prefer to walk away (and skip this tough stuff).

- **A high level of trust.** Everyone in the group needs the assurance that a dissenting view will be respected and listened to. Elders should not be allowed to attend several meetings and never make a comment. It would be the role of the chair of the meeting to pull them into the discussion and assure a fair hearing. Where there are trust issues among the leaders, take the time to resolve them. If issues are deep, with a long history, consider finding a consultant to help the group work through the issues. Develop annual events where the leaders focus on strengthening their relationships and building trust—rather than on work or business. Find ways to maintain and protect the trust among the leaders.

  > *Everyone in the group needs the assurance that a dissenting view will be respected and listened to.*

- **Free from "power plays" that would overturn the approved process.**[7] Leaders in autonomous churches have no higher (earthly) authority outside the local church to overturn their decisions; they are locally accountable and lead by influence more than power. The consensus process can improve their effectiveness in leading because followers choose to follow.

- **Humility.** Open minds and hearts can learn from anyone in any context. Most elders find themselves in new situations facing issues they do not like nor can they avoid.

---

[7] Avery, p. 8.

They approach any issue with very strong convictions but may discover, after further study and thought, that they have been wrong all these years. The line between convictions and stubbornness can be extremely thin. The majority opinion, the tradition, or the newest trend can be wrong for any church. Consensus seeks the shared wisdom of the group. In a postmodern culture where almost everything is questioned, church leaders will be forced to rethink almost everything. Let us keep studying the Word and be willing to be led by the Spirit with humility.

• **A shared mission, purpose, and direction.**[8] A model I use for assessing the health of churches involves four factors: spirituality, relationships, mission, and organization.[9] After several decades of experience with this model, I have not seen one church that ranked "mission" as their strongest factor.

> *Mission is about the energy we give outside the church to make a difference and transform our world for the honor of God.*

tor. In fact, it is almost always last or next to last. This may say something about the churches that invite me to consult, but I think it is typical of plateaued and declining churches. Neither the leaders nor the followers can articulate the mission of the church. Without a clarified

---

[8] By "mission" I am not referring to what a church does when it sends someone to a foreign country, or to a statement that can go in the bulletin each week. Church leaders have wasted hours creating a mission statement that is neither remembered by anyone nor is it used to shape policy. On the other hand, if there is consensus among the leaders about the goals or purpose of the church for the next 5-10 years, it will take much less time to craft a good mission statement with a measurable outcome.

[9] For a detailed explanation of how I use these four factors to assess church health see: Evertt W. Huffard, "From Quick Fix to Healthy Assessment," in *Doing God's Work: A Primer for Church Leaders* (Hope Network Ministries, 2013), p. 29-35.

mission, followers become consumers and leaders become followers. Add mobility to the consumer phenomenon and it is easy to see why American Christians find it so easy to leave a church or "shop" for the church that they like. How do we ever develop maturity to the fullness of Christ when we fail to submit to the mission of Christ or know faithfulness to the people of God? Holy crowds on Sunday will never transform the world, much less our lives.

Possibly the most difficult homework leaders will engage in to make consensus a reality will be to identify the mission of their congregation. To answer, with clarity, why this church is in this neighborhood at this time will give the church a reason to work together to resolve conflict and to love each other and their neighbors. I have heard many elders express how they really want a clear mission for the church but competing voices among the leaders make it impossible to define the mission. A church can live week to week like this but it will turn all the energy of the leaders and the church inward — on itself. Mission is about the energy we give outside the church to make a difference and transform our world for the honor of God. This self-consumption of energy also leaves us weak and vulnerable in fighting a spiritual war. On the other hand, a unifying vision generates energy and unleashes the power of the Spirit in our lives and community. The process of identifying the mission of God for this church will be a great exercise in consensus. The best thing I can do for my children is love

> *Possibly the most difficult homework leaders will engage in to make consensus a reality will be to identify the mission of their congregation.*

their mother. The best thing leaders can do for their church is to love each other — so lead with consensus to execute God's mission for the church.

- **Time** for as many as possible to work through an issue. Relationships always demand more time than tasks! This may be one reason Paul wanted elders to have families. That is where they learn the importance of time in balancing relationships with issues/tasks. Because family defines church more than corporation, relationships have priority over tasks and issues. As in any family, each member has different learning styles and speed of "getting it." Some need time to reflect and process ideas that are contrary to what they have always believed. Have you noticed that one parent may be quicker to accept your choice for a life mate than the other one — but they both eventually get there? While this same decision-making process can be a very slow process in a church, it increases the involvement in executing the decision. If Christians love their sisters and brothers and believe that love is patient and kind, will they not long for consensus?

- **A desire to work together for the honor of God.** Church leaders can have moments of inspiration to know what is best for the church — but these moments may be rare and random. An elder (S1) can be so convinced that the preacher is not as effective as he could be that he would risk criticism, tension among the elders, and mistreat the preacher to impose the change he wants. If an atmosphere could be created where the elders and preacher/ministry team are constantly dedicated to working together, the preacher could possibly conclude that his ministry needs to change or that he cannot give the church what it needs and should be the one to change. A preacher (S2) can be personally committed to changing something in a church that has high priority to him and fears involving others who may challenge or alter his agenda. Through a process of consensus, his own thinking could mature as well as that of his perceived "opponents." In such a context, patience and engagement would be much better behaviors than anger and withdrawal. Outcomes in both scenarios would have been different if the desire to work together were as strong as the desire to bring about some specific change.

A leader might think that kings of Israel or Africa chiefs had it made—they could just decide for everyone and move with haste. It might be surprising to discover that great kings and chiefs led by consensus. For example, how did David decide to move the Ark of the Covenant to Jerusalem after it had been in the house of Abinadab for fifty years? When you read 2 Sam. 6, you get the impression that it was the will of the king to move the ark to Jerusalem. After Uzzah was struck dead, David had second thoughts about taking the ark into his own care in Jerusalem. He left it at the house of Obed-edom the Gittite for three months.

We get a little different picture of the process in 1 Chronicles 13. David consulted with all Israel, including the priests and Levites. He sought consensus. "The whole assembly agreed to do so, for the thing pleased all the people" (13:4). He assembled "all Israel in Jerusalem to bring up the ark of the LORD to its place, which he had prepared for it" (15:3). When the ark was in place, they all came together to honor God with psalms of praise (16:8-36). When all the people said "Amen!" and praised the LORD, they were in one accord, in harmony, all together, united in honoring God. I assume Abinadab even said the amen. It was a great day for consensus in Israel. King David led them by consensus to create a new chapter in the history of Jerusalem as the place where the Lord dwells. The times David failed God and his people could also be viewed as times when he failed to seek or listen to wise counsel and allow the consensus process to protect him from tragic mistakes.

Consensus is not for everyone or every situation.

1. There are mitigating circumstances when the minority must go with the majority opinion or decision. It will usually have negative consequences if everyone's involvement will be necessary to resolve the problem or execute the decision.

2. The larger the group, the greater the opportunity for diverse opinions and the more difficult it is to reach consensus. Decision making groups over 20-25 would have to resort to more voting and expect less commitment to the execution of the change.[10]

3. For a group to be harmonious all the time could also pose a problem. Who would want to be the "bad guy" to bring up a contrary view or rock the boat? Someone needs to be assigned the role of the "Devil's advocate" just to get different perspectives on the problem. The times to anticipate the need for a consensus process would be when the elders try to clarify the mission of the church, to define core values, to set a budget, to hire/fire ministry staff, to change a doctrine/tradition, to discipline a member, to

---

[10] Williams and McLeod would set the limit at a couple of dozen (p. 1).

appoint new leaders, to begin a new ministry, or to create a strategic plan.[11]

Steps to Consensus

1. **Preparation**

   Before a proposal for any kind of change is to be made, begin with private and public discussions where everyone can freely express their opinions. When elders hear a drastic proposal for the first time in a meeting—like firing the preacher (S1) or changing the role of women in public worship (S2)—we can assume inadequate preparation went into that proposal and could expect major resistance. If those making the proposal know the majority opinion would support their agenda, then they may count on voting it through, devaluing dissenting voices and disregarding the possibility of negative consequences. In this case, voting reflects a lack of preparation and minimizes the value of other leaders. Preparation does not require agreement BEFORE the proposal is made. It just reflects the willingness to begin the process with humility and a willingness to listen to other perspectives.

2. **Equipped Facilitator**

   Our two scenarios had chairmen of the meetings who were not equipped to lead with consensus. They could have averted some of the fall-out by not being part of the problem (S1) or not making the problem worse by a sudden "straw vote" (S2). I am of the opinion that one of the weakest factors of churches that are led by elders is the tradition that every elder should take a turn serving as chair of the meetings, without any policy or guidelines or

---

[11] Tree Bressen, p. 214.

stated expectations for that role. This often becomes an opportunity for an elder to push his agendas during the few months he is "in power" — not a good way to build trust with his fellow leaders. If we expect members of the church to serve according to their gifts, so should the elders. Some men are not gifted to lead a meeting. Whether this practice prevails or not, set a policy for the role of the chairman so he will know what is expected of him. This

> *If we expect members of the church to serve according to their gifts, so should the elders.*

would include the need to organize the agenda for the meetings, keep the discussion on task, maintain a godly spirit within the group, involve those who seem too quiet in the discussion, regulate those who talk too much, and bring the discussion to some conclusion or action. He should take responsibility for consensus within the group when conflicts arise.[12] If he does not feel gifted or qualified to do these things, then give him a free pass. He will feel the love!

3. **Develop a Policy (that everyone agrees to and follows!)**
    Few churches have clearly defined written policies. I understand the reservation some may have for doing so because they think it could be creedal. However, for the collective wisdom of the leaders to be communicated to the ministry team and to the congregation (as well as future leaders), it is important for the elders to develop some policies for code of conduct, governance, etc. A policy on

---

[12] Several good resources could equip one to lead by consensus. See the references in this chapter along with: Rob Sandelin, "Basics of Consensus" [available on-line at: http://nica.ic.org/Process/Consensusbasics.php]. I also use a tool called *Team Dimensions Profile©* that has been very effective in helping everyone in a decision-making group discover their role as well as the role of a facilitator.

managing conflict among the elders will build trust and actually reduce conflict. The policy would include the role of the chairman in discerning the issues that need this process. A policy for how disagreement among the elders would be resolved would have really helped George, the elder in S1, avert a crisis in the way the preacher was fired. He had other options. He could have reminded the group that they agreed to make decisions like this by consensus and propose a time to seek the collective wisdom of the leaders. The issue was not the issue! A policy for managing disagreement between the elders and ministry team would have averted the knee-jerk reactions of Tim and a few of the elders. Again, the issue was not the issue they needed to address. In both cases, the train did not get derailed — it just had no tracks to run down or bridge to cross.

> *...for the collective wisdom of the leaders to be communicated... it is important for the elders to develop some policies for code of conduct, governance, etc.*

4. **Designate a Time to Discuss the Proposal**

Ground rules for these meetings need to be understood and followed. These might include things like everyone will: commit to the mission of the church, seek to do what is best for the church, participate openly, listen respectfully, create a safe environment to speak without being interrupted, and respect the collective wisdom of the group. Without these behaviors, a fundamental step of open creative "brainstorming" will not be possible.[13]

---

[13] Avery, p. 45.

The elders in S1 needed a special meeting to discuss only the preaching ministry. The elders and ministry team in S2 needed a weekend retreat to hear everyone's perspective on the role of women, with each person sharing their view. The first goal will NOT be to persuade everyone to "their side" – it would be to listen to each other well enough to be able to explain an opposing view with fairness. As the saying goes, where there are two sides to an issue, the truth lies somewhere in the middle. If everyone is open to the outcome of the process the truth may be found. If consensus cannot be reached in the first meeting, set up a task group, with opposing views represented within it, to work through the issue to seek consensus. If they can reach consensus then make a proposal to all the elders with supporting information. Another option is for all the elders to find time for a second meeting to give more time for consensus to develop. If at the end of a reasonable time consensus cannot be reached, because one or two people are blocking the process, this is the time for another policy to be applied.[14] Most healthy churches have a policy that if an elder cannot accept the decision of the majority, he would either support the collective judgment of the elders or he would resign.

When I became an elder we discussed a similar (unwritten!) policy. We had twenty elders; I was one of the newest five. The senior five elders each told of a time when he was the dissenting voice and could not agree with the majority decision. But rather than resign, he "went along" with it and supported it. He did not speak badly about the decision or the elders outside that meeting. As I remember it, every elder shared how it became clear to

---

[14] See Avery (p. 33) for a discussion of the problem of "tyranny by minority."

him a few months later that the majority did the right thing. He was wrong and grateful that the decision had not gone "his way." Leading a church is a humbling learning experience.

5. **Execute and Evaluate**

Whoever leads the meetings (and hopefully others will too) keeps a pulse on the quality of relationships and summarizes the next steps. Give priority to relationships—because the commitment within the church will be to fellowship, unity, and love. If the next steps involve reconciliation and healing, facilitate that. If relationships are fine, proceed with specific assignments to committees and individuals to work on consensus with the congregation, to communicate well, and to connect it all to the mission of the church.

> *Give priority to relationships— because the commitment within the church will be to fellowship, unity, and love.*

Summary

If you return to the second paragraph of this chapter, you will recall that this discussion of decision making among church leaders would be a third priority for me. From the perspective of my top two priorities, I could write a dozen more pages on the spiritual importance of prayer in decision-making, of shepherds shepherding each other, of how to delegate, of how spiritual influence is more important than power in making decisions, and of submission to one another out of reverence for Christ. But I must stop somewhere.

Leading by consensus honors the mission of God to unite all things in Christ and takes a lot of time and energy. In a time of rapid change within our culture and churches, the need to lead churches by consensus will be counter-cultural but allows the church to be led by the Spirit and maintain the unity of the spirit in the bond of peace.

WHEN LEADERS ARE STUCK
A Guide for Communal Discernment

Grady D. King

8:00 p.m. Wednesday night. Elders and ministers meeting. Everyone is present except one elder. People are tired after a long day of work. There are nine items on the agenda and the most difficult discussion is number nine. It's been on the agenda for months and continually postponed.

9:00 p.m. Six items remain on the agenda. Restlessness fills the room. Someone looks at their watch. Another one checks his phone for a message. And someone takes a restroom break. What everyone knows is that the difficult discussion will not happen, again. Some are relieved. Others are frustrated. The chairman speaks up, *"We can't discuss one particular item without all of us being present."* No one is surprised.

10.00 PM. Three agenda items remain. The meeting adjourns with closing prayer.

The Reality of Stuck

If any of this sounds familiar, then you know STUCK first hand. It's understandable. We take for granted that good men who love God and take their responsibility seriously can come together, have an open, difficult discussion resulting in a decision and remain united. When you think about it, what other organization is called to function like an elder group? Companies have chief executive officers, universities have presidents, schools have superinten- dents, and the armed services have officers—a chain of command. The elder

> *When you think about it, what other organization is called to function like an elder group?*

group, however, is not a hierarchy, but rather, a community of equals. Authority lies not in one's individual position, strength of personality, or longevity of service. Rather, it lies by virtue of one's life and character in Christ. No one elder has the final say—it's a group decision. This is, however, not the experience of many elder groups. Every group has the listeners and talkers, the competitive and the avoidant, the agreeable and disagreea- ble. Being a functioning group is not easy. Group dynamics are complex. Conflict is inevitable and essential. To view conflict as detrimental, something to avoid, keeps the group stuck.

Conflict: Good or Bad?

Stop. Before reading any further, take a moment to reflect on conflict.

- What is my attitude regarding conflict?
- What is my general behavior when conflict arises?
- What is my function in a group in conflict?

Knowing your own conflict style is helpful. Even more helpful is a group understanding of each other's conflict style. TKI is one tool that is helpful for this important relationship dynamic informing decision-making tendencies. The goal is to get unstuck for the sake of the body of Christ and the growth of the kingdom. Communal discernment can be a way to get unstuck. It is not a quick fix and does require commitment, patience, and discipline, coupled with confession of pride and openness to change — all of which is about maturing in Christ, rather than sanctifying our peculiarities as men.

> *The goal is to get unstuck for the sake of the body of Christ and the growth of the kingdom.*

Men will be Men

My wife has a humorous saying that is more truth than fiction — *"Wherever two or three men are gathered, there is a junior high boy."* It is usually in reference to the kind of humor, competitiveness, and spirit that emerges when men gather. There is, however, one common characteristic of men that works against communal discernment. Men are wired to be fixers. It's not all bad, just as being a warrior and protector has its place with leaders. Since men are wired to be fixers, there is typically an impatience with process and poor self-awareness about the need to change the way we do things. One definition of insanity is doing the same things over and over and expecting different results. Although we understand the reality, we tend to do what we have always done and get what we have always got.

The Red Green Show, a Canadian PBS show that ended in 2006, was one of my favorite shows. It was a Canadian version of *Home Improvement* set in the fictional town of Possum Lake, Canada, and followed the mishaps of Red, the leader of the Possum Lodge men's club, and his nephew in their plight to be good handymen. They attempted to fix everything with duct tape and had some amazing successes and failures. Each episode ended in the lodge with the men reciting the man's prayer — "I'm a man. I can change. I guess. Amen." As humorous as this is, it is true, and conflict makes it evident. With conflict comes pressure and frustration. When pressure and frustration are at a high level, the proverbial man-card is often played — *"Hey, we are all grown men, let's just get it on the table, be honest, take a vote, and make a decision."* In baseball terms, what's the batting average of this approach in your group? Has it worked? How was the decision made? Did it unify or polarize the group? What is the residual relationship baggage? Likely, the answers to these questions are less than satisfactory. It is a challenge for a stuck group to make a significant decision.

The Challenge

Godly people coming together to make a decision seems like an innocuous task. It is, however, fraught with challenges. The weightier the decision, the greater the challenge. To believe the primary task is to get everyone on the same page is naive, because it does not take into account the complexities of being human: expectations, fears, motives, intellect, personality, tradition, ego, power, needs, and preferences. All of this is only multiplied and compounded at the congregational level. Yet, all human systems have similar dynamics, and understanding the church as a system provides insight and tools for the process of communal discernment.

Communal Discernment

Communal discernment is a spiritual task dependent upon people who are maturing in Christ, rooted in prayer and the power of the Holy Spirit. Discernment, at its core, is about judging, assessing, and evaluating. It is not voting or holding out for a unanimous decision. It is a process where the Holy Spirit is active in and through disagreement as well as agreement. Discounting emotions and intuition by not bringing them to bear in the discussion (even without an apparent clear rationale) can hinder process and sabotage decision-making. The reason is that unexpressed feelings often take the form of unstated resistance or postponing a decision in the name of gathering more information. Courage to take a stand: state belief, express feelings, and/or share intuitively

> *Communal discernment is a spiritual task dependent upon people who are maturing in Christ, rooted in prayer and the power of the Holy Spirit.*

is an essential part of the process. If communal discernment is about anything, it is about surfacing latent as well as visible anxiety that shapes our decisions. Anxiety begets anxiety and erodes courage. Chronically anxious leaders are leaderless. Our greatest task as leaders is to manage our own anxiety. This is why an outside facilitator is recommended.

Process Guidance

An outside facilitator is advised for the first time working through the process. It cannot be overstated that THE PROCESS itself is essential for healthy discernment. Each part of the process is deliberate and has a purpose in group dynamics. An outside facilitator provides objectivity and active listening. This person can also provide insights into dynamics of engagement, disengagement, pain, and body language.

IF an outside facilitator is not used, then designate a person in the group to coach them through the process with someone who is an experienced facilitator.

The Process

The process is designed as a reflective practice of communal discernment. It acknowledges that everyone makes decisions for a variety of reasons. Decision-making is complex. For the purpose of this exercise, three levels of discernment—biblical, pastoral, and personal—are considered. Each leader reflects on their thoughts and feelings for each level.

A. **Biblical**: What does the Bible say? What about the nature of God? What does God value?
B. **Pastoral**: How will it impact the church? What is my level of anxiety?
C. **Personal**: What is my personal viewpoint? If I wasn't a designated leader I . . .

As leaders, we can be committed to the Bible while differing on the precise meaning of a passage and application regarding an issue. We can also vary greatly as to anticipated congregational response and our own level of anxiety, which impacts the pastoral dynamic. Commitment to a good process is key. The key to good process is specific commitments in the conversation. These include, especially, listening, honesty, and self-control, followed by respect, courtesy, and clarity.

> *Commitment to a good process is key. The key to good process is specific commitments in the conversation.*

Essential Process Tasks for Every Participant

1. *Clarity*: Writing out answers for clear thinking and rationale.
2. *Verbal Sharing*: Articulating thoughts and feelings is about taking ownership of beliefs.

3. *Active Listening:* Eye contact and focus communicates value and engagement.

Personal Reflections for Group Meeting *(Write out your responses for sharing)*

The following questions are designed to till the soil of your thinking and willingness to be fully present in the process. Sharing your answers with each other at the beginning of the meeting is essential. Some of these questions may not be necessary, depending on the nature of the discussion (i.e., searching for a preacher, theological position of leadership, building program, etc.)

1. What did others give up for me to be present for this process?
2. What crossroads is _____ (congregation or group) facing at this time?
3. What possibilities for ministry exist in your local context?
4. What refusal am I postponing?
    *What am I refusing to say, *"Yes"* and *"No"* to?
5. How am I contributing to the problem I am concerned with?
6. What commitments am I willing to make for the future of _____?

The Process Steps

Pre-Work

1. Respond to the personal-reflection section and bring your written responses with you to the group meeting.
2. Identify the key topic for discernment and state it as a central question.

This can be done as group discussion, led by the facilitator or chosen leaders. It is crucial that everyone involved knows the exact topic, stated as a question.

3. Each participant fills out the worksheet, which will be used in the group meeting.

Group Meeting

1. Begin the meeting with prayer and brief period of silence.
2. The facilitator shares conversation commitments (i.e., the ground rules).
   a. Everyone speaks.
   b. Everyone speaks without interruption.
   c. Everyone speaks in first person (I think, I believe, I feel, etc.).
   d. Everyone checks what they heard by saying, "I heard you say... . " and gives opportunity for the speaker to verify or clarify.
   e. Everyone takes a position and provides rationale for their position in the discussion.
3. The facilitator reproduces the levels of discernment on a whiteboard for everyone to see.
4. Each person shares the results of their worksheet, and those are recorded on the whiteboard.
5. A time of silence (5 minutes minimum) for personal reflection and implications is given for each person to make notes, consider additional questions of clarification, etc.
6. Numbers are totaled and averaged for group consensus at each level, and then cumulatively.
7. Identify the points of divergence and restate rationale inclusive of intuitive considerations.
   Consider an acceptable range for group consensus in moving forward.

8. If the group remains stuck, restate the question, take a few minutes for prayer, and call for another consideration of numeric positions and rationale.

    At this point, acknowledge fears, congregational pressure (specific people and/or constituencies), possible member and/or financial loss, and family dynamics, that may impact position/rationale.

9. Once there is a consensus, affirm the person(s) with the greatest divergence as essential to the process and pray for *"unity of the Spirit in the bond of peace"* (Eph. 4:3).

Special Notes

1. Although the focus of this chapter has been on elders and ministers, the process can be used with any group of people — male, female, or a combination. The basic process has been used with as few as 6 people and as many as 24 in one setting.

2. This process is designed for clearly-stuck groups and not intended to be used for every decision. Neither is it intended to convey that a successful discernment means it is a unanimous decision. Rather, consensus means learning to disagree and remain united.

3. The process has been used with elders stuck on who to hire as a preacher, with two congregations co-sponsoring a church plant, and in working through apparent philosophic and traditional differences.

4. A good facilitator trained in group process will know how to make the necessary adjustments for a meaningful experience. The process should be adapted to varying context and needs.

5. This process takes time — generally, a minimum of 3-4 hours for the group meeting, and elements of the process

may have to be repeated. Rushing the process expecting good results is a recipe for increased frustration.

Next Steps

1. Pray for wisdom and growth in communal discernment.
2. Consider having everyone in your leader group read this chapter and approach to communal discernment. Follow up with a discussion.
3. Read one of the recommended books on Church Systems and share your top 7-10 learnings that apply to yourself and/or your group dynamic.
4. Share your list with other leaders and have them do the same. Compare and discuss.
5. Describe how decisions are made in your present leader group using these reflective questions —
   - What is going well?
   - What could be better?
   - What needs to be different?
   - What if . . .
6. What does your leader-group value based on the content of meetings, time, energy, and resources?
7. Make a list of the topics or areas of conflict that your group has postponed discussing and/or making a decision about. Create a chart and label each one related to the mission, growth, and/or health of the church as:
   - Urgent
   - Important
   - Not necessary

WORKSHEET

The Practice of Communal Discernment

Topic: What is the discernment question?

Levels of Discernment

   A. Biblical: What does the Bible say? The nature of God? What does God value?
   B. Pastoral: How will it impact the church? What is my level of anxiety?
   C. Personal: What is my personal viewpoint? If I wasn't a designated leader I . . .

A. _____ BIBLICAL:
(OPPOSED) 1   2   3   4   5   6   7   8   9   10 (SUPPORT)
My Rationale:

B. _____ PASTORAL:
(OPPOSED) 1   2   3   4   5   6   7   8   9   10 (SUPPORT)
My Rationale:

C. _____ PERSONAL:
(OPPOSED) 1   2   3   4   5   6   7   8   9   10 (SUPPORT)
My Rationale:

The vast majority of church leaders do not have a good process for making decisions and typically, are not patient or disciplined in following a process. Discipline and patience are essential for healthy decision-making. Granted, not every decision requires a process of this nature. But if you are stuck as a leader group and it is draining your spirit and any notion of moving forward, then why not try a different approach?

It is a process that has been utilized and tweaked each time it has been used. I look forward to hearing your experience with this process and how God is moving you forward for the sake of the kingdom.

May God bless you richly in leading God's people.

SPIRITUAL FORMATION

WHO'S DRIVING THIS BUS?
Surrendering to Rhythms of Staff Spiritual Formation

Rhesa Higgins

He couldn't sit still, fidgeting his hands and crossing, then uncrossing, his legs. His cheeks were flushed with embarrassment and he refused to meet my gaze. With eyes directed to the floor, tears began to leak and words rushed out.

"I can't remember why I do this anymore. At some point in my life, I became a minister because I sensed a connection with God. Now, I feel like I put on my 'God-suit' every day and hope nobody notices it doesn't fit anymore.

"I pray only when other people are around and listening. Even then, I don't know what to say. I study scripture only so I can teach and preach. And it isn't like I planned to be at this place or even want to be at this place. I couldn't tell you how I got here or when it started. I miss God. And I feel like a failure because I can't lead my church to be better disciples. I don't know how to be a disciple myself! I am a fraud. I am a failure. I don't know what to do."

This scene is not an anomaly. Several times each month, different ministers walk into my office and repeat a version of this confession. They are burned out on church work. They are exhausted. Their families are hurting. They have misplaced their souls.

> *Then Jesus went to work on his disciples. "Anyone who intends to come with me has to let me lead. You're not in the driver's seat; I am. Don't run from suffering; embrace it. Follow me and I'll show you how. Self-help is no help at all. Self-sacrifice is the way, my way, to finding yourself, your true self. What kind of deal is it to get everything you want but lose yourself? What could you ever trade your soul for?"*
> *Matt. 16:24-26 (The Message)*

Ministry is hard work. There are so many explanations for why it is hard. I won't reiterate all of them here. However, there is one challenge to ministry life that I want to focus on. Ministry requires an individual to combine vocation, social connection, and spirituality into one place in their life. This reality presents the difficulty of being a professional Christian, in every aspect of life and in every waking moment of the day.

> *Ministry requires an individual to combine vocation, social connection, and spirituality into one place in their life.*

As a spiritual director, I see ministers often who have lost touch with their own individual sense of faith, spirituality, and relationship with God. They have felt forced to become the one who always knows the right answers and next steps and is readily available to hear someone else's pain. These are qualities that congregations and elders expect from their ministers. However, spirituality requires space to be vulnerable with God. True relationship with anyone, especially the Holy One, is squelched by guardedness. Where is it safe for ministers to be authentic before God and what could that even look like?

One logical place is together with ministry staff. The following rhythms are described for a ministry staff of two or more (including any support staff). If your congregation doesn't employ this many ministers, I encourage elders to seek ways to join with their minister in pursuing relationship with God. The rhythms are broken into sections of time: weekly, seasonally, yearly, and every 5 years.

Weekly

Pray together
Once a week, for at least 45 minutes, bring the whole staff together for the sole purpose of prayer.

The temptation here is to spend this time collecting the names of those in your church who are ill or who are grieving. There can also be pressure to pray for your church, its future and vitality. These are good, holy, and important prayers, but they are not what I am talking about for this one section of time a week.

Be with God, for the sake of each other. I recommend that you begin this time with silence.

- Breathe deeply and come to a place of rest in God's presence for 5 minutes.

- Then, read a psalm or a prayer from the *Book of Common Prayer*. Rest again after hearing it in silence for 2 or 3 minutes.
- Read the same passage a second time, listening for God's invitation to you as an individual. Allow for a few moments of silence.
- Share your responses, then read it again, listening for how you want to respond to God's invitation.
- Again, rest in silence for few moments as you honestly respond to God.
- Then, as desired, share this response aloud.

This is an ancient practice called *lectio divina*. It is a simple way of being in community with God's word without anyone needing to be the spokesperson for God. I lead a staff through this type of experience every week. What we have learned together is that listening to God in this way requires trust in each other to be safe ears, trust that God has a word for us, and trust that we can come to God as ourselves and not just the ministers for the sake of others.

This practice costs nothing but time. However, it yields bountiful fruit in stronger, trusting relationships among your staff as well as healthier ministers who can give from a full well instead of a dry one.

Practice Sabbath Together

It is commanded in scripture that we honor the Sabbath to keep it holy. Most ministers break this commandment regularly and wonder why they burn out. Ministry staff works on Sunday. Therefore, there must be

> *... it is not healthy for your soul to be engaged in ministry to others 24/7. There must be some space for rest.*

another day of the week that they are given off. Many churches have either Monday or Friday as this time. I recommend that all of the staff takes the same day in order to protect that day. For instance, our church office is closed on Friday. The congregation is invited to recognize their ministers' need for time away and there is no one trying to contact a fellow staff member for an unfinished task.

Anyone who has served in ministry for any length of time knows that quite often ministry happens on days off anyway. A member is ill or passes away, requiring your attention. This is the nature of our work. However, it is not healthy for your soul to be engaged in ministry to others 24/7. There must be some space for rest. Help one another honor this commandment and the benefit it brings to our lives.

Seasonally

Learn Together
Several times in a year, choose to study something together. Perhaps it will be a recent book written about a topic that is facing your church. Maybe focus in on a specific book of the Bible as you are drawn to it. My recommendation is that you learn as a group for a month at time with space for "learning rest" on each side. If you study together in January, take off February and March. I believe this space between learning topics allows your staff to pursue learning related to their specific ministry or personal lives. Your purpose in studying together is transformation and learning, together. Healthier fruit will be yielded if there is space for other learning, as individuals, to take place as well. Then, shared learning isn't mimicking what one person thinks. It is more nuanced and diverse, and therefore richer.

I also recommend that you purposefully limit this kind of studying you do as a staff so that it won't take the place of other ways of connecting with God. Learning information is so important, but it is only one piece of the puzzle. Praying together, fasting together, and resting together are also important elements of your spiritual formation. Leave room for them by studying less.

Fast Together

At least twice a year, fast together. Fasting is a practice that calls us back to God, calls us to come more wholly to God. It asks us to notice where we are resisting God. Are there places in our lives where we assume we can handle this, and don't need God to meddle? Are there places in our lives where we don't want God poking around for fear of the pain that could be inflicted? Are there places where we never considered inviting God?

For the one who seeks to live the life of a spiritual leader, fasting is a key practice! It requires us to remember that we are not our own and we are not an entity unto ourselves. In other words, we are broken. We are limited. We are needy.

When we have identified these places where we resist God, then we consider how to practice surrendering them. This is where fasting can be a transformational experience. For instance, if I am aware that I use food, especially sweets, to soothe feelings of stress, then going without sweets for a time to become aware of those feelings is a healthy practice of making space for transformation. The fast from sweets isn't about losing weight or gaining other health benefits. It is about surrendering to God my own inadequacy to rule the world.

> *For the one who seeks to live the life of a spiritual leader, fasting is a key practice!*

Or, if I am aware that I spend a great deal of my waking hours concerned with money—Do I have enough? Have I spent too much? Could I save more here?—then I might need to consider the possibility that I am resisting God's sovereignty over money. How can I surrender that? My financial situation may not change by fasting from my debit card, but my perspective on it might.

In each of us exist areas of our lives where we have learned to handle things on our own. We learn habits and traits that help us cope with fears. We present our strengths as covers on the places in us where we don't want anyone to have reason to come looking. Fasting is an invitation to peek under the covers and invite God to join us in our fear.

I invite you to just let this question float around in you, along with your staff: Where am I resisting God?

> *Where am I resisting God?*

Your first answer to the question may be true, but it is unlikely to be deeply true. Sit with the question. Take it with you to prayer. Ask to see more clearly. Seek to see beneath the resistance—why do you resist here?

Whatever resistance you find, consider how to lessen your dependence on it for a set time. I recommend longer than a week but less than a month to begin with. Decide ahead of time how you will fill the hole that you create. Perhaps you will pray the Lord's Prayer each time you are confronted with the resistance. Perhaps you will look at a certain picture on your cell phone. Be diligent in journaling through this practice so that you stay aware of how God wants to meet you in your fast.

151

Fasting asks us to realize that we are all addicts. We are addicted to things that have become our idols. If we lay them down for a time, we may discover that they are just pieces of wood after all.[1]

Set the parameters that make the most sense for your staff. I prefer to let them choose for themselves something they will fast from. Some may choose to give up watching TV, some may choose to give up sugar, some may choose to give up wearing makeup. Keep the timeline reasonable.

Finally, for one of these fasts, consider fasting for the sake of congregation. For instance, fast together for two weeks in March for the sake of asking God to bring His harvest on Easter Sunday. Or, fast together in August to hold up your children who are heading back to the mission field of their schools.

Yearly

Retreat Together

Once a year, for at least two days, get away as a group. You are not retreating to get more work done but instead to enjoy living in community. Eat good food, play fun games, spend time in silence, worship together, pray together, build relationship together as you practice Koinonia.

> *You are not retreating to get more work done but instead to enjoy living in community.*

I believe that it is important to actually "get away" for this time. Does a member of your church have a more remote vacation home or cabin that your staff could borrow? Have each staff member take charge of planning one meal and invite others to assist in cooking and cleaning up. Turn in cell phones at the

---

[1] I am indebted to Sean Palmer for this insight.
(http://www.thepalmerperspective.com)

beginning of the time in order to pay attention to each other and to God. Resist the urge to over-plan this time. Instead, turn your desire to control the time over to prayer. Ask God to fill the spaces with joy, rest, connectedness, and fulfillment.

This experience is not a waste of time. On the contrary, this experience is about deeper trust with each other and in God. Ministry is impossible without trust!

Every 5 Years

At least one-month sabbatical, NOT TOGETHER

This is a lot of together! After every 5 years of serving your church, on a rotating basis, ministers should be blessed to be away from the community for at least one month. They are seeking to restore connection with their own truest selves, with their families, and with God — outside of the church community. This is necessary and holy rest that sustains a minister for a lifetime of being poured out for the sake of others. Sabbatical is not vacation time. It is work of a different kind.

During Sabbatical, wise ministers work to untangle the combination of vocation, social connection, and spirituality that ministry creates. This unweaving involves our egos and our first answer to how we know ourselves. It is very hard work to loosen the knots that have held a façade together so very well. However, it is also very healthy work that invites a minister to dare to wonder how to connect with God outside of their vocation.

> *If you want a vibrant, dynamic local church body, invest in the health of your leadership!*

There are a lot of people who worry about the state and future of the local church. They point to declining memberships and staff that doesn't stay in place for very long. Culture, mobility, and social contexts are all influences on these statistics, but I don't want to argue about their meaning or offer multiple solutions. I believe the health of the local church depends on the health of its ministers. If you want a vibrant, dynamic local church body, invest in the health of your leadership! Offer permission to be vulnerable, authentic seekers of God. Create space to be with God for the sake of relationship. Allow time to weave together staff friendships. These are investments in the kingdom of heaven. These are invitations to trust the Driver of our bus to get us where He means us to go.

Cheat Sheet

Weekly
- Pray together for 45 minutes.
- Practice Sabbath together.

Seasonally
- Learn together 4 times a year.
- Fast together 2 times a year.

Yearly
- Retreat together for at least 2 days.

Every 5 Years
- Offer each staff member a one-month Sabbatical.

BEST PRACTICES FOR WORSHIP MINISTRY
Getting the Most Out of Our Worship to God

Bret Testerman

The Dilemma

I was recently asked to meet with a group of elders from a small, somewhat conservative congregation. They were concerned, concerned that they were losing an all-important battle of retaining the younger demographic of their church. By young I don't mean teens. I mean young couples under the age of 40, most of whom have children. This church, though small, actually had quite a few of these young couples. Maybe as much as 35% of their congregation was made up of these families. But the concern was real.

You see, this same congregation had probably lost a similar amount from the same demographic group to start-up church plants that had exploded in the local area over the last few years.

These new churches had a lot to offer a young family, great children's programing, relevant preaching, a lot of activities for young families, and a dynamic worship experience. In addition, these churches had a lot of financial resources to put into these programs, which raised the excellence barometer considerably. What these elders really wanted to know is, "How do we compete with that?" They felt discouraged and burdened, as shepherds of this flock, to make sure they provided every possible opportunity to keep these younger families engaged, and they knew that what they had to offer wasn't very compelling.

They also felt the pressure of knowing there were two opposing and real forces they were caught between. On the one hand, they didn't have a lot of resources. They felt that in order to create an attractive culture for these young families, they needed money and expertise to put the necessary polish on their church. On the other hand, they had the limitations of an older generation from their congregation that was resistant to change. What could they do? How do they make everybody happy?

It's a scenario that many churches face, "How can we continue to use the same forms that we've always used and hope to get different (better) results?" The truth is, we can't, and I'm not even sure that God wants us to. Our forms should be constantly shifting and changing, even ever so slightly, so that they can be more effective (functional) at bringing our people before the throne to God in worship and carrying out his mission. I don't mean large-scale, reinventing-the-wheel types of change. I just mean making slight tweaks here and there to be more effective. The focus of this chapter will be to suggest some ways to gain better vision and tweak some of

> "How can we continue to use the same forms that we've always used and hope to get different (better) results?"

our old worship forms so we can be better at stewarding the opportunities God has given us as church leaders. [1]

A Biblical Call to Change

The apostle Paul was certainly familiar with change. In fact, he was a catalyst of change, constantly examining and shifting his forms based on the context of his work and calling. It was Paul who said, "To the Jews I became like a Jew, to win the Jews"..."To those not having the law I became like one not having the law, so as to win those not having the law"..."I have become all things to all people so that by **all possible means** I might save some" (1 Cor. 9:19-23).

Paul had not sold out to a certain way of doing things but was constantly tweaking his methods to make sure he was being effective. Why? "I do all this for the sake of the gospel, that I may share in its blessings." God was in on this *function-over-form* strategy also, for it was God himself who changed Paul's name from the Hebrew name Saul to the Greek name Paul. Why

> *Paul had not sold out to a certain way of doing things but was constantly tweaking his methods to make sure he was being effective.*

the name change, you ask? Because Paul was uniquely qualified for a special ministry of God. Paul explains it like this in Acts 22:3—"*I am a Jew, born in Tarsus of Cilicia, but brought up in this city (Jerusalem). I studied under Gamaliel and was thoroughly trained in the law of our ancestors. I was just as zealous for God as any of you are today.*"

Yes Paul, a Jew, was born in Tarsus, a Greek city, but studied in Jerusalem under Gamaliel, a Pharisee and doctor of Jewish law.

---

[1] For a great conversation about form vs. function, see Tim Woodroof's book *A Church That Flies: A New Call to Restoration in the Churches of Christ.*

And it was this interesting combination of Jewish and Greek origins that uniquely qualified Paul to be God's ambassador to the Gentiles. And so God changed his name from the Hebrew name Saul to the Greek name Paul so that he might be more effective in his ministry to the Gentiles. Functional forms trumped traditional forms.

The challenge we often face as church leaders is that at any given time we are not just ministering to one group of people. In fact, the majority of our churches are filled with multiple groups of people whose preferences are defined generationally, ethnically, culturally, and by their traditional religious backgrounds, to name a few.

One group may be more established in the congregation. Some from this group may have been at the church for 40 years or more, and many have had multiple generations of their family who have been members. Often the people in this group are older and care very deeply about the current forms the church uses, regardless of how little function they may offer.

Other groups may not care too much about the traditional forms. They are more functionally oriented in their approach to forms. They want the preaching to be relatable and add value to their lives. They want their children to build deep relationships with other Christians they can journey through life with. And they want to experience something in worship that is engaging and helps connect their hearts with the heart of God. They haven't been a part of the congregation nearly as long as some of the others, but they bring a lot of value to the church because they are full of energy and highly involved. They have become the "life-blood" of the congregation. This group tends to be more active in sharing their faith and therefore wants the forms that are used to make sense to those who are unfamiliar with the church. In other words, if they're going to invite their friends to church, they don't want to be embarrassed because the church seems out of touch.

These are two prominent groups that are found in most churches. And the truth is, there are many other groups and subgroups that fill in the gaps. So who do we cater to? How do we decide the direction we are going to take and what the steps are going to be? These are perhaps the most critical questions we can ask and conversations we can have as church leaders.

> *If people can't see what God is doing, they stumble all over themselves. But when they attend to what he reveals, they are most blessed. Prov. 29:18 (The Message)*

Vision, Mission, Values

The reality is that we cannot allow preferences to drive decisions about what forms will be used or how functional they will be. As we just discussed, the challenge that lies before us with regard to preferences is real. Every group of people that make up the church has different preferences. In fact, every member of a congregation has their own set of preferences that transcend the groups they belong to and are influenced and shaped by their own background. These preferences can unknowingly speak to their flesh and keep them focused on themselves rather than the active work of God. If leaders allow the preferences of one individual or group to drive their decision-making process, then they alienate every other group in the congregation and compromise the mission of God. So what becomes the fuel that drives our decision-making process? What do we use to help us find our way through this essential expedition?

> *...we cannot allow preferences to drive decisions about what forms will be used...*

159

I've always loved Eugene Peterson's interpretation of Prov. 29:3 that we've always quoted this way — "without vision the people perish." Notice his nuance: "If people can't see what God is doing, they stumble all over themselves. But when they attend to what he reveals, they are most blessed." This is so true! If people don't have a vision for the things of God, then they become internally focused and care only about themselves and what they want. But when they see his vision and engage in his mission, they reap the blessing of bearing much fruit.

It is the job of those God has called into leadership to give the people this vision and help them paint themselves into it. We need to show them God's vision for our church and help them see how they fit into that vision. Therefore, vision becomes the catalyst for the work of God. It helps us to define and understand the mission that God has called us to. And it provides the lenses so we can see what's important, thus giving us values to work from. Once we have defined vision, mission, and values, we can then form a strategy or strategic plan for how the mission is going to be executed. All of these steps are critical prerequisites to any conversation about worship forms and the practical functionality of those forms.[2]

Turning Over A New Leaf

Once the hard work of defining vision, mission, and values has been done, then we can use those things to help us in developing a strategy for execution. This is where we begin to make the sudden tweaks in our forms because our vision has given them purpose. In other words, we are not just making arbitrary changes to how we do things. This is not change for the sake of

---

[2] To drill down further on these ideas of vision, mission and values, see "Vision: A Peek into the Future" by Tim Woodroof and Jon Mullican, in this book.

change. We are letting our vision inform us of changes that need to be made in our forms so they can be effective. We are being intentional about how we do things so our mission can be accomplished.

For example, in the scenario I mentioned earlier, once this group of elders worked through their vision, mission, and values, they were able to overcome the obstacles that had bottlenecked their process earlier. They were able to clearly communicate their vision to the congregation and explain how this vision compelled them to update the current forms they were using. And most importantly, they were able to solicit buy-in from the entire congregation by helping them to see the mission that God had called them to.

> *This is not change for the sake of change. We are letting our vision inform us of changes that need to be made in our forms so that they can be effective... so our mission can be accomplished.*

You see, a clearly-communicated vision about God's mission delivered by godly leaders and infused with the Holy Spirit compelled the members to take their eyes off themselves and their preferences and be open to change for the sake of God's calling.

So you might be wondering, what kinds of tweaks could you make? Based on your vision, mission, and values, what are the changes you should make to your worship gatherings? How can you be more intentional about connecting with younger families and creating a worship culture that is vibrant and engaging? The truth is, each church will have a different answer to those questions. But going through this process will bring you to the place where those questions can be answered in a way that will be right for your church.

The rest of this chapter will focus on providing options for some of those questions. Not every one of these ideas (forms) will be something you choose for your church, because your vision, mission, and values are leading you in a different direction. It is my hope, however, that there will be something here that will prove to be a good resource for breathing new life into a current form or introducing a new form altogether. I also want you to consider some new practices that can help bring impact to your gatherings. I will try to provide a broad enough spectrum of ideas so everyone, from the most basic church to those farther down the road, can find something applicable.

Worship Design and Execution

Every preaching minister needs a partner in planning worship. Whether they know it or not, they are more effective if they have someone (it must be the right person) they can dream with or throw ideas up against the wall with just to see what sticks. Sometimes just having another perspective to help unpack an idea is a gift. Quite often the best person for this role is the one who is leading the church's music (for this conversation we will refer to him as the worship leader). There is a synergistic relationship that happens between a preaching minister and a worship leader in designing worship that is God-honoring, ministers to the hearts of the people, and is filled with the Holy Spirit.

In the culinary world you see a similar relationship between a Master Chef and the Sous Chef. It is the Master Chef who has the painstaking task of determining the main course for the meal. Every other decision will be based on this. In addition to deciding on the main course, the Master Chef decides the flavor profile of the meal. These are the flavor combinations that will be created with herbs and spices and carried throughout the entire meal. It is the flavor profile that gives each dish its unique personality in the context of the whole meal.

Once these critical decisions are made, the Master Chef meets with the Sous Chef to discuss the sides that will go with the meal and how the meal will be garnished. The Master Chef then communicates to the Sous Chef his ideas for the main course, the kind and cut of meat they will use, how it will be cooked, and what flavor profile he will create. This becomes a foundation for creativity with regard to deciding what sides will be prepared. It also helps determine what complementary flavors there are that can be used in the sides to help bring out the savory flavors of the main course. They then discuss how they can best present (plate and garnish) the meal so that it looks like the savory meal that it is.

This metaphor helps us to understand the relationship and roles the preaching minister and the worship leader take on as they work together to create an experience in worship that has trajectory and purpose. The preaching minister decides what the sermon *(main course)* will be, what text will be used, and what he will draw out of the text and emphasize *(flavor profile)*. This last part is critical because most texts have many directions one could go in, so clearly defining the flavor profile is necessary.

Once these decisions are made, the preaching minister and worship leader meet to plan the details of the worship experience. The preaching minister shares his ideas for the sermon, what text he will use and what he intends to draw out of the text. This gives the worship leader a foundation to begin sharing ideas from about songs they could use, Communion ideas, or other elements that could be used to help bring out the savory flavors of the sermon. Ideally you create an experience where a thread of continuity is woven from the beginning to the end, and every element works together to take the worshipper on a journey to a destination, which is closer to God.

When every phase of this process is bathed in prayer and infused with the Holy Spirit, you can then prepare your teams or those participating to execute the plan in a way that honors God and encourages His people.

Creating A Worship Narrative

As mentioned before, the goal of Worship Design is to create an experience where a thread of continuity is woven from the beginning to the end, tying every element of worship together. We call this "creating a Worship Narrative." To go back to our earlier metaphor, the Worship Narrative speaks to the main course and flavor profiles and how those are developed and executed. And while the preaching minister and the worship leader may plan every detail of the service, there are others who come into the picture as we begin to talk about execution.

Communion meditations will be given, prayers will be offered, and announcements will be made. Some churches may even use a Praise Team or others who might participate in some way. On any given Sunday there may be a variety of other worship expressions used to move the message forward. Then, in many churches, there's a team of technical people who help make sound, lights, and media work together to that same end.

> *When the entire process is prayerfully planned, carefully communicated, and thoroughly rehearsed, it can then be skillfully presented in a way that honors God and encourages His people to draw near to him in worship.*

164

All of these people must understand the nuances of the Worship Narrative and the design that went into it if you expect to accomplish your desired outcome with the plating and presentation of the main course. The preaching minister and the worship leader must find ways of sharing this vision with the various groups of people who will be working together to execute the planned Worship Narrative. When the entire process is prayerfully planned, carefully communicated, and thoroughly rehearsed, it can then be skillfully presented in a way that honors God and encourages His people to draw near to him in worship.

Simple First Steps For Creating Change

Perhaps your church is one that has worked through its vision, mission, and values and has simply chosen to stick to its roots. Or maybe you need to take baby steps at improving your worship forms. The question I often get from church leaders is, "What are the simple things we can do to improve our worship?" Though there is much to be gleaned by these churches from the section below called "Nuts and Bolts," here are some simple first steps that can help get your church more engaged.

1. *Invest In A Leader* – Even if you're not in a position to have a paid worship leader, that doesn't mean that you shouldn't approach the job with excellence. Find the best volunteer you have and ask him if he will work alongside your preaching minister to plan and organize the worship each week. That doesn't mean he has to lead each week. It just means he becomes the point man for the worship ministry – planning, organizing, and communicating with those who are participating. If he shows good leadership skills but doesn't have a lot of music background, then help him learn the basics. The more

you invest in your key volunteers, the more you will get in return.

2. *Create a Culture of Excellence* — "Whatever you do, work at it with all of your heart, as working for the Lord, and not for man" Col. 3:23. – God deserves our best. He deserves excellence. It brings honor to him when we serve him with excellence, and yet how do we measure what that means? Excellence in worship doesn't mean expecting perfection and allowing only paid professionals to participate. It doesn't mean that everything must be scripted, sterile, and removed from the active presence of the Holy Spirit. It doesn't mean that the purpose is creating an entertaining show. What excellence in worship does mean is that it is always:

   a. Prayerfully Planned — When services of worship are a God-led endeavor, they will be humble, beautiful, meaningful, and spiritually rich.
   b. Thoroughly Rehearsed — Rehearsal helps the leaders to focus on God and the message instead of technique and fundamentals. It prevents embarrassing distractions due to poor execution.
   c. Skillfully Presented — When people's gifts are used artistically and skillfully to praise God, it is a pleasing offering to God (1 Peter 2:5; Matt. 22:37) and the rest of the body will praise God as these offerings are made.

3. *Get Rid Of The Hymnals* — I don't mean to literally get rid of them. But you would be surprised at how much more dynamic your singing will be if you get people looking up and get their noses out of the book. Moving into the digital age with media-driven worship music will give

your worship leader so many new options at creating song flow that is fluid instead of having to stop in between songs to have people turn the page. And getting rid of the hymnal doesn't mean you have to give up music. If you are a group that feels strongly about needing the sheet music, then tools like the Paperless Hymnal are great for you.

4. *Get Creative With Communication* — One of the side benefits of moving into the digital age with media is that you can present all of your announcements digitally. Rather than having all of your announcements read publicly during the service, create slides with your announcement information, and create a slideshow that plays before and after the service. You can even attach mp3 files of your favorite worship songs to this presentation and have a nice music bed that plays through the sound system while the announcements are scrolling. This allows you the opportunity to mention only the most important announcements during the service.

5. *Add Intelligibility To Your Sound* — I often talk to sound techs that are scratching their head because while they have plenty of volume, they can't seem to bring intelligibility to the mix. This is important stuff. We have the greatest message in the world and many of our members can't understand what is being said because the system has lost its intelligibility or clarity. You can try to EQ more highs into the mix but all you're doing putting a Band-Aid on the real problem and risking feedback. The truth is, sound systems weren't meant to last forever. Most professional-level speaker manufactures say that 8-10 years is the lifespan of the modern speaker. That means that if your sound system is 10-12 years old, then

you may need a makeover. Though all of this equipment continues to get better, the components wear out over time, and even though you continue to get sound out of it, cone fatigue sets in and your speakers lose their sharpness. The good news is that sound equipment is not only getting better, it's getting cheaper, making upgrades much more possible for even the smallest church.

6. *Change The Template*—Even after 40+ years, I can still tell you what the service template was each week for the small rural church I grew up in. It was more predictable than the time. This predictability, however, can work against our desire to engage people in worship. Make adjustments to the order of worship and highlight different aspects of the worship at different times.

For example, the communion doesn't always have to go before the sermon. Sometimes, if the topic is right, it would actually be better if communion was served after the lesson or as a response to the lesson. And why do we so often connect the offering to the communion? I understand all the pragmatic reasons for it, but sometimes the offering would be more meaningful if it stood alone or was coupled with just the right scripture or song. In other words, be intentional when planning where the different components of your service will happen.

7. *Create Better Flow*—I remember when we used to announce every single aspect of the service. Maybe you still do. "And now Brother Joe will come up and lead our opening prayer." "Please turn to number 728b." As I mentioned earlier, we followed the same template every week, and yet somehow we still felt like we needed to tell everybody what was happening next. Well, you would

be surprised at how much more fluid the flow would be if you eliminated all of the transitional chatter. If there's good planning and good communication, all you need to do is let brother Joe know when you want him to pray and what microphone you want him to use, and it should be a mostly painless process. Give it a try.

8. *Connect the Musical Dots*—Speaking of flow, one of the blessings of digital song slides is that you don't have to stop between each song and allow people to turn pages. This allows you the creative license to develop groups of songs that can be done together as a medley. Just make sure that you select songs that are in the same key and are in a similar meter and tempo so that the transition from one song to the next goes smoothly. And if this is new to you, make sure that this is thoroughly rehearsed.

The Nuts and Bolts

For a moment, let's take a look at some of the various elements that might be used to help create this narrative and garnish the main course of our meal. Some of these elements will take on a more profound role in our assemblies than others. And outside of music, prayer, and communion, which will be done weekly, frequency is a discussion to have regarding the other elements that will become flavor profiles in our meals. Again, your vision, mission, and values should drive any decisions that are made about what different forms you choose to integrate into your gathering.

Music—Music is a language that gives voice to the heart of God's people in worship. Throughout the history of Israel we see worship that was expressed through the writing and singing of songs. These songs expressed everything from gratitude and thanksgiving to anger, frustration, and even lament. The human voice is the one instrument we all have in common to share these sentiments, and so music is one of the most important forms of our worship. When we are choosing a catalog of songs that we will use in our corporate worship, there a few things to consider:

1. *Frequency*—Paul Baloche, a worship leader and worshipologist, says that at any given time a church's song catalog should be limited to 40 songs. The rationale is that the church participates more when you limit the amount of songs that they sing over a period of time. 40 songs gives you enough to support a theme without too much repetition. Because Restoration-Movement churches have a time of communion every week, I stretch that number to 40-50 songs. These songs should include a blend of popular worship songs and choruses, as well as some hymns and communion meditations, and should consider the following variables as well.

2. *Seasons*—Churches go through seasons where certain themes tend to permeate their conversations. For example, I did some consulting and interim worship leading with the Providence Road Church in Charlotte, North Carolina a few years ago when their leaders had just rolled out a new vision statement of "Fearlessly Following Jesus." So as a congregation we were beginning to unpack what it means to fearlessly follow Jesus in our lives. Therefore, the song catalog included a good number of songs that supported that narrative. As you go through different seasons, the song catalog should reflect those seasons. For example, if a church was to go through the unexpected loss of a prominent member, you would need to interject some songs into the catalog that would help the church express their loss. These don't need to be

permanent additions but should stay until the church has adequately lamented. In general, if the preaching minister sets a preaching calendar for the year, then the song catalog should support the preaching narratives.

3. *Theology*—One could argue that music is the greatest conduit we have for infusing theology into our people. Because music connects our heart and mind, it is not only an emotive expression of our faith but an analytical one as well. When choosing songs, contemplate the theology that is expressed in the songs. Try to stay away from choosing songs *just because they're fun to sing*. If a song doesn't have solid theology, then it's just taking up space in your catalog. There are enough good songs out there that have good theology and resonate with the hearts of people.

4. *Familiarity*—Christian Radio has given new life to the role music plays in our worship experience because we have access to good Christian music 24/7. In addition, many radio markets' Top 10 lists are being dominated by worship music. Consider the playlist of your current Christian radio station. If they have a lot of worship music in heavy rotation, then this should be a factor in what you choose. There are few things that will engage your church in singing more than leading the songs they "jam to" in the car.

5. *Sing-ability*—When looking at song possibilities, consider how easy it would be to sing the song with the congregation. Some really popular songs have a rhythm or meter that is just too difficult to sing with large groups. We may do well to sing them by ourselves in the car but done

corporately they would just not take flight. Singing songs that have simple melodies will help your worship to soar.

Prayer — There are always going to be times when we naturally pray in our services. Before our communion or offerings we will almost always have prayer. But prayer can be used strategically to help connect the heart of a worshipper to the heart of God when developing a narrative or meta-narrative.

For example, if you were working on developing the vision statement of Fearlessly Following Jesus as a narrative, you might sing the Randy Gill song "We Are Not Afraid" because it carries that refrain of "we will be fearless for you" throughout the chorus and thus supports the narrative. But if you followed that song with a prayer and ask God to give us the strength not to fear but to boldly live on mission as disciples of Jesus Christ, then that would not only support the narrative, it could also support a meta-narrative found in the church's mission of Come, Connect, Grow, Go. Especially if that song is done after the lesson and is the last song out the door then that prayer could be used as a charge on the GO meta-narrative.

As a word of caution, with regard to strategy, praying as a means to get the praise team on and off the stage is not a God honoring strategy. Prayer should be used only to speak to God in a way that shares an honest communal sentiment and helps move the narrative forward and connect the pieces together for people. That doesn't mean you can't bring the Praise Team out during a prayer. Just make sure that's not the reason you're praying.

Communion — We are people who naturally forget. I'm really bad at remembering names and need frequent reminding when getting to know new people. I think that's why Jesus said that when we gather we should remember him and what he has done on the cross. This is a time of intentional focus on his grace, mercy, and provision demonstrated on the cross. However, if you are not intentional about creatively providing new thought to this memorial, it can become a time of ritual and disconnect. This is a place where the preaching minister and worship leader can work together to creatively find new ways of sharing a familiar story. There are literally dozens of ways that you could bring life to this time, but it takes real creative energy. Testimonies, videos, special music, choral readings, dramas, and a host of other worship forms could be used to provide a specific context for this time. If your church uses its members to lead this time of sharing, then the preaching minister or the worship leader will need to work with them in developing and executing the theme. One might also consider bringing the Bread and Juice together and doing only one thought and one prayer. This would make things much easier on the one sharing and would improve flow with regard to music being shared during this time.

As a resource, the Christian Standard, a magazine put out by the independent Christian churches, has a section in each edition called Communion Meditations. These can be found on their website ChristianStandard.com under Features > Communion Meditations.

Tithes and Offerings — At most churches tithes and offerings are taken each week as a standard practice for their members. However, one might consider how we preference this time of giving and make sure that there is a deep theological connection to giving. From my experience, there doesn't seem to be a lot of thought that goes into helping prepare people's hearts for giving back to God. I think this time in our assemblies could be greatly improved with some thoughtful, scripture-based vignettes on why God calls us to be givers. It also might be worth emphasizing the fact that this is something that we are asking of our members so visitors don't feel obligated to do something they don't understand or haven't committed to. To improve this time, there will need to be a commitment to working with the volunteers who are leading the prayer and meditation.

As a resource, The Rocket Company has giving-talk scripts as a part of their Giving Rocket program. They have samples free for download at therocketcompany.com.

Media — In today's culture the average person spends at least 4 hours watching TV each day. With the younger generation you also have gaming media as a big influencer of culture. So it makes sense that media should play a big role in the tools we use to create our narratives of worship. There are literally dozens of small companies creating media pieces that address specific themes of worship. Be selective and use a video only when you can find one that is a perfect set-up for the narrative you are creating. At times a short (2- to 3-minute) video clip can be used, in place of a bumper video, to begin a preaching segment. There are also some great videos that can be used at the beginning of a service as a call to worship. Communion is a place when you might use a video, instead of a song, for a meditation piece. There are all kinds of creative ways to use media to move your narrative forward.

As resources, WorshipHouseMedia.com, SermonSpice.com, and ShiftWorship.com are portals where all the small independent media producers sell their media. If you are looking for still media or backgrounds, Heartlight.org is a great resource.

Movie Clips — Though they share the same medium, Movie Clips are delineated from Media as tools that we can use in worship design for a couple of minor reasons. Movies can become blockbusters and therefore are thought of differently by people than a media piece that they've probably never seen before. Great cinema can capture and connect the hearts of people to a film for decades. *Up, Amazing Grace,* and *Braveheart* are great examples of movies that move people. What red-blooded American male could ever forget the scene in *Braveheart* where William Wallace rallies the men to fight for their FREEDOM? So play movies to their strength. As you're communicating a message from scripture, use a movie clip that a large cross-section of your congregation would be familiar with to drive that point home. If you find a movie clip that would be less familiar, make sure that you set it up well by setting the scene for the clip. In many cases, the preaching minister is the most likely candidate to identify the need for a movie clip since he is creating the sermon, and movie clips are most often used during the message portion of the service.

As a resource, ScreenView.com is provided by the same licensing group that brings you CCLI. Though it requires a separate licensing fee, it is well worth it for the resource it provides. They have very easy-to-use search tools for finding clips that will fit a narrative you are creating. Also, if your church is a part of the Willow Creek Association, they also have some great resources for this.

Choral Readings—Our churches value God's word and the power found in the Bible. But the scripture has a lot of dimensions that are often missed when read as a monologue. The Bible is filled with characters and dialogue between characters. Therefore, there are times when it is best to read the Bible dramatically as a choral reading. A choral reading is just a way of taking the scripture and dividing it up into its natural parts to be read as dialogue.

When doing a choral reading, first think of the character voices that are needed. Then think through the members of your congregation and discern who might best represent that character. Consider age, gender, and vocal strength when casting. This is also a good way to use a greater cross-section of your church by using people from different ages, races, and cultures. There are also roles like narrator that can be done by either gender. When looking at a scripture you are considering, look at all of the natural ways there are of dividing the passage up into parts. Anywhere from 2-4 parts is best, depending on what the passage calls for. These will need to be created and casted a few weeks in advance to give time for learning and rehearsal.

As a resource, let me recommend a three-volume set by Michael Perry called *The Dramatized Old Testament* (2 volumes) and *The Dramatized New Testament* (1 volume). Perry does a good job of breaking the scriptures up effectively. These books use the NIV translation but could be modified to fit any translation preference.

Scripture Reading—Sometimes scripture readings should just be a monologue. In such a case, identify a scripture that will help set the tone for the narrative of the day. Find a translation that is easy to follow and best communicates the sentiment. Then think about WHO would be the best person to do the reading (see section on Involvement and Integration below). Where in the service should the reading take place? Is there a particular song that it should follow? Many times it is best executed by someone who is already on the stage—a singer, or even the worship leader himself. How do we segue in and out of the scripture reading? All of these questions should be weighed out during your worship planning.

Drama—While not many churches use this form as a way of developing narrative, I wanted to include this material for those who might. Life is drama. Perhaps that's why one of the most effective ways to set up a message is through drama. If done well, drama can be a great way to engage the audience in a conversation because drama is something they understand. But doing drama well takes a lot of work and is perhaps the most complicated process in worship planning. So here are a few things to consider before deciding to use drama:

1. *Script*—It all starts with a good script, and if you happen to have an excellent scriptwriter in your church, then enlisting their help is preferred. Going back to our metaphor of the Chef and Sous Chef, meal preparation starts with identifying the main course. Once that is done, you can develop all the sides to complement that main course and carry out the chosen flavor profile. If you have a good scriptwriter, they can sit down with the preaching minister and discover all of the many layers and nuances of the main course and write a script to fully complement and garnish that main course. If you don't have a scriptwriter, then the next best thing is to buy scripts. However, it is very likely that any script that you would buy would need to be adapted so it can help you move forward the specific narrative you're creating.

2. *Talent*—There is a reason why nobody has ever won an Oscar for his or her role in a B-movie. Bad acting is just bad. If you think drama is something that you're going to use periodically, then make sure you have good actors. Even if the talent you have still needs work there are plenty of small community theaters that actors can cut their teeth on and learn the needed skills. These theaters are also filled with actors that might love coming to your

church if they knew you valued drama and a medium. But if you have the available talent, then there's no better way to honor God than by putting that talent to work and blessing the congregation.

3. *Direction* — Every good drama has a good director. This person must be able to read the script and envision every nuance of how the story unfolds. If you don't have someone with experience directing a drama, then try to enlist someone from the local community theater group or a drama teacher from a local school.

4. *Costume* — Usually costuming is determined by the scriptwriter based on their vision, or the director based on their interpretation. But once the costuming has been set, then you need somebody to find or make the necessary wardrobe pieces. Finding someone who sews well is a must. Good costuming can immediately set the context of a drama before even one word is said. This also is also another great way for people to use their gifts.

5. *Makeup* — Good makeup is critical to role execution, because so much of an actor's effectiveness depends on non-verbal expressions like facial gestures. Makeup helps the audience to be able to see and follow all of the facial expressions. Another reason for makeup is that fact that lighting can make some skin complexions look pale and so a good makeup artist can help give each actor the boost they need for their complexion.

6. *Sets* — Like with costuming, sets are determined by the scriptwriter or the director. It's helpful to have someone in your church that does woodworking and is willing to be on your team. You also need someone who could

paint and help develop and execute a set design. A good set communicates so much about the circumstances the characters find themselves in.

7. *Lighting* — Good lighting is used to draw you into the drama and focus your attention on the message. It is important to have someone on your team that understands how to use lighting effectively in this context. You also must have the equipment to make it happen.

8. *Sound* — Sound for theater is different than sound for music. With drama your goal is not to amplify the voice at high decibels but rather to help boost the conversation so that the audience can hear each line clearly and with intelligibility. Having a soundman that knows how to EQ voices for intelligibility is important in this regard. There's nothing worse than muddy voices that you can't understand. This is also an area that requires the right equipment, preferably high-quality headset microphones.

The good news is that drama is a *high investment-high reward* thing by its very nature. There are few things that can draw people in more than great drama. But if you can't do it with excellence, then don't do it. There are other things that are easier to create and can accomplish similar results. But if you have all of the above tools available, then drama is a great way to include a lot of different people in your services.

Because of the steps involved, dramas need to be planned at least 6 weeks in advance. Your scriptwriter will need three weeks to write a 3 to 5 minute drama. This process will require weekly or bi-weekly time to make sure the script captures the essence of the message. Once the script is finalized and the director is selected, then another 3 weeks will be needed for casting and rehearsals. Once the drama is cast, the director should sit down with all the actors to read through the script. During this process the director will help the actors understand their vision for the execution of the roles. After this first read-through, memorization begins, and by the last week of practices every actor must be off script. The last couple of rehearsals should be in full costuming and makeup with the set in place and lighting and sound staff involved.

The Willow Creek Association has a lot of dramas in their catalog ånd is a good resource for this material. They also allow you to view the drama before purchasing. Dramashare.org also has a lot of dramas and resources to look at. Skit Guys (www.skitguys.com) also have a number of good dramas shot on video that you could just show as a media piece if you want the effect of drama without all the work that goes into drama.

Spoken Word—Spoken word has been around about as long as there's been poetry. But as an art form it has gained a recent surge in popularity because of the way a handful of artists have developed their craft. Spoken word requires two things to be effective—good writing and good delivery. The ability to craft words that impact and engage people's hearts is rare but necessary for good spoken word. Then you must deliver those words in an emphatic way that drives the message deep into the heart of the listener. Because of its popularity there may be people in your congregation who do spoken word. This would be a great ministry to develop because it can include a lot of different people groups, especially the youth. Like dramas, spoken word will require plenty of lead-time for someone to write and prepare for presentation.

Some good artists to look at for spoken word are Taylor Walling, David Bowden, Amena Brown Owen, and Jason Tomlinson. Samples of their work can be found on Vimeo or YouTube.

Testimony — The Bible is a story. It's the story of God and his relationship and interactions with his people. But the story continues to unfold because God is still at work in the lives of his people. Testimonies are a way for us to hear about God's activity in the lives of people that we know and consider part of our church family. Always keep your ear to the ground for stories that people share from their lives. When you are developing a narrative, think about the story in scripture and ask yourself if there is anyone in your congregation who has a similar story. Hearing the same story from a friend helps make the Bible more real to the listener. The preaching minister might need to take the lead when planning a testimony because he can first interview the person, hear their story, and discern if it will help to move the narrative forward.

If you decide to move forward with a testimony, the preaching minister should write down the aspects of the story that he wants the person to share. There are often far too many details to share in the limited time you have, so every word counts. Script out your leading questions and the response you want the participant to focus on. This will help minimize rambling that can happen if everything is left open-ended. If the testimony is effective but you are afraid that rambling might distract from it, then you might consider videotaping the testimony. That way you can include the parts that you want and cut out the rambling.

Greeting/Welcome — There is really an opportunity to set the stage for the entire service during this initial welcome. However, it can easily become something that is pretty routine if you don't give appropriate energy and thought to it. If your church has a connection card that they want people to fill out then this is an opportunity to highlight and give instruction to that. If you do a stand-and-greet, then this could be the time to do it.

However, I know there has been some discussion with regard to recent studies that show that visitors hate stand-and-greet times. This is certainly something that should be discussed. Don't miss the opportunity to frame or provide context to the service during this time. A few comments, an appropriate scripture reading before you usher them back into singing, can be a catalyst for great worship time. In general, this time in the service should be brief and efficient.

Response Time/Baptisms — There may be no time in our gathering where God's Spirit is more evident than when people respond to Him. This time encapsulates everything that has been happening in the heart of the worshipper as we have led them through all of the songs, prayers, communion, scriptures, and sermon. When the Spirit of God works through all of that to bring about a conviction of need, then the Bible says the "angels rejoice" and God's people are encouraged.

This is a great time for the preaching minister to take the lead in receiving those who respond and then involving our Shepherds and prayer team to minister to individual needs. The preaching minister can then discern if someone needs to be taken to another room for more prayer and conversation and if the need or prayer concern is something that needs to be shared publicly. If it is shared publicly it would work best if the preaching minister shared with the congregation and either prayed or had an elder do the prayer.

Often Baptisms are planned in advance and extra songs or refrains are placed in the end of the service to accommodate the preparation time. However, there are times when people spontaneously respond and request Baptism. Make sure that you have a music piece that you can come back to when that time comes. It could just be a chorus of celebration that the worship leader is always prepared to sing or a refrain of a song that you've already sung that addresses God's faithfulness and goodness.

Creating Flow

When you look at the different elements that you have planned for a service, of course you want each piece to be as impactful as possible. One thing that allows you to have the desired impact are the transitions going into and out of each element. When you look at the entire service, on a macro level, good flow is the polish that helps give your service the highest level of impact. Having good flow in your service is not difficult. It just takes intentional thought to how everything works together. Here are a few rules that will help make your services flow better.

1. *Always Have A Plan* — Know how you're getting from point A to point B. Look at how one element ends and how the next one begins. Then plan out a segue that intentionally and meaningfully moves between the two. And it's a good idea to write this down — this will help with the next step.

2. *Inform All Involved* — After you plan your transitions, make sure EVERYONE involved knows the WHAT, WHEN, HOW, and WHY. If people catch the vision for the kind of moment you're trying to create, they'll be

more apt to follow through on the instructions you give them.

3. *Keep It Brief* — Transitional elements should be short. Why? They're not the main focus, you're just connecting the dots. And brevity is an absolute must for a *talking* transition. Always follow rule #1: Planning (and writing) out your verbal segue keeps it shorter AND makes it more focused and effective. One should avoid segues that are off-the-cuff.

4. *Keep It Simple* — The more complex a transition is, the more easily it can fall apart. Look for the simplest route from point A to point B. There are times to make a segue more complex, but it needs to serve a purpose and be a meaningful part of the worship journey.

5. *Always Practice Segues* — It may seem tedious at times, but have a run-through where all those involved practice the segues. This gives you the peace of mind of knowing that everyone gets it. And it also reveals those segues that don't work like they were planned.

Involvement and Integration

When planning your worship, and looking at all of the elements that will make up a given week, give careful thought to WHO would be the best person to serve in different roles. Those giving communion meditations, sharing prayers, performing dramas, and giving testimonies should, when possible, represent the tapestry of members that make up your church. One of the beautiful things about your church is the different races, cultures, genders, and ages that make up the body of believers.

Giving careful thought to WHO might be best to serve is critical. However, one should not be scheduled to serve just because they fit a certain demographic. They must be the right person even before you consider race, culture, gender, or age.

Each church has different ideas about how women can serve in their services. My prayer is that everyone who has been called to lead God's people have studied this carefully and from many perspectives, bathed it in prayer, and requested the perspective and insight of others. However, no matter where your leaders land on this issues, their position should be honored and taken into consideration when integrating members into the assembly.

Developing Meta-Narratives

We've already talked about creating worship narratives. However, for every narrative there are meta-narratives that support that narrative. Often the meta-narrative might be something regarding the church's overall vision or mission statement. A subtle reference to the church's vision statement during a sermon or as a segue between different elements helps the church see what you are doing in light of the vision statement. Ending a service with a charge to GO and be the presence of Jesus helps tie everything back into the church's mission statement of COME, CONNECT, GROW, GO.

These meta-narratives can be the glue that helps bind everything together and makes sense of what we are doing. It's not difficult to tie meta-narratives into what you're doing, but it takes intentional thought. As you are looking at all of the sermons for a series, it is important to identify the overarching narrative for the series. Once the narrative is set, you can begin to notice other subtle themes that are woven into the texts. These subtleties can become your meta-narratives. For example, if your overall narrative is a focus on grace from the Gospel of Mark, then some of the meta-narratives might be love, discipleship, or redemption.

Book Ends

How you begin and end a service is critical. How you start sets the stage for what will happen in the next 60-75 minutes. It's the *main course* or narrative that helps us to determine what we should do and how we should do it. Most often one would start a little more upbeat with a Call To Worship, which would include some modern praise choruses or hymns and perhaps some scripture reading. Then maybe switch gears a little bit as we move into the Communion. However, there might be times when you start with something more subtle like the Doxology. Sometimes a media piece can help bring focus to the beginning of a service. Give thought to the tone you are trying to set and choose the elements that best help you to accomplish that. Consider the fact that often a high percentage of the people are not yet in the auditorium when the service first starts so stay away from starting with things that are foundational to the rest of the service.

One of the values that I often talk about when helping churches develop a Theology of Worship is that we don't see our gathering times as the culmination of what God is doing but as a catalyst to fuel the mission of God as we go out and live lives of worship by being the presence of the living God in our community, workplaces, neighborhoods, and homes. When we end our gathering times we have the opportunity to remind God's people that how they live as disciples of Jesus matters. Give thought to how you can use the time of corporate worship to catapult the church into action and live out the narrative that was discussed.

Anomalies

Periodically there are things that need to happen during the course of a service that don't really have anything to do with the narrative you are trying to create for that day. Perhaps the Elders want to dedicate a new set of deacons, or maybe you're going to do baby dedications or praying over a group that is leaving on a mission trip. These anomalies provide an opportunity for you to help the church see everything God is doing as a part of the overarching vision of your church. How one navigates in and out of these segments can determine how effective they are at providing value to the listener.

Announcements are another anomaly that happens more frequently. There are details of events and things that affect the entire church that need to be communicated when we are together. The key is to find an opportune time to make these announcements where it won't interrupt the flow and distract from the narrative. As always, giving thought to who should do the announcement and the segues in and out are an important variable. A great idea is to do your announcements while the offering is being passed. Another thought would be to have the majority of announcements be done on video if you have someone with gifts in making videos.

For recurring announcements, like events that your church does on a regular basis, you could write a script and have your connections deacon record it to video and then you could set it to a music bed. Perhaps he could even have a couple of other people involved in his ministry record one using the same basic script and they could be rotated. Events that are planned in advance could also have announcement videos made and these could be put together in one congruent announcement roll. Pre-service announcement slides could be done that same way. This video could then be played during the offering time and could provide a segue to the worship leader/praise team coming back on to lead. There are many possibilities of what could happen with announcements that could make them more effective.

Planning Center

The preaching minister and worship leader have the most collective time on stage and therefore probably have the best sense of how the service could be best planned in order for it to truly be a savory meal. The Planning Center (planningcenter-online.com) is the greatest tool they have for helping manage all of the details that make up each week's assembly. Below are quick descriptions of the various ways the PC can help your worship planning be effective.

- The PC allows you a quick reference to how often you've used various elements in the past so that there's not too much repetition.
- The PC allows you to manage, schedule, and communicate with all of the various volunteers that will be participating in each week's service.
- The PC can manage all of the media that you play during the assemblies as well. Even if the media is ultimately going to be played with ProPresenter, by uploading it first to the PC you can communicate with your Tech Staff what pieces will be used and they can then take them from the PC and put them into ProPresenter.
- In the PC you can manage all of your music files, creating multiple arrangements for each song, and then upload MP3s and PDFs for each arrangement. This allows each music team to have the resources they need to prepare for rehearsals.
- There are notes that can be added to each section of a worship plan and assigned to specific people in the PC.

So, for example, the preaching minister could put instructional cues in the sermons section of the plan that the media operator could use as a guide for changing slides. You could also give lighting cues to your Lighting Tech if you planned lighting changes during your music set. There's also a section called Communion Coordination where you could give ideas to the people leading Communion Meditations. That way, once you've invited them to participate in a given service, they can go right to the section that applies to them and see the communication and details that you have for them.

- Probably the greatest asset the PC is to worship planning is the fact that you can visually see every detail that you have planned. As you're thinking about flow you can visually see how everything connects. And the ability to shuffle the deck by dragging and dropping elements into different places is invaluable.

These things are really just scratching the surface on what the Planning Center is capable of. It would be a great investment for the church to have the preaching minister and worship leader get some training on the Planning Center so that they can be able to use its many layers as worship planning becomes more involved and complex.

Get Started

This is just a starting point for helping a preaching minister and worship leader learn to work together to design dynamic corporate worship. The important thing is to begin to incorporate some of these flavor profiles (elements and processes) into the meals that you create so that God's story is told in a way that helps transform lives to be more like Jesus and to live on mission for him.

HABITS THAT CAN GIVE LEADERS ENERGY AND ENDURANCE

Jim Martin

Many church leaders are tired. Many ministers and elders describe themselves as being *worn out*. A few years ago, I was in conversation with the former president of a large seminary. He was now working with another seminary in a far less strenuous role. In this role, he typically preached at a different church each Sunday. I asked him, "What are you seeing in the churches across the country where you are the guest speaker?"

He replied, "Jim, I am seeing many, many tired people in these churches. Some are exhausted." He spoke of how many of these people seem to lack any kind of margin in their lives. Sometimes entire congregations are exhausted after having been through a grueling process, crisis, or church fight.

Across the country, there are many tired church leaders. Some leaders are drained due in part to the hectic pace of their congregation. Some churches do appear to be extremely busy. The leaders may feel like they are spinning many plates and may wonder how much more they can take. In some churches, leaders say "no" to hardly any request. Consequently, more and more programs are initiated, which of course means there are that many more programs that must be maintained, resulting in energy being depleted.

Meanwhile, other leaders have very poor habits. Some have poor spiritual-formation habits. Others may have poor ministry or relational habits. Still others may have poor habits when it comes to basic "street smarts" that are necessary to navigate within a congregation.

Good habits are very important. In fact they are critical.

While God is our ultimate source of energy (Phil. 2:12-13; Eph. 1:17-19 and 3:16-21) for perseverance and sustainability, our habits can either contribute positively to our energy or deplete our energy.

If leaders are not aware of the quality of their habits, they might be leading in a manner that is not sustainable for the long term.

Henri Nouwen once observed that ministry is service in the name of the Lord.[1] That being true, we certainly don't depend upon our own strength and might in order to go the distance. At the same time, our

> *If leaders are not aware of the quality of their habits, they might be leading in a manner that is not sustainable for the long term.*

---

[1] Nouwen, *The Living Reminder*, p. 12.

habits and practices really do matter. I have found it helpful to frame such habits under several different headings.

1. *Spiritual-Formation Habits.* Our habits have a way of helping to form and shape us into a certain kind of person. Ideally, our habits reflect a life well-lived. One habit that church leaders might pay attention to is making choices that help one live as a healthy individual within a congregation.

This is so important for church leaders. There are many stories about church leaders who, for one reason or another, do not take their own formation seriously. These stories are far too common. Adultery. Theft. Plagiarism.

Some are attentive to their own spiritual disciplines, yet their spiritual life and their emotional life seem to be disconnected from each other. Consequently, a minister can be a person who has an M.Div. or other advanced training while remaining very immature in his marriage. Or, an elder might perceive himself to be seasoned and experienced as a shepherd but has a volatile temper that his family knows all too well. Peter Scazzero reminds us in his excellent book, *The Emotionally Healthy Leader,* that one cannot separate one's spiritual life from one's emotional/relational life.

2. *Self-awareness Habits.* Healthy people are self-aware. They are aware of their thinking and their emotions. They develop habits that reflect that they understand the need to manage themselves. However, when we are unaware of our emotions, we may find that what lies beneath the surface

> *Healthy people are self-aware.*

(emotionally) can bubble up to the surface when triggered. For example, a man may feel deep hurt over the absence (emotional if not physical) of his father. He may have wondered if perhaps he had done something to cause his father to want nothing to do with him. Consequently, when a group of elders talk with him about changes they would like to see him make, he may hear their comments as if they were about to abandon him. While the requests may actually be minor, he receives this admonition as much stronger than they intended.

3. *Relationship Habits.* We all bring particular habits into our relationships. Some of these habits were developed in our family of origin. Some we developed along the way. These habits can impact the relationships we have in the body of Christ.

One relationship habit that we should cultivate as church leaders is the habit of paying attention to others. This may be challenging. Our culture is constantly attempting to get our attention. Texts. E-mails. Facebook messages. Tweets. Advertising. Television, etc. Many Christians have difficulty engaging in a simple conversation without constantly checking their phones. Yet, Christian leaders have the opportunity to model before the congregation what it means to pay attention to someone.

Perhaps a good beginning is to practice solitude in one's devotional life. Starting off the day alone, with the devices off, can help a person begin to focus on another. Without such a discipline, we can live as scattered people flitting from one activity to the next while we are fully present with no one. Other practices which might be helpful include eye contact, using another's name, and listening to the details of another's life.

4. *Ministry Habits.* Some people use this word *ministry* to refer to the many things they do at the church building. Others may use the word to refer to the church programs they are involved in. Christian leaders need to pay attention to some basic habits related to ministry.

For example, one habit that might be helpful to many church leaders is to make the commitment to stop unnecessary costly behaviors. Serving as a preacher or elder can be very difficult. These roles can require much time and energy. What heightens the difficulties is when we engage in costly behaviors that are unnecessary and even depleting. For example, when leaders regularly complain and are cynical, it can be very costly to the leader and to others as well. When leaders come together and one is typically negative and cynical, these behaviors have a way of draining the energy out of the group.

Contrast this to the minister or elder who comes together with the group of leaders and is typically ready to report on what God is doing in the church. Perhaps this elder tells a story about what God is doing in the life of a particular family. As a result, the leadership group feels energized and encouraged.

> *The leader who leads from conviction imagines what God might do if only we would trust in him.*

Another example of a ministry habit that can be costly occurs when a leader leads out of anxiety instead of conviction. This is costly behavior. Those who lead out of anxiety are more worried about who might be upset than those who might be blessed. This leader might be wringing his hands wondering what the leadership team will do if this or that happens. The leader who leads from conviction imagines what God might do if only we would trust in him.

5. *Practical Habits.* There are certain habits that might best come under the category of "street smarts." These street smarts can be wonderful habits for leaders. They often surface only after years of serving.

Lately, I have been asking groups of church leaders for suggestions about "street smarts." Typically, they immediately respond with some real nuggets that are worthy of becoming habits. Here are some of their answers:

- "Pick your battles."
- "Make the effort to remember people's names."
- "There is often another side to the story you just heard."
- "Show an interest in the children."
- "Listen well."
- "Be very careful in making announcements."
- "Don't repeat what was told you in confidence."
- "Remember how far someone has actually come."
- "You never know what someone in the congregation is actually going through."
- "When you need to have a difficult conversation with someone, don't go alone."

So where do we go from here? A few suggestions:

1. Consider specific actions that you might implement under each one of these categories.
2. Seek to identify negative depleting habits.
3. Start practicing one habit that in some way contributes in a positive way to energy and endurance.

These and other actions, practiced regularly, may help church leaders to develop more energy and endurance for their work.

THE IMMANUEL EXPERIENCE
Longing, Lifestyle, and Mission with Jesus

Phil Ware

Longing

Philip said, "Lord, show us the Father and that will be enough for us."
(John 14:8)

Can you believe Philip's audacity? "Lord, just show us God, and we will be fine!"

Philip hits the nail on the head for many of us. Our mortality guarantees that we will face challenges we can't handle. If we could only know God was there with us, we might survive our hard times.

Over decades of ministry, I've learned that people with a dying loved one need to know that God is with them in their helplessness and grief. When I have prayed with them, I've asked the Lord to make his presence known to them in tangible ways. When circumstances are too big for us, all of us need to know we are not alone. We call on the One who is bigger than our catastrophes, disasters, diseases, addictions, and heartbreaks.

Rather than criticize Philip for his audacious request, I've learned to make the same petition but hopefully with a bit more humility. Plus, Philip wasn't the first of God's people to make this kind of bold request. Remember what Moses told God about leading his people:

> The LORD replied [to Moses], "My Presence will go with you, and I will give you rest."
>
> Then Moses said to him, "If your Presence does not go with us, do not send us up from here. How will anyone know that you are pleased with your people, and with me as their leader unless you go with us? What else will distinguish your people and me from all the other people on the face of the earth?"
>
> And the LORD said to Moses, "I will do the very thing you have asked, because I am pleased with you and I know you by name."
>
> Then Moses said, "Now show me your glory." (Ex. 33:14–18)

Moses knew that without the LORD's presence, trying to lead his people was futile. He demanded to experience God's glory. And the LORD honored Moses's request (Ex. 33:19-24) just as I have seen God reassure those facing life's most difficult moments with his presence.

We know this yearning for God's presence burns in the hearts of his people. We are aware because we have the same yearning. Life crashes in on us. Our strength, ideas, hope, money, energy, health, wisdom, and coping abilities are exhausted. Out of our weakest moments, we have seen God sustain us. We have experienced his presence mysteriously strengthening us and moving us forward when fear, despair, worry, and dread had frozen us in our helplessness.

We also know this yearning for God's presence lies in the heart of each believer because of our songs. Read or sing the great Charles Myles hymn, "In the Garden":

> I come to the garden alone,
> While the dew is still on the roses,
> And the voice I hear falling on my ear
> The Son of God discloses.

> Refrain:
> And He walks with me, and He talks with me,
> And He tells me I am His own;
> And the joy we share as we tarry there,
> None other has ever known.

Or remember the powerful words of Mary A. Lathbury in "Break Thou the Bread of Life":

> Beyond the sacred page, I seek Thee, Lord;
> My spirit pants for Thee, O living Word!

Not only do these older songs anticipate the intimate words of our modern hymnody, but they also speak to a deep yearning that we have as disciples for Jesus to be real to us. In recent years, many have attributed this yearning for "God experiences" to millennials, X'ers, Gen Y, and Gen Z young adults. "They just want more sizzle, pop, and emotion in worship!" We know better. This longing for God to show himself exists in every disciple's heart—a longing that often goes unstated until life's realities seem impossible to navigate. We ache for Jesus to come to us in our storms to calm the winds and still our raging seas. We long for David's experience of the Lord as our Shepherd to lead us, guide us, calm us, accompany us, and prepare a place in his presence for us. But where can we go to satiate our God-longings?

Matthew

Why do we allow this yearning in our hearts to experience God's presence to lie dormant during our everyday lives as disciples? Why do we wait to search for the Lord's presence until our world falls apart? Does Jesus come to us only in the storm? Is the presence of God revealed only when we are in distress? Why don't we emphasize the Lord's promise to be present and real to us in our lives as his disciples?

> *Why do we allow this yearning to lie dormant in our lives as disciples?*

Two decades ago, I heard a biblical scholar say something like this:

> For eighteen centuries, Matthew was the Gospel of the church. However, in the nineteenth and much of the twentieth century, Matthew has been largely ignored.

My life in church and my neglect of Matthew in my personal study verified this speaker's observation. I began pouring myself into Matthew's story of Jesus. Why had Matthew's story of Jesus fallen into such lack of use? Why had I pursued the power and excitement of Mark, or the social justice themes of Luke, or the personal conversations of Jesus with people in John? What had I missed in Matthew? Why had I neglected his story of Jesus?

As I read Matthew, I noticed a key theme. He addressed our yearning to experience God's presence in our lives. Matthew introduced this theme early in his gospel. Only Matthew has these words and this name for Jesus – notice the underlined words in the quotation that follows:

> But after [Joseph] had considered [divorcing Mary privately because of her pregnancy], an angel of the Lord appeared to him in a dream and said, "Joseph son of David, do not be afraid to take Mary home as your wife, because what is conceived in her is from the Holy Spirit. She will give birth to a son, and you are to give him the name Jesus, because he will save his people from their sins."
>
> All this took place to fulfill what the Lord had said through the prophet: "The virgin will conceive and give birth to a son, and they will call him Immanuel" (which means "God with us"). (Matt. 1:20–23)

Matthew helps us know from the beginning of his story of Jesus that God is present in the work and words of Jesus. Disciples can experience "Immanuel" in the life and teachings of Jesus Christ! He is "God with us"! From the beginning, Matthew's story of Jesus points us to a lifestyle and mission focused that leads us to experience God's presence.

Mission

But how does this help us with our yearning for God's presence?

How does this help us speak to the restlessness of our younger members and the coming generations discontent with church life confined to pews and classrooms?

How does this help us as church leaders find a mission that sustains and fulfills the longings of our people's hearts and helps us fulfill the mission the Lord gave us to do as his followers?

If we are willing to listen, Matthew tells us. He points us to three other Immanuel sayings in Jesus's ministry. As Jesus enters the final phase of his mission on earth, he begins to move toward the cross warning his disciples about what is ahead and calling them to follow him:

> *From that time on Jesus began to explain to his disciples that he must go to Jerusalem and suffer many things at the hands of the elders, the chief priests and the teachers of the law and that he must be killed and on the third day be raised to life. (Matt. 16:21)*

Matthew shows us Jesus spending his time on the way to the cross preparing his disciples for life without his physical presence. He is teaching them to live as his disciples in his church. Yes, on the way to the cross Jesus will heal some who have deep needs. He will also confront his religious enemies. But, the focus of this final part of the Gospel is Jesus teaching his disciples about their lifestyle and their mission after he is gone. Of course, Jesus's words are for us as well. That is why Matthew wrote them.

Jesus is Immanuel, "God with us," in Matthew's story of Jesus (Matt. 1:23) — Matthew's first Immanuel saying. In this final section, Jesus promises to be Immanuel, "God with us," in three additional sayings:

- *"For where two or three gather in my name, there am I with them"* *(Matt. 18:20).*
- *"Truly I tell you, whatever you did for one of the least of these brothers and sisters of mine, you did for me"* *(Matt. 25:40).*
- *"Therefore go and make disciples of all nations, baptizing them in the name of the Father and of the Son and of the Holy Spirit, and teaching them to obey everything I have commanded you. And surely I am with you always, to the very end of the age"* *(Matt. 28:19–20).*

While Matthew does not use the term "Immanuel" in these three passages, the concept is present. Jesus's focus in these passages is on how to do life and live out mission as Jesus's disciples. The context of each Immanuel saying calls us as Jesus's disciples to live out his mission expecting the Lord to meet us as we do.

> *The context of each Immanuel saying calls us to live out his mission expecting the Lord to meet us as we do.*

The first Immanuel saying in this last section of the Gospel comes from Matthew 18. This chapter is about living the principles of the kingdom of heaven in our church families. When we guard our influence to keep others from stumbling, when we forgive from the heart radically despite its cost, when we go in search of the brother or sister who has wandered away, and when we practice loving church discipline, Jesus lives among us. We experience Immanuel, "God with us"!

The second Immanuel saying in this last section occurs in chapter 25. Jesus calls us to practice genuine compassion for those in need. When we serve the hungry, the thirsty, the stranger, those in need of clothing, people who are ill, or those confined in prison, then he promises to be present. We are not only doing his work and accomplishing his mission; we are serving him. We are serving Immanuel! We experience Immanuel as we serve.

The third Immanuel saying in Matthew's last section are Jesus's final words of the gospel, found in Matthew 28. We know this as "The Great Commission." Jesus challenges us to make disciples by crossing cultural boundaries to reach all people, by baptizing those who believe in him, and by teaching the newly baptized to obey the teachings of their Lord. Jesus promises that when we do these things he will be present. We experience Immanuel, the Lord's power and presence as we live his mission for us in the world.

Real

One of the most significant challenges for most of us as church leaders is to help our congregations live out of our sense of mission. I ask church leaders, "How would your neighborhood and community be different, what would they lose, if you weren't there?" Surprisingly, many don't know how to answer that question. Nearly all, however, want to know how to attract young families and keep their young people. Somehow they don't see disconnect. They want a quick fix. They are looking at what other churches do that is successful, not realizing that living out the Lord's call to mission must be at the heart of their efforts to keep those they are losing or reach those they not reaching.

Unfortunately, some congregations have made a mad dash to offer special experiences for those who are younger to attract and keep them. We live in an experience-habituated and experience-saturated culture. The emergence of virtual-reality experiences compounds this saturation. However, experience for experience sake is just another form of addiction. Without intentional, missional, and lifestyle purposes, our church experiences become little more than an experience for experience sake. The truth is, however, that we don't have enough bright lights, moving music, great video presentations, and social media apps to keep the "experience junkies" in our congregations. Experience "fixes" are all around and delivered in ever-increasing frequency and quality. Most churches cannot compete!

> *Without intentional, missional, and lifestyle purpose, our church experiences become another form of addiction.*

However, if we understand all addiction as some form of God-hunger—a need for God to be real, a longing for God that we've short-circuited with counterfeit God-experiences—then we can address three issues related to experiencing God in one missional move:

- We can provide an avenue for folks to satiate the yearning to experience God's presence.
- We can engage our experience-driven generations with opportunities to experience Immanuel, "God with us," and not just have another counterfeit spiritual experience.
- We can live out the call of Jesus to be his people of righteous character, gracious compassion, and passionate mission.

As we look at our budgets, our vision/mission statements, and our slate of activities and ministries, we must ask:

Why are we doing this? This activity or ministry may be good, but is it of God? Providing this experience may keep folks hanging around, but are their lives being changed because they have had an encounter with Immanuel?

In our desire to fix what may be broken, to keep those we fear we are losing, and to reach those we are not reaching, let's return to Matthew for guidance.

For some folks, Bible study — especially the study of Jesus — can provide remarkable moments where Jesus is real to them. They feel as if they can hear his voice and smell the dust of the Galilean countryside in his garments. They can be caught up in the euphoria of his miracles and convicted to their core by his loving rebukes. Bible study for information is nothing more than a data dump, but they read to pursue Jesus, asking the Holy Spirit to make the Lord real to them as they seek to discover Immanuel, "God with us" in the Lord's story.

For other folks, life in genuine community grabs their hearts and connects them to God like nothing else. They could be participating with brothers in sisters in meaningful worship. They could be challenged to forgive someone who feels impossible to pardon and finding that the Lord is empowering them do what feels impossible. It could be going in search of someone who has wandered and winning back a friend and bringing back them back to Jesus. In the context of community, Jesus becomes Immanuel, "God with us."

Still others find spiritual exhilaration when they help others. They feel closest to Jesus when they are demonstrating God's compassion through acts of kindness. Their costly and sometimes dângerous service resonates with the Holy Spirit deep in their hearts as they live out the gracious compassion of their Lord. Even though many who receive this mercy, love, care, and support are not as responsive as they would hope, they continue to serve. They find God's holy power helping them. In the context of compassionate care, Jesus becomes Immanuel to them, "God with us."

Finally, when Jesus' disciples risk stepping outside of their culture to reach others, they often bump up against their insufficiency. In their insufficiency, they discover the Lord is making them better than they are. They miraculously have the right words. They find themselves in the right place to make a spiritual connection with someone who is seeking the Lord. God opens doors of opportunity, and the Holy Spirit opens the doors to people's hearts. As they see new children born into God's family, they are energized by the sense of God's holy power and presence as Immanuel, "God with us."

Matthew reminds us that we must live out of Jesus's call to lifestyles of righteous character, gracious compassion, and passionate mission. And when we intentionally do this to honor the Lord, Jesus shows up and we experience Immanuel.

Now

While many of us have participated in one or more of these four dimensions of the Immanuel experience, not many of us have connected it to our mission as Jesus's disciple. Fewer congregational budgets are built around these four ways for people to experience the Lord's presence. We find it easier to reach for a quick fix or try one of the latest fads or bestselling church-help books. Shouldn't we at least take some time to walk with Jesus in the Gospel of Matthew and see if we can find ways to experience Immanuel?

But where do we start?

A church change begins with a core of the congregational leaders changing. This can begin by this core group of leaders reading one chapter from one of the gospels every day for a year. They pray, asking the Holy Spirit to help them to hear what the Lord wants them to KNOW, FEEL, and DO that day based on their reading. On a regular basis, this group gets together during lunch, coffee, or small-group gatherings. They share what the Lord is doing in their hearts and what they have put into their practice in their lives.

About three months into their journey with Jesus, this group begins to focus on the four Immanuel sayings in Matthew. Does what is said here ring true to them and to what they have found in their journey with Jesus? They discuss what would happen if the congregation, or some part of it, began to pursue and live out these four ways experiencing Immanuel with passion. They share their Immanuel experiences and invite others to do the same.

> *A church change begins with a core of the congregational leaders changing.*

Finally, this group begins to look at their church mission, event planning, and budgeting. They are honest about where they spend their words, time, and money. They focus on giving people in their congregation an intentional opportunity to live out the lifestyle and mission of Jesus. They carefully examine how they spend their money, time, and words in congregational life and recalibrate their budget. Are they only having more activities or propping up old ministries that have long run out of steam and interest? Then they do the important work of aligning the ministry efforts to their sense of mission. They make sure all their church events and ministries intentionally are planned to provide a pathway to one of the four Immanuel experiences through mission and lifestyle.

Epilogue

Does this work? If so, where?

Some congregations find it hard to give up so many of their traditional and expected activities to realign with Matthew's vision of the church. Many congregations even have a hard time finding a significant group of leaders who will do the intentional Bible reading for a year. Finding churches that follow Matthew's vision is hard. Church transformation from the inside out can be slow work, so churches choose to go with fads, seminars, and copycat programs. Deep inside, however, we know that we must not ignore the importance of spiritual passion, discipline, and devotion. Matthew reminds us that when a core group of leaders commits to a clear mission that enables their people to experience Immanuel, then transformation comes.

If you look at healthy, vibrant, growing churches, you will find at least two or three of Matthew's Immanuel principles at the core of their mission and practices. They might not be called Immanuel principles, but these churches have built their lifestyle and mission around these biblically-rooted practices.

Look also at successful missional community movements — aka house churches, missional families, or missional groups. (Beware, there are missional movements in more liberal denominations called missional movements, but I'm referring to those who share a similar approach to Scripture that most of our restoration-movement churches have toward Scripture.) The growing groups emphasize three or four Immanuel principles as foundational to their mission and culture. They build their

> *...when a core group of leaders commits to a clear mission that enables their people to experience Immanuel, then transformation comes.*

operational practices around these principles. My study on Matthew's Immanuel sayings and my investigative work into missional communities (3DM, Verge, and For the City) helped me see this coalescence. Matthew used the Immanuel theme for more than just a structural framework for his story of Jesus. He is presenting Jesus' plan for growing disciples. Of course, this shouldn't surprise us, based on Jesus's closing words in the Gospel of Matthew!

My prayer is that you will find a group of committed disciples who will begin a yearlong Jesus journey with you. My hope is that you would find a group of fellow church leaders who will dedicate a year to the journey, prayerfully re-calibrating your approach to your lifestyle and mission as disciples of Jesus.

Jesus wants to be Immanuel to our yearning hearts. Jesus calls us to live out his lifestyle and mission in the world and promises to be present with us as we do. The Holy Spirit indwells and empowers us to know the will and follow the direction of our Lord Jesus. Let's never settle for just doing church. Let's experience Immanuel and help our churches do the same.

CHURCH HEALTH

Bonding Agents, Pastoral Presence, and Congregational Health

Randy Daugherty

Sometimes instruction comes when you least expect it and in ways that you don't expect. Several years ago, during a church planting effort in the country of Ghana, I was blessed with an invitation to visit a Liberian refugee camp. I walked into the camp assuming the role of a teacher. Before the day was over, I was the student and they were my teacher.

I sat for a few hours and listened to young and old alike tell heart-wrenching stories of the events that led to their eventual placement in a refugee camp in Ghana. A thousand people lived together in this small camp.

A few years earlier, they escaped potential genocide by fleeing to the west coast of Africa and boarding a ship. The ship made port twice between Liberia and Ghana, hoping to find safe harbor. At each stop they were rejected. Finally, Ghana agreed to receive them.

When they arrived at the refugee camp they had nothing but the clothes on their backs. They built their own housing from bamboo. The government agreed to provide them food rations each month, but these usually lasted for only two weeks. They finished out the month by foraging in the forest for berries, nuts, and small animals. It was customary for the younger ones to fast for 5-8 days so they could have enough food to share with older ones, and especially the sick people.

I was stunned by their story, their survival, and the most genuine experience of community I've ever seen. I asked a fifteen-year-old boy how they deal with the challenges and uncertainties that come with their way of life. He looked me straight in the eyes and said, "Sir, we lived through unspeakable horror; we lived together in the belly of a ship for eleven days. Life experiences, God, and brotherhood have sewn our lives together." Yes, he was fifteen!

Meanwhile, back in America...

About a year ago I received a call from Thomas. I met him a few years ago at a retreat. We exchanged emails a few times over the years about different things and had a few coffee conversations. He is intelligent and well read. When we met years ago, he struck me as someone who possessed a passionate faith and a deep love for pastoral ministry. But the voice on the other end of the phone sounded tired and frustrated. "Paul said that anyone who desires the office of a bishop desires a good work," he said. "I'm not sure that's true. I didn't sign up for this."

I asked a few probing questions in response. He was ready to talk!

This is the gist of what he said:

We are stuck in a proverbial traffic circle. We know it's true but nobody wants to talk about it. I'm not saying we aren't doing some things as a leadership and as a congregation. We do a lot of things. We have a lot of activities and moving parts. But we aren't really connecting with our people. To be completely honest, I don't have relationships with anyone. In fact, as an eldership we are professional but we aren't connected to each other beyond the tasks that we perform.

We don't know our staff and their families as human beings. They are nothing more than employees. I go to meetings. I weigh in on the occasional issue and deal with a crisis here and there.

I just feel like we are maintaining a system. I guess that is important. But something is lacking. I don't feel like we are really engaged with our people or they with us. We rarely share any pastoral-care stories. It's like there is a "gap" between the assumptions we live by about our leadership of this body and of its health and the actual truth about our leadership and what is happening within our congregation. It's the elephant in the living room that nobody wants to talk about. I'm not sure we even know how to talk about it. I'm just really disillusioned about my service and where we are right now as a congregation.

The "Altered" State of Our Union

Recently, on a flight to California, I was reminded how calm and serene everything looks from 35,000 feet. But eventually we landed in the middle of *reality*.

Church is like that, isn't it?

Alan Roxborough, author of *Joining God, Remaking Church, Changing the World*, describes what we are experiencing as the "great unraveling." Doesn't sound too comforting, right? It's a time of disorientation due to cultural changes and changes within churches and families that is providing us an opportunity to rethink what it means to be a Christian today, to be healthy as churches, and what Christian community should look like. It's easier said than done. But it must be done.

We gather in assemblies and classes every week. We attend events together — occasionally. We have the occasional potluck. But we have surrendered some critical ground.

Nominal spirituality is on the rise. We come together in our privacy. Small-group participation is on the decline (not to mention what actually passes as quality small-group interaction!). We have lost the art of hospitality. We listen to lessons on a weekly basis but we don't know how to sit together and talk about kingdom matters. We do congregational assessments, but intellectualize and smooth the rough edges of discovery, choosing instead to live in cordial proximity to ruggedly-honest conversations about   the state of our union and "what's next." We have, at least in some instances, become enamored with data collection and the promise (illusion?) that analysis of the same will be the answer to what ails us. Most often, though, the journey into healthier ways of being doesn't complete. Why? In short, we are disregarding what is learned from diagnostics because we don't want to cross pain thresholds that stand between who we are and who the Spirit is nudging us to become as leaderships and as a people.

We are making mechanical, organizational, and cosmetic changes but overlooking the larger issue of what's actually happening (and not happening) spiritually *within people and families.*[2]

A few months ago a friend told me about a call he got from a woman who had no electrical power in her house. She told him she flipped switches in every room. Nothing. She checked the wire coming from the street to the house. All good. She called the electric company about power outages. All good. Exasperated, she said, "Is it possible the wiring in my house is bad?" My friend asked, "Have you checked the breaker box?" She said, "What's that?" The rest is history.

> *We are making mechanical, organizational, and cosmetic changes but overlooking the larger issue of what's actually happening (and not happening) spiritually within people and families.*

Bulbs. Switches. Cords. They are important. But they are secondary to the flow of electricity. Electrical power in a house is a more fundamental issue that must be addressed before other things that are a part of the transfer of electrical power can function properly.

---

2 I think James Thompson, *The Church According to Paul: Rediscovering the Community Conformed to Christ,* p. 247, makes an excellent point: "The church is the new humanity, which is now being transformed. Paul's mission is to proclaim Christ and invite people into this community . . . . Their mission is to grow up and to work together to complete the building that is under construction . . . . Paul never mentions the numerical growth of his congregations . . . . While Paul undoubtedly wanted the churches to grow, he gives primary attention in his letters to the transformation of communities into the image of Christ (Rom. 8:29). Legitimate growth occurs when the transformation of the believers is a light to people in darkness."

Remember my friend Thomas? Sometimes we pretend the lights are on when they really aren't because we are too enamored with the false comfort of some conventional defaults.

Some of these default habits and behaviors might be:

1. Denial, avoidance, comforting ourselves with nostalgic memories of the past, excuses, and of course, blaming something or somebody for the state of our union.

2. Ignoring a more diagnostic approach to where we are and focusing on professionalism, hip technology, special events, celebrating wider ministry offerings and programs, and rhetorical fixes (e.g., give the room an "atta boy" and assume all is well.).

3. Assuming that website development and vision statements are representative of where our people are spiritually and who we are as a congregation.

4. Endless analysis and data gathering that eventually dies a slow death in the grip of waning interest.

It is difficult to break free from such defaults and into a more diagnostic and intentional approach that distinguishes symptoms from causes. But this is precisely what needs to happen for any system — our system — to reimagine what health looks like for both leadership and congregation.[3]

I think Edwin Friedman (*Leadership in an Age of Quick Fix*) is spot-on when he says the way out cannot be obtained by "developing some new method for 'tinkering with the mechanics,' or

---

[3] See chapters 2-3 of Tom Rainier, *Autopsy of a Deceased Church*, for a stimulating conversation on this point.

by redoubling our efforts to try harder. The way out, rather, requires *shifting our orientation to the way we think about relationships* from one that focuses on techniques that motivate others to one that focuses on the leader's own presence and being."[4]

Friedman's point is a critical piece in setting the trajectory for conversations about congregational health in general and pastoral functioning and care in particular. We need to stop pretending in our leaderships and congregations that this is an optional point or something that needs to be trimmed up and refined. We need to come together over this ground as humble students. Larger conversations about leadership functioning, congregational health, and who we claim to be can gain genuine traction toward refreshing possibilities only as we get convicted on this point.

I am in no way an expert in chemistry. But I ran across something recently while reading about the phenomenon of chemical bonding that offers a powerful parallel for us to consider.

Chemical bonding lies at the very core of chemistry. It is what enables about one hundred elements to form the more than fifty million known chemical substances that make up the physical world: "A chemical bond is an "effect" that causes certain atoms to join together to form enduring structures that have unique physical and chemical properties." Extract chemical bonding from life and our world would change dramatically, to say the least! It is the glue that holds stuff together and makes things happen.

What has been said thus far and what is now offered is not suggested as a "fix-all." It isn't a recipe for success. At a

---

4 Edwin Friedman, *A Failure of Nerve: Leadership in an Age of Quick Fix*, p. 3.

minimum, it is a contribution to future conversations about responsible pastoral and relational functioning that can help us create the kind of "bonding effects" that will result in reimagining new habits and norms for what health looks like in leadership and in our congregations.

Bonding Agent #1: Practicing Divine Encounter

It is easy for leaders and congregations to become lost in the mechanical and tactical aspects of church life. Meetings, decisions, thinking, and norms can be slowly eclipsed by *second-order* things. We just keep the church machine running and assume everybody has a solid connection between theological reference points and ministry.

Before Isaiah began his ministry, he was given a vision of God's majesty and power (cf. Isa. 6). This encounter with the living God became the *reference point* for his ministry. He preached and ministered out of the impression created by this vision. He was God's prophet to the people — not the people's prophet.

I've often wondered how many times throughout his very challenging ministry he revisited the "temple vision." As situations, challenges, and trials clawed away at his mind and heart, it was this temple experience that gave him comfort, strength, and courage to be God's man no matter the circumstance.

> *"Are the leaders of the future truly men and women of God, people with an ardent desire to dwell in God's presence, to listen to God's voice, to look at God's beauty, to touch God's incarnate Word and taste fully of God's infinite goodness?"*
> – Henri Nouwen

Paul does ministry "in the presence of the Lord or in the sight of Lord" (2 Cor. 4:2; 6:1; 8:21). He talks openly about God's presence as a reminder to himself but also a reminder to his readers. God's presence is a critical reference point for us, too. Henri Nouwen is on target when he addresses this idea:

> *It is not enough for God's people of the future to be moral people, well-trained, eager to help their fellow humans, and able to respond creatively to the burning issues of their time. All of that is very valuable and important, but it is not the heart of Christian leadership. The central question is, "Are the leaders of the future truly men and women of God, people with an ardent desire to dwell in God's presence, to listen to God's voice, to look at God's beauty, to touch God's incarnate Word and taste fully of God's infinite goodness?"[5]*

It is tempting to give this a nod and say, "Yeah, we got it. Next!" But doing so would be symptomatic of why we sometimes don't have lights in the house.[6] We need to check this breaker within ourselves! Living before the Lord as persons and as a leadership says much about our humility and the filters that inform how we discern and do ministry together. Sharpening our awareness of ministry before the Lord should come through our prayers, reading scripture together, and how we occasionally frame

---

[5] Henry J. Nouwen, *In the Name of Jesus,* 2002.
[6] Alan Roxborough, *Joining God, Remaking Church, Changing the World,* pp. xiv-xv, speaking about a fundamental malformation that has occurred among Christians in North America over the past half century, says: "We have come to see our sources of hope everywhere except in the reality of God's presence and action in our world. We might have claimed to be God's people, but we have accepted what might be called 'modernity's wager' — on some level, we think life can be lived without God, that if we or our churches are to be saved, it is up to us alone. This might sound strange if you regularly attend worship, but it is about the most basic convictions that have driven our actions . . . . We've become practiced at personalizing and psychologizing biblical stories for the purpose of self-help and generalized moral teaching for being good citizens. We lost sight of the story that runs through Scripture about God's actions in the world. What we actually need is to imagine that God is up to something. Imagine that God is active in the midst of what seems to be an unrelenting unraveling of not just our churches but our way of life in North America."

conversations about ministry and congregational life. We need to hear it and not just assume it is there. Paul didn't. Neither should we.

Bonding Agent #2: Checking Our Vital Signs

In terms of our physical health, it is important that we take our blood pressure on a regular basis. It is an indicator of personal health and can give us a heads-up that we need a more thorough physical.

The same is true for church leaders. We can drift into ministry slumps while ignoring what is happening *within us* as persons. None of us is beyond the reach of this kind of personal assessment. We must ask ourselves, Am I tired, angry, discouraged, hopeful, confused, hurt, afraid, engaged?[7]

I recall a few years ago attempting to have this kind of conversation with some elders. A few minutes into the conversation it became painfully obvious that nobody wanted to engage in this kind of personal and group assessment. After three or four attempts at opening the conversation...crickets! The reasons for this are certainly symptomatic of other health issues.

The larger point is this: If we can't take our own pulse as leaders and as a leadership, how can we do this with the people we serve? Setting an example speaks volumes about our human-

---

[7] One of the greatest ministries that elderships can provide for their ministry staff is careful attention to this kind of "listening and assessing" for ministers. Sadly, it is too often the case that ministers pine away under heavy clouds of emotional duress because no one genuinely cared enough to "check their pulse." I suspect that many of the men and women who are no longer connected with ministry posts would be if they had leaders and members who ministered to their hearts. It's helpful, too, if ministers are open to this kind of honest conversation!

ness, our honesty with God and ourselves, and our willingness to be transparent with each other.

Assessing ourselves and assessing our health as a leadership is critical to the kind of presence we bring to the life of congregation.

Bonding Agent #3: Being More Intentional with Spiritual Formation

Scripture presents a picture of Christ-followers as people who are part of a community that is intentionally developmental. Jesus said "everybody" is to pick up their cross and come follow!

Eph. 4:15-16 says we are to grow up "in all aspects into him who is the head, even Christ from whom the whole body being fitted and held together by that which every joint supplies causes the growth of the body for the building up of itself in love." A major purpose of leadership is to help Christians engage in this experience of building up (Eph. 4:12).

> *Scripture presents a picture of Christ-followers as people who are part of a community that is intentionally developmental.*

More increasingly, our default here is to operate from the assumption that preaching and teaching is "one-stop shopping" for spiritual formation. We look at aesthetic facets of our health barometers like attendance, giving, ministry machinery, stopping right at the surface and saying all is well.

But, the jury is in. The ground is shifting in our congregations in some serious ways and I'm not talking about worship styles, latte bars, and women's role. This goes beyond aesthetics — it's about faith survival and family health.

Recently, I listened as an elder shared his confusion over a recent decision that revealed the leadership's preference for . . . *distance.*

The congregation had completed a thorough congregational diagnostic that revealed high interest from the congregation for more interaction with the shepherds. The matter was discussed and a course of action was chosen. They announced on a Sunday morning that the minister to the senior members would be increasing his visitation schedule! (Yes, this really happened!) An opportunity for learning, ministry, the re-establishment of pastoral care health initiatives, and faith nurturing was . . . deferred.

We can no longer afford ourselves the hypocritical luxury of decrying things such as attrition, low involvement, and nominal spirituality while we sit and watch from our meeting rooms! Forget the light bulbs for a minute—Where is the breaker box!

Early in his ministry Jesus called twelve men to be his disciples. He spent a great deal of time with the Twelve. They traveled with him. They listened to him teach. They had countless conversations between villages. They sat around campfires and talked for hours. His life was bound up in theirs. He called them friends. He knew them! His ministry was about *message and presence.*

It is impossible to present a holistic picture of Jesus's ministry apart from this relational component. It was a critical piece in how his *message gained traction* in their lives. Bonding!

Paul offers a similar model. He lays his life before the churches as a template for what their relationships and ministry should look like. He reminded the Ephesian elders that his ministry for three years was "house to house" (Acts 20:17-20). His was a ministry of presence and modeling (Acts 20:31, 35).

Some of the most endearing and descriptive pastoral language is found in his first letter to the Thessalonians. Concerned with some possible misunderstandings about his motives and ministry, he spends a good bit of the letter laying these to rest. But tucked away in his assurance are insights into spiritual formation.

In 1 Thess. 2:7-8 he says,

> But we were gentle among you, like a nursing mother taking care of her own children. So being affectionately desirous of you, we were ready to share with you not on the gospel of God but also our own selves, because you had become very dear to us.

What a beautiful picture! He helped them engage the gospel and grow in the Spirit by being involved with them in relationally intentional ways that helped formation gain traction.

Some pressing (and helpful!) questions are knocking on our front door. What should more intentional conversations about spiritual formation look and sound like in our congregation? What do we know about our people . . . *really*? What mechanisms do we have in place to discern how our people and families are doing . . . *really*? What kind of interactions and contexts do we need to create that can help people grow in the Spirit? What kind of feedback loops do we need to put in place to give us a barometer on where our people are in their spiritual walk? How can prayer, small groups, mentoring groups, book clubs, and even home visits be used toward this end?

Bonding Agent #4: Letting the Church Inside

How many times have we learned something new from another person because we decided to have a conversation with them? Or, asked a particular question? Or, listened five minutes longer? Most people know this as both truth and experience. Why isn't this second nature for us as leaderships and congregations?

Some of Paul's letters insinuate previous conversations with churches. His letters impart teaching about what to do with particular situations as well as provide theological underpinnings for living out the Christian life. But, flying at 30,000 feet and looking down on Paul's letters, one can see them as an open conversation between Paul and the churches. The bearer of the letter was charged with reading the letter and then "processing" the contents after the reading. They didn't listen and go home. They heard and processed together. And, yes, church lasted more than 2 hours on those special Sundays!

I wonder how congregational health and leadership effectiveness would be improved if leaders *created space* for people to come and talk openly about things that are on their hearts, dreams they have about the church's future, concerns they may have, and a litany of other possibilities? And what if this wasn't a crisis-initiated event but instead a normative experience? At a minimum, creating these kinds of learning spaces requires humility, an eagerness to learn and relax into the adventure of learning, and the courage to see fresh ways of traveling together as a community.

Opportunities to discover and embrace a new imagination for our congregations "will not happen through a teaching series, reading a popular book, or having a weekend retreat." Alan Roxborough continues, "It happens as a group of very ordinary men, women, and young people begin to take on new practices, in particular the practices of listening, discerning, experiencing, reflecting, and deciding. Together, these steps make up a journey."[8]

This involves engaging good leadership and community diagnostics. Does it take time? Yes. Can it be messy and difficult on occasion? Yes. But we should not fear this uncharted territory. It is a piece of the spiritual-bonding experience that can create some tangible expressions of healthy ministry.

Bonding Agent #5: Breaking an Impasse. A Word to Church Folk

Everybody knows what an impasse is. It's a stuck place. Something is either blocking the way forward or some event has created the impossibility of forward movement. Impasses can disrupt a drive to work, a ballgame, holiday travel, and the shortest route to our vacation spot. Ask anybody who comes upon an impasse if they are having a "happy moment." Make sure you are standing five feet away!

There isn't a road crew in the United States that learns about an impasse and says, "Oh well. It was bound to happen. That road probably needs to be blocked anyway. Let it be!" No. They move into action. They remove the obstacle or fix the situation. Whatever it takes!

Churches experience impasses, too. They aren't static experiences. They eventually evolve into an accepted norm. And, they disrupt the flow of healthy juices within a body of Christians.

---

[8] Roxbourgh, p. xiii.

Too often leaders and congregations live on opposite sides of an impasse. Things happen. Disagreements fester into hardened attitudes. Trust swoons. Criticism walks the hallways and sits comfortably in the assembly as the Lord's Supper is passed. Life together in the Spirit becomes brittle and strained. But there is a better way.

If you are reading this as a Christian who isn't wearing elder shoes, I invite you to consider a few things. They are things that can help us build bridges across impasses.

Open your heart.
Plaque buildup in our physical arteries can reduce the flow of blood, reducing the ability of our heart to function properly. We can start exercising, eat better, kick some habits that have contributed to plaque build, but the reality is...our arteries are clogged. We can't have true health improvement and feel better until we get them open. The same holds true for our spiritual hearts.

There were things the Corinthians should have said to Paul. They created the distance. They are the ones who needed to mature. They should have reached out to him. But, Paul reaches across the "impasse". . . . again. He lays all that aside and opens his heart.

> We have spoken freely to you. Corinthians our heart is wide open. You are not restricted by us, but you are restricted in your own affections. In return (I speak as to children) open your hearts also. (2 Cor. 6:11-13)

Remember the Liberian refugees? The bond they share with each and the "way" they engage each other is breathtaking. But we might quip, "Yes, but their story is extraordinary. They lived through unspeakable horror and experienced inhumane conditions on the way to starting a new life together."

That is true, but it's also true that *we share a narrative together, too.* We crossed out of darkness and into light. We were transferred out of dominion of Satan and into the kingdom of God. We claim to live in the cross story and to have experienced resurrection as individuals and as a community. Our narrative is extraordinary, too. It should also — above all other concerns — be the defining truth in our lives, leaderships, and congregations.

So much of what congests and paralyzes congregational systems often comes down to this question: Will we allow "our story" to once again become the centerpiece in our thinking? Will it feel strange? Perhaps. But doing so is first order of business in removing the chains that bind our affection, setting us free — all of us! — into the experience of *open hearts* and community health.

Choose to become the voice of encouragement and strength.
It's more than a trite notion. We have promoted "cordial" treatment of one another to the category of a fruit of the spirit. I checked the list. It's not in there (cf. Gal. 5:22-23). Our connection to each other in the Spirit *necessitates behaviors and actions* that indicate our submission to the Spirit. If we claim to wish the best for each other then we should "sound like it." 1 Thess. 5:12-13 is a powerful text.

> *Our connection to each other in the Spirit necessitates behaviors and actions that indicate our submission to the Spirit.*

We ask you, brothers, to respect those who labor among you and are over you in the Lord and admonish you, and to esteem them very highly in love because of their work. Be at peace among yourselves.

His words aren't a holy suggestion. *Respect. Esteem. Peace.* Such should be normative for us.

Too often, we forget that leaders are wrapped in skin, too. They get tired. They hurt. They get discouraged. Sometimes they have grueling bouts of loneliness (and so do their wives). They make missteps along the way. But they need *you*. They need *you* to be a voice of encouragement in their lives. Their hearts need to hear *your* prayers for them. They need *you* to walk alongside them in patience and understanding. They need *you* as conversation partners and fellow journey men and women.

Get engaged.

Too many Christians are sitting on the sidelines. We come to the assembly and drop in a few dollars. We attend the occasional event and . . . see you later. We are gathering. But are we *engaged*?

I recently sat in a small group and listened to a woman share her thoughts about the congregation. She said she had been there for about a year. After a long pause, one of the ladies asked her, "What is your name?" I watched in amazement as over half of the group introduced themselves to her. This congregation was less than 150 members.

Others shared passionately about people who had left the congregation over the past four years. I asked a few probing questions about what caused the departures. Various reasons were offered with the preface, "I think it was mainly . . . " or "I think it was because such-and-such happened." Then I asked, "Who in here had a conversation with any of the "departed"? Crickets! Nobody. Nada.

Interestingly, this same group had just minutes earlier shared about how much they wanted new people to come into the congregation! I said, "You aren't ready for new people until you re-engage some critical aspects of your faith." I received some strange looks for sure!

It is tempting to stand off in the distance and look at leadership, congregational health, and what the way forward looks like from the vantage point of what needs to change within the system. "They need to" or "We need to" is often the beginning place. But what about "I need to?"

We need to take some cues from the life of Nehemiah. When his Jewish brothers brought word of the depressed situation in Jerusalem, Nehemiah didn't deflect it. He didn't promise to give it some thought and summarily dismiss them with a smug, "I'll get back to you." He didn't bury the situation in endless analysis. *He got engaged.*

> *As soon as I heard these words I sat down and wept and mourned for days, and I continued fasting and praying before the God of heaven. (Neh. 1:4)*

And *then* he went to see the king, got permission, and headed west!

I like these words from Peter Steinke:

> *Health is promoted by personal activity. Health comes from measures that each person can effect.*

Measures that each person can effect. That's what Nehemiah did. He took the situation into his heart. He embraced the burden of the call and moved into action. He became an instrument in

God's hands that resulted in helping his people calm down around a strategy, rally around hope, and get a wall rebuilt.

I think the same is true for us, too. As we think, process, and look at the systems we are part of, the question for each believer is, "How does God want and need me to be engaged?"

> *How does God want and need me to be engaged?"*

Whatever else we might consider to be critical to the way forward, how we answer that question stands head and shoulders above it all.

A Parting Word!

As I write this, I'm sitting in a second-story loft enjoying a breathtaking view of the Colorado mountains. A few days ago I was traveling through desert country in New Mexico. Nothing against the desert, but I much prefer this view. It is magnificent! Sometimes we need a *better view*. We need our vision lifted. We need to allow our perspective to be "reset" within the larger view — magnificent view! — of who we are in Christ. Faith can easily become a journey with a desert perspective.

Paul constantly reminds early Christians to live inside the larger framework of what God is doing through the gospel and through their lives of faith and service. Consider these words from Eph. 1:16-23:

> *I do not cease to give thanks for you, remembering you in my prayers, that the God of our Lord Jesus Christ, the Father of glory, may give you the Spirit of wisdom and of revelation in the knowledge of him, having the eyes of your hearts enlightened, that you may know what is the hope to which he has*

called you, what are the riches of his glorious inheritance in the saints, and what is the immeasurable greatness of his power toward us who believe, according to the working of his great might that he worked in Christ when he raised him from the dead and seated him at his right hand in the heavenly places, far above all rule and authority and power and dominion, and above every name that is named, not only in this age but also in the one to come. And he put all things under his feet and gave him as head over all things to the church, which is his body, the fullness of him who fills all in all.

He travels into the majestic mountain peaks of who they are in Christ and summons them to travel with him high above tree line. It is this fresh vision that helped early believers find renewal and strength for their journey — *together.*

We need to travel above tree line, too. We can't and we won't do much that is worth doing without it. It is *there* that we are refreshed, softened, humbled, and reminded that our labor is not in vain in the Lord.

Now, grab a friend and make the hike. It's worth it. Our churches are worth it. And, the way forward will be a much better journey for leaderships, families, and congregations who do so.

A Proactive Shepherding Model That Works

Charlie Herndon and Jimmy Adcox

If you are a Shepherd, you know the sense of responsibility you feel for your local family of believers. You serve because you love God and you care about the church and its mission. You believe God wants you to be a difference maker and have stepped up to the plate in faith, feeling completely inadequate for the task. How can a few shepherds know the flock, be proactive in offering spiritual care, and become more than boardroom decision makers? How can elders move from reactive intervention ("there must be a problem") to proactive blessing and encouragement ("these men care for my soul and bless my life with Christ")?

What if there was a simple process that could help you have ongoing, significant spiritual conversations with the people of your church? What if you knew the sheep—their stories, their longings, and their trials? What if you could pray with them and bless them as individuals and families proactively? What if you could develop powerful spiritual connections with people in your church at a heart and life level? What if you felt the weight of shepherding lightened because you no longer felt paralyzed and guilty about the seemingly impossible task of knowing your families and engaging with them spiritually? What if you had a doable, systematic strategy for ongoing spiritual conversations with the flock? It is not as difficult as you might think.

The shepherding tool proposed in this chapter was piloted in the Donelson Church of Christ in Nashville, Tennessee. I (Jimmy) discovered this simple tool in conversation with Charlie Herndon at a funeral where we shared some common friends. Charlie is a former minister and currently a shepherd at Donelson. His spiritual life spills over onto everyone he meets. Much of what you will find in this chapter was shaped in the Donelson Church. The experiences and observations cited at the end of the chapter came after 254 interviews with 414 members of the Donelson Church of Christ family. Charlie has co-written this chapter with me. When we speak about our experiences in first person, we will identify ourselves.

The Southwest Church where I serve in Jonesboro, Arkansas is implementing this plan as well. We are excited to find a simple tool that creates spiritual conversations that are natural and helpful. Our church has warmly received it and our shepherds are enjoying and being encouraged by the connections and blessings this process brings. And what a relief to know a process is underway that will potentially touch the lives of our 600

> *We may know our members by name and may even know their attendance patterns, but how well do we know them and how well do they know us?*

families over a relatively short period of time! In just three short months our shepherds have already had significant spiritual conversations with over fifty families.

Jesus said, "I am the good shepherd; I know my sheep and my sheep know me" (John 10:14). We may know our members by name and may even know their attendance patterns, but how well do we know them and how well do they know us? Do we know their stories and where they are in their walk with God? Do they know we love Jesus and we love them in the Lord? Progress toward this is surprisingly easy and mutually edifying.

The Simplicity of the Plan: "Invite people in and facilitate a conversation to get to Jesus"

This simply amounts to asking a person or a couple in our flock to sit down with two shepherds, tell us how they are doing, and let us pray with them. [Some Southwest Shepherds have opted to engage their interviews as husband-wife teams.]

If our people are not glad to do that, what does that say about them and about us? The truth may be that we are not coming across as approachable. This is all the more reason to have these interviews and change the perception.

We found that most were glad to meet with us. A few were reluctant and excused themselves. That's fine. A shepherd can watch for an opportunity to chat with them and assess their well-being. They know they were invited. To gain confidence, start with a few families you know who will be easy to interview. The interviews were very enjoyable and mutually beneficial.

Setting Up Interviews

The most challenging part of this effort may be contacting the members and scheduling the interviews. Both Donelson and Southwest secured a very capable volunteer to schedule the interviews. In order to make this process as doable as possible, most of the visits are made before or after services or during Bible classes.

It is important to announce your plans to the church before contacts are made. The announcement should make it clear that our shepherds want to get to know you better, encourage and bless you, and pray for you. You might jokingly remind them that if they get a call about meeting with an elder, they shouldn't assume something is wrong. You are looking forward to getting to know and blessing everyone at your church. You might also let them know that it will take some time to meet with everyone in the church, so ask for patience. If someone would like to have the visit early in the process, let them know who to contact.

You might also decide if you want to give priority to any particular group, such as new Christians, new members, deacons, or perhaps people you have concerns for. This is a very non-threatening way to engage people in conversation that you suspect may need the connection. Perhaps the oldest members deserve priority. They will bless you.

How the Interview Begins

After greeting the guests and chatting a minute, thank them for coming and state the purpose for getting together. Decide which elder will facilitate. It could go something like the following:

"We would like to begin with a reading from scripture that is our focus as elders and shepherds of this church. In 1 Peter 5:1-4, Peter tells us we are to be examples and overseers, which we understand and find challenging. But he also says to be shepherds of God's flock. Jesus said, *'I am the good shepherd; I know my sheep and my sheep know me.'* We want to get better at being shepherds. Knowing your names and knowing you are present from week to week is not enough. We believe that to know the sheep better we need to spend some time face to face and see how you are doing. That's why we invited you in today."

This sets the tone for this being about our fellowship in Christ.

The Flow of Conversation

The plan is basically sharing why we are having these visits with our people, learning about their family for a few minutes, and transitioning into their story of faith. So ask them, *"How long have you been at this church, why did you come here, and why have you stayed? Who have you built relationships with? Who do you admire and appreciate? Who do you credit from the past for pointing you to God and following Jesus?"* This is the pivotal question. We want to know whatever they will share about their spiritual journey and how they are doing in the Lord today.

Discussion about family and faith stories leads to conversation about their current life with God. These questions include, *"How would you describe where you are at this time in your relationship with God? Where do you feel the greatest need to make progress? What do you think you need to do at this point to grow stronger and closer to God?"* This creates a great opportunity to encourage and console in the Lord. Close with prayer, on your knees, huddled, holding hands, or whatever feels appropriate. Make this a heartfelt and blessed moment.

These conversations convey that you as a shepherd want the same things for them that God wants. Paul revealed his main concern in saying, *"I will continue with all of you for your progress and joy in the faith"* (Phil. 1:25). Similarly, he wrote, *"My dear children, for whom I am again in the pains of childbirth until Christ is formed in you"* (Gal. 4:19). This is a powerful way for shepherds to share their spiritual longings with each person in their flock and it reveals the shepherd's heart for their members' life with Christ.

Important: By setting the tone early and directing the conversation, we make this visit about valuing their relationship with God and their fellowship with us. If they have a need to vent on some matter, we requested a separate meeting for that. We had maybe two or three who did that.

The Value of Conversations in the Lord

Our elders (Jimmy) have commented about how easy and tempting it is to focus on the information questions and leave little time for the spiritual conversation time—especially the conversation time about how they are doing in their life with God. This process is about more than getting better acquainted. This is about helping people walk closer to the Lord. This is shepherd work. If you feel awkward at first asking such personal questions, it might be helpful to remember the following:

1. Early conversations about their spiritual history lead naturally into this conversation.
2. People will choose their own level of transparency. You are not being intrusive.

3. Caring for the spiritual needs of your flock is why you are a shepherd. Don't be afraid to go there.
4. Spiritual conversations can have a transforming influence in people's lives.

The most meaningful conversations I (Charlie) have had throughout my life have been about our relationships with God and his Son, Jesus Christ. Though it seems that most Christians are hesitant to initiate the conversation about their faith, I have found all believers are willing to talk if prompted. Even better, I would say most enjoy sharing their faith when they feel free to speak. I am referring to conversations about our walk with God and admiration of Jesus, not debating issues or pointing out the problems in the church.

> *Though it seems that most Christians are hesitant to initiate the conversation about their faith, I have found all believers are willing to talk if prompted. Even better, I would say most enjoy sharing their faith when they feel free to speak.*

A text that comes to mind is Philemon 6.

> *"I pray that the faith you share with us may deepen your understanding of every blessing that belongs to you in Christ."*

Whenever I express my heart to others about my journey with Jesus and ask about their relationship with God, I am refreshed and often surprised by what thoughts come to me and to the other person. It reinforces to me the importance of Christians developing relationships where mutual sharing of faith occurs. The beauty and power of the church is that we live in a community where we can actually walk and talk by faith.

I have always sought out men and women of genuine faith and love for God because I wanted to know more and grow more. I need to know there are believers I can go to with my struggles or just to be refreshed in Christ. As shepherds of God's people, we must progress in being perceived as men who know Jesus so that our sheep will come to us when needed. It requires that we, like God, take the initiative to connect with them and influence them to trust God and keep their eyes on Jesus.

Our people should find in a conversation with us that there really is something valuable to be gained by taking Jesus seriously throughout life. The words from Paul about fullness in Christ must be found in us if we expect others to pursue it. Peter wrote about inexpressible and glorious joy in those who believed in Jesus and loved him though they had never seen him. Wouldn't there be evidence of that in elders who have followed Jesus so many years?

If we are not finding it easy to talk with each other about life in Christ, are we really going to find it easy to share our faith with the world? Shepherds of God's people are not only able to talk about life through Jesus, they are eager to get with the sheep and feed them! They expect us to point them to Jesus. We should always assume their faith is genuine and speak from the Spirit in us.

The Shepherd's Mindset during Interviews

As shepherds of God's flock, people assume we are men who have walked with Christ for many years. From our years of surrender and submission to the will of God, we have come to know the Lord more personally and intimately. We have gained considerable knowledge of the Bible over the years, but more importantly, we have been granted the knowledge of God himself as he has made himself known to us. We have experienced fellowship with him, and with his Son, Jesus Christ.

We identify with the words of Peter, who wrote:

> *Though you have not seen him, you love him; and though you do not see him now, you believe in him and are filled with an inexpressible and glorious joy, for you are receiving the goal of your faith, the salvation of your souls. (1 Peter 1:8-9)*

And as it was said of Peter, so is it sometimes perceived of us, that we have been with Jesus. We have looked at him, listened to him, and practiced his teachings so long that others who believe in him and desire him actually feel closer to him when they are with us. It may be difficult for you to perceive yourself in this way. It doesn't mean you have arrived in your spiritual life with God, but it does mean that you have life experiences with God that can bless other people.

People want to believe we can actually help them grow stronger in their faith in God and in their love for God. We can help make the mystery of the gospel more real and alive, and more believable. They hunger for us to lead them to a deeper and more fulfilling relationship with God. They trust us as sheep trust the shepherd. Therefore, when we invite them in for an "interview" or a "spiritual check-up," it seems we should take seriously what it means to be in the mind of the Spirit and believe that the Lord himself is in our midst as we listen to them, as we exhort and encourage them, as we love them with the love of the Lord, and as we pray with them.

> *...when we invite them in for an "interview"... we should take seriously what it means to be in the mind of the Spirit and believe that the Lord himself is in our midst...*

Blessings in Working this Plan:

1. Every participant appreciated the visit (sometimes shedding tears).
2. Everyone returns to the body with more respect for their shepherds.
3. We have more credibility to stand before the church to speak or lead.
4. We feel more connected as we move about the church and interact.
5. We have progressed at working together as shepherds and have a shared experience of counseling and blessing our people.
6. Interviews provide opportunities for us to share from our journeys in the Lord.
7. We have a reason to get in front of some we have been concerned about to assess their well-being and to be God's instrument to renew them.
8. We have learned of spiritual gifts and abilities that need to be used.
9. We have heard inspiring stories of God's faithfulness.
10. We have been humbled by the struggles and hardships some have endured through life and crosses they continue to carry.
11. We know who people are closest to in the church when needs arise.
12. We know who they appreciate as examples in the church.
13. We get to remind and reinforce in others what is most important—our "progress and joy in the faith" and "Christ being formed in us."
14. More of our people are coming to us for prayer at other times now.
15. We have a "point of reference" if we need to approach them in the future.

16. We now have something in place to welcome a new family.

17. This provides a possible interview with a visiting "church seeker."

18. Because the church knows we are doing this, someone can be seen meeting with us without feeling like others will think they have a problem.

19. It provides a great opportunity to personally validate and appreciate people.

20. It provides us with names of those in the church who are appreciated and might be good for us to pursue for ministry or leadership.

21. Asking people about their journey of faith helps them express their faith, helps us see where they are in spiritual maturity, and makes the basis of our fellowship more about our common bond of Jesus.

A Doable Plan

There is an exponential power in systemically working this plan. In our Southwest Church, with twenty shepherds spending time with three families per month around worship times in teams of two, each individual or couple in our church can be engaged in conversation about Jesus with our shepherds every 20 months. The same can be accomplished in 10 months with elder/wife teams. And even if three interviews per month is not achievable, you will be surprised at what can be accomplished through consistency over time. You will be amazed at how meaningful and fulfilling such spiritual connections with the flock will be.

> *This plan doesn't require great expertise. It is all about shepherds who walk with Jesus walking alongside sheep who are aspiring to do the same. God works when that happens!*

This plan doesn't require great expertise. It is all about shepherds who walk with Jesus walking alongside sheep who are aspiring to do the same. God works when that happens! It is not unusual to hear about leaders not being in touch with the people. These conversations change the perception that we are a board of directors in a back room, making decisions and running the organization. We become like Jesus, who said, "I know my sheep and my sheep know me."

Where Do We Start?

1. Process through this plan with your fellow shepherds.
2. Have all the shepherds practice this approach 2-3 times with couples who would be easy to interview, and then get their feedback.
3. Commit the effort to the Lord and announce the plan to the church.
4. Recruit someone to contact the members, schedule the interviews, and make assignments with the shepherds.
5. Compassionately and boldly engage and bless your people.
6. Share with all the shepherds what was experienced in the interviews, and follow up as needed.
7. Work the plan and see what God does in you and your church.

Appendix One

KNOW THE SHEEP – KNOW THE SHEPHERD

INTERVIEW OUTLINE

A. Welcome – Update "Family Data Record."

B. Share the objective of our meeting.

1. **Relationship With Your Shepherds.**
   a. Begin with reading Peter's words to elders (1 Peter 5:1-4).
   b. We want to follow Jesus, who said . . . (John 10:14).
   c. Our responsibility as examples, overseers, and shepherds who know the sheep.

2. **Relationships Within Your Family.**
   a. Who are the grandparents, parents, and siblings still in their lives?
   b. Who are their children/spouses? Where do they live?
   c. Who are their grandchildren?
   d. Good to inquire regarding who shares their faith in God.

3. **Relationship With God.**
   a. Who at Donelson have you become close to?
   b. Others at Donelson you have come to appreciate?
   c. Who would you most likely go to for spiritual support?
   d. Who has been the biggest influence on your relationship with God?

e. How would you describe where you are in your relationship with God today?

*HAND OUT : "Our Prayer For You" (See Appendix Two)

f. Where do you feel the greatest need to make progress?

g. What do you think you need to do to grow stronger, or what do you do to stay close to God and strong spiritually?

PRAYER—What could we pray with you about as we close? (It may seem appropriate to move in closer, lay hands on them, hold hands, huddle up, or kneel before them. Find an appropriate way to make this a sacred moment.)

Appendix Two

OUR PRAYER FOR YOU

"Your Progress and Joy in the Faith" (Phil. 1:21-25)

1. **That you will trust God that by grace you have been saved!**
   "For it is by grace you have been saved, through faith – and this not from yourselves, it is the gift of God – not by works, so that no one can boast." (Eph. 2:8-9)

2. **That the word of Christ will dwell in you richly!**
   "Let the word of Christ dwell in you richly as you teach and admonish one another with all wisdom, and as you sing...with gratitude in your hearts to God." (Col. 3:16)

3. **That you will pray about everything and be anxious about nothing!**
   "Do not be anxious about anything, but in everything, by prayer and petition, with thanksgiving, present your requests to God." (Phil. 4:6)

4. **That you will know the surpassing love of Christ for you!**
   "And I pray that you, being rooted and established in love, may have power, together with all the saints, to grasp how wide and long and high and deep is the love of Christ, and to know this love that surpasses knowledge – that you may be filled to the measure of all the fullness of God." (Eph. 3:17-19)

5. **That you will love others until God's love is made complete in you!**
   "No one has ever seen God; but if we love one another, God lives in us and his love is made complete in us." (1 John 4:12)

6. **That you will persevere in every trial so that you may be mature!**

   "Consider it pure joy, my brothers, whenever you face trials of many kinds because you know that the testing of your faith develops perseverance. Perseverance must finish its work so that you may be mature and complete..." (James 1:2-4)

7. **That you will trust that the Holy Spirit intercedes for you!**

   "And he who searches our hearts knows the mind of the Spirit, because the Spirit intercedes for the saints in accordance with God's will." (Rom. 8:27)

8. **That you will trust God to provide a way out when you are tempted!**

   "No temptation has overtaken you except what is common to us all. And God is faithful; he will not let you be tempted beyond what you can bear. But when you are tempted, he will also provide a way out so that you can endure it." (1 Cor. 10:13)

9. **That you will know that God is working all things out for your good!**

   "And we know that in all things God works for the good of those who love him, who have been called according to his purpose." (Rom. 8:28)

10. **That you will do the good works God created you to do!**

    "For we are God's workmanship, created in Christ Jesus to do good works, which God prepared in advance for us to do." (Eph. 2:10)

11. **That the Spirit God gave you will bear much fruit in you!**

    "But the fruit of the Spirit is love, joy, peace, patience, kindness, goodness, faithfulness, gentleness, and self-control." (Gal. 5:22)

12. That you will believe God works in you to will and to act for him!

"...for it is God who works in you to will and to act in order to fulfill his good purpose." (Phil. 2:13)

"...until Christ is formed in you."
(Gal. 4:19)

Appendix Three
INTERVIEW INFORMATION SHEET

Member(s) Interviewed: _____ Date: _____

Interviewing shepherds: _____

Living Grandparents: (his)   (hers)

Parents & Siblings:

F- _____   S- _____   S- _____
M- _____   S- _____   S- _____
F- _____   S- _____   S- _____
M- _____   S- _____   S- _____

Children/Spouses & Grandchildren:

C- _____   _____   _____   _____
C- _____   _____   _____   _____
C- _____   _____   _____   _____
C- _____   _____   _____   _____

1. Who are those you have become especially close to at
    Donelson?

    _____   _____   _____

    _____   _____   _____

    _____   _____   _____

2. Who are those you have come to appreciate at Donelson as
    examples?

    _____   _____   _____

    _____   _____   _____

    _____   _____   _____

3. Who would you go to for spiritual guidance or support if you needed it?

4. Who has had the greatest influence on your relationship with God?

5. How would you describe where you are at this time in your relationship with God?

6. Where do you feel the greatest need for progress or improvement?

7. What do you think you need to do this time to grow stronger in the Lord?

8. NOTES: Perceived prayer needs / Follow-up?

TRIAGE FOR MARRIAGES IN CRISIS

Jon R. Anderson

You just got a call from someone who says his or her marriage is in trouble:

> *My spouse just told me he wants a divorce. I didn't see this coming. I mean, I know we didn't have a perfect marriage, but I had no idea he thought things were this bad! I don't know what to do! I tried to tell him that we could get counseling or something, but he says that it's too late and that he's already made up his mind and wants me to start moving forward as someone who's no longer married to him. I feel incredibly helpless! Why would he, all of a sudden, spring this on me without giving me the opportunity to make things better?*

Or maybe it's this one:

I've just found out that my wife has been having an affair. She says she's sorry and that it's over and that we should move on and put it behind us. I've told her I forgive her, but it doesn't seem that simple. I don't think she understands how devastating this is to me! I think we need more help, but she seems to think I just need to be better at forgiving. Am I just crazy, or what? I don't know how to deal with this.

Here's the other most common example:

We need help! We've tried everything . . . books, seminars, even counseling, but things just seem to be getting worse. And now my spouse is recommending that we try a separation. That doesn't feel like the answer to me, but she/he seems convinced, and it doesn't look like I have much say in the matter. What do I do?

These scenarios are textbook examples of the three most common issues that would constitute a marriage in crisis. However, *any* marriage that appears to be deteriorating is very likely to be in crisis. The sad part is that it is unlikely you will even know a marriage needs help before it gets into a crisis mode. So, as a rule of thumb, it's best to assume that the marriage is in crisis when only one spouse initially comes to you for help.

> *...any marriage that appears to be deteriorating is very likely to be in crisis.*

Once a marriage is in "crisis mode," it is very difficult for even the most skilled marriage therapist to make any progress meeting with both spouses. And it is equally difficult getting both spouses to attend more than a few sessions with the same counselor. Furthermore, many of the best-known marriage experts, such as John Gottman and Willard Harley, would argue AGAINST counseling or therapy as the *first* step with a couple in crisis. So, if some of the top marriage therapists in the country don't claim to have much success with using therapy or counseling as the *first* step, why would I, as a church leader, with some lesser amount of experience in that realm, believe I could do any better? This was one of the lessons I wish I had learned decades earlier as a therapist. I could have saved a lot more marriages and wasted countless fewer hours conducting sessions that only seemed to ultimately make matters worse. This all raises the question: So then, what do you do?

Here's the short answer: Have the spouse who is coming to you (or whichever spouse seems more willing to save the marriage) get in touch with someone who conducts reputable and effective marriage intensives. A list of recommended intensives is included at the end of this chapter, but one of them, *Love Reboot,* my wife and I conduct almost every month. Most of these organizations will be happy to coach that person on how to approach their spouse in a way that makes it more likely for them to be willing to attend.

> *... many of the best-known marriage experts, would argue AGAINST counseling or therapy as the first step with a couple in crisis.*

Marriage intensives are typically developed by marriage therapists who understand that counseling and therapy, as a FIRST step for couples in crisis, is not only ineffective, but it may actually make matters worse, or even speed up the deterioration of the marriage.

Now, my experience is that most people don't swallow the short answer whole, with a trusting smile. So, let me try my best to explain just some of the dynamics that are at play here . . . .

Relationship

I wish working with *marriages* was about working with *relation-ships*. How nice it would be to have the couple show up for the first session, drop off the relationship at my office, and then return a few months later to pick up a now healthy, thriving relationship. The problem is that there really is no such thing as a relationship . . . at least, not as something tangible. We can't tell a relationship to start working harder. We can't provide tools and practices for the relationship to go home and work on. We can't provide concepts and paradigms that will hopefully change the way a relationship thinks.

The only real things we have to work with are two *individuals*. But individuals tend to see their relational challenges as, at best, something wrong with the relationship, and, more commonly, as something wrong with the "other" in the relationship. If we can't somehow provide an environment for each person to focus on their own part in the relationship, we won't make progress. Unfortunately, the environment of the counseling office provides the opposite. One reason for this is *Triangulation*.

Triangulation

Triangulation is the term for describing the inherent relationship that exists between a couple and the therapist. Like a triangle has three sides, there are three different people in this relationship, and each person brings with them an entirely different agenda than the other two. The therapist brings the agenda of trying to help each individual get better at relating to the other.* The husband has his agenda of what his wife should be doing differently, and the wife has her agenda of what the husband should be doing differently. Each person, from the very begin-ning of the very first session, will be attempting to somehow make his or her own agenda the one that is followed by all three. If the therapist seems to lean more toward the husband's agenda, intentionally or not, the wife is displeased with the process. If the husband perceives that the therapist is more on the wife's side, he begins to think that the therapist is incompetent and, therefore, wasting their time. The therapist is hamstrung with the ongoing mental gymnastics of trying to appear unbiased, even when one of them makes a ridiculous statement or is clearly in the wrong. Effective intensives remove the triangulation by removing the counselor/client relationship. Instead of placing themselves in the role of advocate or mediator, the therapist conducts a group as teacher and facilitator of a process.

It is my experience that many counselors and therapists do not have the experience and/or training to avoid the trap of attempting to work on the *relationship* instead of facilitating individual change within each *spouse*. This usually leads to the therapist becoming more of a judge or mediator, leaving both spouses feeling somewhat cheated and seeing the counselor as incompetent.

Cognitive Dissonance

When someone is considering ending a marriage, especially if that person is a "church-goer," they have likely been attempting to come up with a good excuse to do so, without violating their own personal value system. So, it is likely that they have thought through all the arguments against their choosing divorce. If the counselor begins to question that person as to why they believe they are justified, they will come prepared with an answer that is acceptable, at least to them.

The only way to change that person's mind is to bring to light a new perspective that contradicts their current mindset. But that new perspective cannot be *overtly* directed at that person. Like many truths we learn in life, most of them are not learned from someone telling them to us directly, especially if that new perspective contradicts the reasoning they have constructed. When that person is dealing directly with a church leader, who they believe is going to attempt to "guilt" them into changing their mind, their defenses against considering that perspective are even higher. However, if that person believes they somehow discovered that new perspective on their own, they are much more likely to consider it. Once they have considered it, the former

> *... if a person believes they somehow discovered a new perspective on their own, they are much more likely to consider it.*

arguments that they have constructed for their case are no longer the main argument for their case, and they must now construct new ones to remain comfortable with their decision to end the marriage. The group setting of the marriage intensive provides an atmosphere where that person can observe others making the same flawed arguments for their own cases. They are then able to see the lies more for what they are. This creates Cognitive Dissonance.

The simple explanation of Cognitive Dissonance is that it is the mental gap that exists between someone's value system and their behavior. When our value system does not align with our behavior, our mind will not allow that gap to continue to exist. It will figuratively and literally "drive us crazy" if we don't do something about it. So, we are left with three choices:

1. Change our behavior to realign with our values.
2. Change our values to line up with our behavior.
3. Do some of both.

The first choice is the only one that brings true mental peace. A well-designed marriage intensive helps the individual discover that true peace and then devise a plan to continue in that peace.

Limerence

Limerence is the scientific term for the concept that our culture normally calls "in love." I choose to embrace the term "limerence" because it describes something that is often void of *real* love. A good definition of limerence is *"the illusion of full acceptance."* It is highly likely that one of the spouses in a crisis marriage is involved in a roman-

> It is highly likely that one of the spouses in a crisis marriage is involved in a romantic relationship with someone else.

tic relationship with someone else. Some experts put it as high as 80%, although it may be even higher since someone who has not been "found out" to be in an affair is likely not going to admit to it. So, many of the couples who come to you in crisis mode are likely to be dealing with an affair and one of the spouses is in limerence with someone outside the marriage.

There is so much to be said about the phenomenon of limerence, but we don't have the space for that discussion here. However, a person who is involved in an extra-marital affair is virtually unreachable in the context of a counseling office or when face-to-face with a church leader. A person in limerence is convinced that the extra-marital relationship was meant to be and that the extra-marital relationship is the only one that will satisfy them.

Limerence, on average, lasts for 6 to 18 months. Many factors decide how long it will last, and the weightiest factor is how much the couple experiences the realities of life together. If a couple immediately moves in together and starts sharing financial and domestic issues, the limerence will be shorter-lived. On the other hand, if the couple sees each other only for brief, sporadic escapades, they won't be dealing with "real life" together as much and the illusion of full acceptance will linger longer.

In Love Reboot workshops, we expose limerence for what it really is. For most of our participants who attend while still involved in an affair, that segment of the workshop is what causes the biggest paradigm shift, resulting in the creation of a new cognitive dissonance, which cannot be closed by the former lies they have been telling themselves.

This limerence presentation would not begin to be heard in a counseling setting. This is primarily because the person in limerence would feel much more defensive due to being singled out or blamed for the current state of the marriage. This dynamic can be more clearly illustrated by an experience many of us have had as spouses:

You've been telling your spouse something for years and it seems to continually fall on deaf ears. Then, one day, your spouse announces to you a new great truth they just discovered. That great "truth" turns out to be the very thing you've been telling them all along! Why did they hear it from someone else and not from you? Well, when someone is directly addressing us with a "truth" that they believe would help us to be a better person, especially when it's our spouse doing so, our human nature is to be defensive and dismissive. However, if we hear that truth in a sermon, spoken to a numerous audience, then we don't feel singled out. We receive the message much more willingly.

What You Can Do

Address the Relationship, Not the Marriage

Instead of attempting to save the marriage, work on strengthening the relationship. The two spouses will always have a relationship with each other, whether or not they stay married. If they share children, this relationship will continue to be a part of their everyday lives. Divorce does not end a relationship. It only re-defines it. So, encourage the reluctant spouse to focus on making the relationship better, regardless of whether they stay married or not. Help them to understand that this is for their own sake, as well as for the children.

> *Instead of attempting to save the marriage, work on strengthening the relationship.*

If someone tells you that they want to end the marriage because the relationship is so destructive, let them know that that is precisely why they need to get help. But they might also say that they get along well with their spouse, it's just that they aren't getting their needs met or they are unhappy. That's where you can explain to them that the other spouse is still going to feel betrayed and hurt and the year-long process is going to be torture for everyone if the relationship is not well tended to.

Don't Suggest. Prescribe!

If my foot was rotting and my primary-care physician, after a thorough examination, told me that I had diabetes and I ought to consider having my foot amputated... I would likely ask what my alternatives were. If the doctor said I could try fish oil, by golly, I'm going to try fish oil, even if she told me it is unlikely to work and things would likely get worse. No, the doctor is not going to *suggest* or *recommend* amputation, He's going to *prescribe* it. In other words, he's going to tell me what he's going to do.

Likewise, when a member of your flock is having a marriage crisis, don't *recommend* he or she attend a marriage intensive...*tell* them to do so. Ministers and elders too often are afraid to do more than recommend or suggest, especially when it comes to marriages. This is likely in part because we have no guarantee that our suggested help will work. What if they go and spend all

> *...when a member of your flock is having a marriage crisis, don't recommend he or she attend a marriage intensive... tell them to do so.*

that time, effort, and money, and they still divorce? I'll look bad and it might jeopardize my ability to work with either or both of them in the future!

Using the medical analogy, the doctor knows that cutting off the foot is not going to cure the diabetes. Even worse, the patient might die on the operating table. Likewise, marriages in crisis are triage and emergency-room cases, and the hard truth is that some are not going to survive the treatment. But sending a crisis marriage to counseling or some enrichment course, instead of an intensive, is tantamount to making an appointment with a primary-care physician for next week when you are bleeding to death. The bleeding must be stopped *before* any medication, diet changes, or exercise regimens can be prescribed. A marriage in crisis is "bleeding out" relationally. So, the first step *must* be a marriage intensive, the ER of marriage help.

Use Existing Momentum

It is likely that each spouse will take on two opposing roles:

1. I want out.
2. Please save us.

It is likely that the "Please save us" spouse will be the one who initially seeks you out. Even people who have been relatively decent spouses will say things like, *"I know I'm not perfect and there are some things I need to do better, but my spouse isn't even willing to give me another chance."*

Use this willing attitude to help them focus on themselves. When they approach their spouse about getting help, have them speak in terms of *me* instead of *we*. One of the most common mistakes one makes is to say to their spouse, *"We need help."* The other spouse is likely to hear this message as, *"We need to get you fixed."* A better approach would be to say something like, *"I know I haven't been an ideal spouse but I need help. I want to learn how to help you feel more loved and accepted. If you will go to this couple's workshop with me, I promise not to bring up your faults. Instead, I will work only on myself."* In cases where the other spouse appears to have their mind made up that the marriage is over, the following phrase is usually a good add-on: *"Whether or not you choose to remain my spouse, I want the best for you, and that depends on the two of us having a good relationship together."*

In the event that you are able to address the "I want out" spouse, don't attempt to use "God hates divorce" tactics. That will be the approach that they will be best-prepared for. You may believe it will outweigh any reasoning they have, but they will already have an answer for it that has satisfied their own conscience. So, leverage the existing momentum! Try some version of the following statement:

> *I want the best for you. You don't believe this marriage can work. But you understand that, whether or not the two of you stay married, you will always have a relationship with each other. So, for your own sake, do what it takes to make that relationship as good as it can be, going forward. I know you will want to be able to look your children in the eye, and yourself in the mirror, and say that you have done everything you can to make the relationship stronger and better. Furthermore, if your spouse doesn't feel like you're on their side, it is unlikely that they will be cooperative throughout the divorce process and beyond.*

Recap—What You Can Do

- Address the relationship, not the marriage.
- Don't suggest. Prescribe!
- Use the existing momentum.

Recommended Marriage Intensives

Love Reboot—www.GrowingLoveNetwork.org
210-823-5282   Jon@GrowingLoveNetwork.org

A New Beginning—www.savemymarriage.com
Marriage Helper 911—www.marriagehelper.com
The Clearing—www.clearingretreat.org
The Smalley Institute—www.smalley.cc

SUSTAINABLE YOUTH MINISTRY

Greg Anderson

Jim was a superstar youth-ministry candidate. He aced his coursework in school, knocked it out of the park during two internships at his home church, and was highly recommended by peers, professors, and mentors. New City Church had just let go of their third youth minister in five years. This time, however, they were committed to finding the right match. Once they saw Jim's resume, checked his references, and interviewed him, they knew they had found their guy. Jim asked about a job description, and the search team chairperson replied, "We want to get you here first and then co-craft a job description that totally plays to your strengths." Jim's mentor advised against the ambiguity, but Jim was drawn to the Spirit-led nature of the conversations and decided it was a "God thing." A job offer was made, Jim accepted, and he began his new position a month later. Within six months, Jim began to realize the severity of the church leadership's poor health. He was blamed for things he had nothing to do with and began to notice more and more scrutiny of many of his decisions. Surely, he had folks who encouraged him, but there were plenty of others who always griped about something.

Within 18 months, Jim was exhausted. He began reaching out to friends to let them know he was open to the Spirit's leading if another opportunity opened up. Less than two years after his hire, Jim submitted his resignation. With renewed enthusiasm and a brighter outlook on life, he transitioned to his new job. New City Church's leadership team bemoaned the poor job universities did to prepare youth ministers for the rigors of the real world. Both Jim and New City Church were firmly convinced, "Things will be different this time."

While the scenario is fictitious, it represents some of the major challenges facing youth ministers and the churches they serve. The purpose of this chapter is to focus on sustainable practices youth ministers and church leaders can employ that may contribute to long-term sustainability. I begin by examining a holistic, personal development framework for youth ministers. As the chapter progresses, I process key questions and practices youth ministers and church leaders can embrace to maintain healthy relationships.

Holistic Personal Development

Even though youth ministry has been around since the 1950's, it remains something of an enigma. Slowly but surely that is changing as youth ministry is coming into its own. Practitioners are recognizing limitations of various approaches and are engaging parents more and more as key contributors to childhood and adolescent faith-development. Similarly, empirical studies are helping seminaries and universities better understand how to equip youth ministers for service in the midst of a postmodern worldview. The challenges are great, and the stakes are truly high. Personal development will not cure all ills. However, it will position youth ministers to be prepared to effectively serve parents and teens while taking care of family and self. In this chapter, I challenge youth ministers to pursue the following characteristics of a holistic personal-development framework:

- Living Into Holistic Personal Health
- Adopting a Leadership Philosophy
- Creating a Contract with Self

Living Into Holistic Personal Health

Component 1: Spiritual Health—It is no accident that taking care of yourself spiritually is at the top of the list. I encourage you to schedule time to feed your soul. Learn to use calendar software correctly and literally schedule one-on-one time with God. This will position your administrative assistant to honestly report, "He/she is with someone." Even though that may sound a little funny, I am quite serious. Schedule an hour each morning to pray, meditate, contemplate, and get into a rhythm of practicing these and other spiritual disciplines. Set aside time to read and study the Bible—not for class prep, but for your own spiritual feeding. My hunch is you would not skip three meals a day and expect to physically survive long-term. The same principle applies spiritually.

I recommend purchasing *Celebration of Discipline* by Richard Foster and *The Good and Beautiful* series by James Bryan Smith, which will lead you to other spiritual health resources both ancient and modern. Immerse yourself in these books and get into the habit of practicing spiritual disciplines.

Not only will taking care of yourself spiritually help you personally, it will also help those within your circles of influence, especially members of your family. When parents and teens come to you with problems, you will have a rich well from which to draw. The Apostle Paul warned against "quenching the Spirit" (1 Thess. 5:19). Heed his counsel if you want to withstand the rigors of ministry while creating a theological framework that serves others well.

> *Not only will taking care of yourself spiritually help you personally, it will also help those within your circles of influence, especially members of your family.*

Component 2: Emotional Health — In an interview with Manfred F. R. Kets de Vries (the Raoul de Vitry d'Avaucourt Chaired Professor of Leadership Development at INSEAD in Fontainebleau, France, and the director of INSEAD's Global Leadership Centre), Diane Coutu, asked, "You've studied the psychology of leaders your whole life. How do you identify the successful ones?" (p. 66). Kets de Vries replied, "The first thing I look for is emotional intelligence — basically, how self-reflective is the person? In general, emotionally intelligent leaders tend to make better team players . . . they are more effective at motivating themselves and others" (Coutu, 2004, p. 66).

Daniel Goleman (2000) defined emotional intelligence as, " . . . the ability to manage ourselves and our relationships effectively" (p. 39). He further observed that emotional intelligence consists of five fundamental capabilities: self-awareness, self-regulation, motivation, empathy, and social skill. According to Goleman, each capability is composed of specific competencies. I provide a brief overview here:

- *Self-Awareness* — Self-awareness, along with self-regulation and motivation, determines how an individual manages self. Self-awareness is "knowing one's internal states, preferences, resources, and intuitions" and is comprised of three emotional competencies: a) emotional awareness, b) accurate self-assessment, and c) self-confidence.

- *Self-regulation* — This capability is defined as the ability to manage the internal states, impulses, and resources of self and is comprised of the competencies of self-control, trustworthiness, conscientiousness, adaptability, and innovation.

- *Motivation* — Goleman (2000) defined motivation as emotional tendencies that guide or facilitate reaching goals. Motivation includes the competencies of achievement drive, commitment to the goals of the group or organization, initiative, and optimism even in the face of setbacks.

The remaining capabilities determine how individuals handle relationships.

- *Empathy* — The heart of empathy is sensing the emotions of others, understanding their perspectives, and taking active interest in their concerns. Wolff, Pescosolido and Druskat (2002) observed empathy was a key aspect of emotional intelligence that enabled thought processes and skills in self-managed teams by providing an understanding of the emotions and needs of others in an organization. Empathy includes the competencies of understanding and developing others, adopting a service orienta-

> *It is critical that youth ministers and church leaders continue to grow their emotional intelligence capacity as leaders.*

tion, leveraging diversity, and practicing political awareness.

- *Social Skills* — Goleman (2000) defined social skills as
adeptness at inducing desirable responses in others. This
capability is comprised of influence or persuasion, clear
communication, the ability to manage conflict, leadership, being a healthy change agent, networking, collabo-
rating, and team building.

It is critical that youth ministers and church leaders continue to
grow their emotional intelligence capacity as leaders. This will
prove especially true as you navigate a myriad of relationships,
value perspectives, and needs of individuals ranging from
lifelong members of the church who may be living in a half-
million dollar house to a homeless person you meet for the first
time. Growing in emotional intelligence will also contribute to
vision, mission, values, and vocabulary for your ministry.

Component 3: Mental Health — My counsel here is short and
sweet — take good care of your brain. This is extremely challenging in today's world. Media outlets in multiple forms beg for
your attention 24 hours a day, seven
days a week. While you certainly can
use various types of media to contribute to mental health, it is critical that
you "unplug" often and intentionally.

> *Your teens do not
> need you to be hip
> and trendy. They need
> you to be rock-solid
> in your faith.*

Choose one day a week that is "media-free day" and never break
that rule. Sit and meditate, or take a long walk in the woods.
Carefully choose what is and is not allowed to enter your mind
through your senses.

No matter how you want to spin it, movies and video games
with graphic violence, nudity, and obscene language are not
good for your mental health. You may think, "But, I need to

know what my teens are watching and playing so I can relate to them." Your teens do not need you to be hip and trendy. They need you to be rock-solid in your faith. I am not suggesting you refrain from these things as a badge of honor. I am suggesting that you take care of your mind. I think this is why Paul counseled us to "take captive every thought" (2 Cor. 10:5) which allows the peace of God to "guard our hearts and minds in Christ Jesus" (Phil. 4:7).

Component 4: Physical Health — Take care of yourself physically. Watch what you eat. Exercise. Play. Stay active. Get an annual physical. Brush and floss daily and get your teeth cleaned every six months. If you struggle with weight, use the calendar tip I mentioned earlier and schedule exercise time. Get on a treadmill, put on your headphones and listen to Scripture, or pray for students and their families by name while you walk and talk with God. I realize there are many pressures on you to cover many other bases, and I also understand that it is easy to get off schedule. That is why effectively managing your calendar is so very important.

Adopting a Leadership Philosophy

Component 5: Leadership Philosophy: Servant Leadership — As you contemplate growing a sustainable youth ministry, I encourage you to consider adopting a leadership-development framework to provide boundaries and vocabulary for your approach to leading your ministry. There are many types of leadership frameworks you could study, including transformational leadership, moral leadership, authentic leadership, situational leadership, etc. While all of these approaches merit investigation, I personally encourage you to plumb the depths of servant leadership.

In the modern era, perhaps no other name is more closely identified with servant leadership than that of Robert Greenleaf (Canales, 2006, 2014; Dierendonck, 2011; Ebener & O'Connell, 2010; Spears, 2014). In 1970, Greenleaf published *The Servant as Leader*, the first of multiple works on servant leadership (Spears, 2014). When examining the relationship between this particular theory and Christian ministry, it is worth noting that Greenleaf was greatly impacted by his religious upbringing (Banks & Ledbetter, 2004; Bekker, 2010). Regarding the servant-leadership characteristic of persuasion that Greenleaf would ultimately weave into the servant-leader framework, for instance, Spears (2010) observed that persuasion over coercion was rooted in the belief system of the Religious Society of Friends. This religious body was also known as the Quakers, the community of faith Robert Greenleaf belonged to (Canales, 2006; Tidball, 2012).

The servant leader's motivation is serving his or her followers, positioning them to become servant leaders who continue the trajectory until an organization's culture is transformed (Reed, Vidaver-Cohen, & Colwell, 2011). Greenleaf expanded his message by articulating ten key characteristics of servant leaders. The competencies and their traits are listed in Table 1. The servant-leadership characteristics are in no particular order (Canales, 2014).

Table 1

Greenleaf's Ten Characteristics of Servant Leadership

Listening	Intentionally focusing on the thoughts, heart, joys, pains of others.
Empathy	The most successful servant leader exercises empathy with others. Empathy can respond to positive and/or negative emotions.

Healing	One of the powerful forces for transformation and integration.
Awareness	Remaining highly alert and reasonably disturbed; not seeking solace; having inner serenity.
Persuasion	Trusting persuasion over positional authority in organizational decision-making.
Conceptualization	The ability to create a future orientation providing vision and mission.
Foresight	Understanding past lessons, present realities, and the probable consequences of future decisions.
Stewardship	Holding institutions in trust for society's greater good.
Commitment to Growth of Others	Believing others have intrinsic value beyond noticeable workplace contributions. Being deeply committed to everyone's growth.
Building Community	Sensing the significance of loss in recent human history due to the shift from the local community to the larger institution as the primary shaper of lives leading to a desire to build organizational community.

Canales (2014), asserting that his definition fits perfectly within the values of Christian youth ministry, defined servant leadership as, "A process of modeling Jesus' attitude of humility, service, respect, and love, which leads the followers in promoting the mission of the group, organization, or institution" (p. 44). As a religious practitioner and scholar, Canales affirmed servant leadership in both articles as a pragmatic, methodological leadership theory modern youth ministry is well suited for (Canales, 2006, 2014).

Canales (2014) specifically noted how servant leadership could effectively contribute to a healthy youth ministry framework. He encouraged youth ministers to study the writings of Greenleaf in order to engage servant-leader concepts and philosophies; to conduct a multi-week series on the topic for all within the youth ministry's circle of influence; to plan a servant-leadership project along with older teens in order to empower teens to lead service-learning experiences; and to offer a video-based series featuring films that showcase servant-leadership-based themes.

Without a leadership development framework, you may default to meandering from resource to resource or be enamored by the latest and greatest fad. I am certainly not suggesting that you study a largely secular model as a replacement for being shaped by the power of the Holy Spirit. However, I am suggesting you consider exploration of a framework that may provide a transformative trajectory for "how" you live out "who" you are becoming as a Christian leader.

Component 6: Leadership Philosophy: Basic Etiquette — I now want to offer some very practical counsel: Learn and practice basic workplace etiquette. By "workplace" I do not just mean the church building. As a minister, your "workplace" is everywhere you go. Do not leave a mess for someone else to clean up. Say "thank-you" and write thank-you notes intentionally and often. When events are over, do not bark at teens to do their part while standing off to the side with your arms folded. Instead, politely invite them to serve with you, roll up your sleeves, and pitch in. Show up on time for meetings. Do not make promises you cannot keep. Do not show up to work if you are sick and contagious. Learn how to properly answer the phone, take detailed notes, and successfully transfer calls. Always let your administrative assistant or another staff member know where you are if you are out of the office during a workday. If you make a change that impacts other people or ministries, let them know. If a parent hosts a devotional and you decide to have a potato-chip-eating contest, make sure you first get permission and second you do not leave that house until the last crumb is in a vacuum cleaner that has been properly put away. If you are taking fifty people to Sonic after small group, call ahead and let the manager know. I could go on and on here, but I pray the point is well taken. "Do to others as you would have them do to you" (Luke 6:31) is more than a simple suggestion. Practice the golden rule again and again and enjoy living into thoughtfulness, respect, hospitality, and grace.

Creating a Contract With Self

Component 7: A Contract With Self — A great mantra I received several years ago when trying to overcome some major obstacles was, "Make a plan. Work the plan." A contract with self can help do just that. To create a contract with self, you need to set aside time each day for a few weeks to articulate the contract. Here are some questions that may help you get started:

> *Make a plan.*
> *Work the plan*

- How will you live into ministry? For instance, will you commit to holistic personal development? Will you practice spiritual disciplines? If so, which ones? How often?
- What is non-negotiable for you? For instance, "I will not counsel a teen one-on-one behind a closed door" may be a contract rule that is very important to you, your spouse, and others within your circle of influence.
- What are your life goals? Do you want to grow in a particular skill-set? Do you want to pursue an advanced degree?

This should not be a foreign concept to believers. Jesus himself observed:

> *"Is there anyone here who, planning to build a new house, doesn't first sit down and figure the cost so you'll know if you can complete it? If you only get the foundation laid and then run out of money, you're going to look pretty foolish. Everyone passing by will poke fun at you: 'He started something he couldn't finish.'" Luke 14:28-30 (The Message).*

I could say much more, but let me share some of my personal "contract with self" categories that showcase what I mean. The list could be much longer and could include many more categories. These simply represent a starting point. (If you really want to plumb the depths of learning contracts, study Adult Learning Theory or Andragogy by Malcolm Knowles). Keep in mind—the purpose of this exercise is to clarify expectations between the Lord, and self, which will position me to better clarify expectations with others. This is, "making a plan and working the plan." Please do not think I am using "work the plan" language to insinuate attempting to earn salvation, nor am I advocating superimposing your plan on someone else's life. What I'm referring to is setting a trajectory that provides a God-honoring, sustainable future.

Portions of my contract with self:

- I commit to lifelong learning.
  - o I will successfully complete a Doctoral Degree in Organizational Leadership
  - o I will continue to attend at least one academic/ ministry-related conference annually.
- I commit to integrity.
  - o I will keep no secrets from my wife.
  - o I will not counsel one on one with a member of the opposite sex.
- I commit to mentoring.
  - o If invited and the timing is right, I will enter into a mentoring relationship with two to three men per year.
  - o I commit to being mentored.
  - o I will purposefully seek out mentoring relationships to help me live into holistic personal development.

Some Practical "Next Steps"

I want to wrap up with a handful of next steps that will provide a solid foundation for sustainability:

- Make sure you have a job description that is updated annually. If you don't have one, work with your leaders to develop one. How can you do your job if you do not know what your job is?
- Engage in annual evaluation of your ministry that is based on your job description. How can you grow as a

leader if you never receive feedback on how you are doing?

- Communicate, communicate, communicate! If this is not your strength, form a team of volunteers that can help you keep parents, teens, and church leaders informed of the "who, what, when, where, why, and how" aspects of your ministry.

- As a church leader, never use "we expect you to work for us" language with your ministry staff. Make sure "we invite you to work with us" is the rule and not the exception.

- As a youth minister, grow your library. Do not buy books for the sake of filling shelves. Budget for them, buy them, read them, reflect on what you read, and integrate what you learn.

- NEVER keep secrets. Find a trusted counselor or mentor who is willing to walk through your pain points with you.

- Do not isolate. Reaching out to your peers is important, but it is equally important to reach out to those who have been in ministry a while. Their wisdom and insight may protect you from many pitfalls.

Obviously, there are many other topics we could cover in relationship to sustainable youth-ministry practices. This chapter was designed to serve as a starting point and will hopefully contribute to a robust dialogue with your family, team, and church leaders as you live into your calling.

References

Banks, R., & Ledbetter, B. M. (2004). *Reviewing leadership: A Christian evaluation of current approaches* (Kindle). Retrieved from Amazon.com. Grand Rapids, MI: Baker Academic.

Bekker, C. J. (2010). Prophet and servant: Locating Robert K. Greenleaf's counter-spirituality of servant-leadership. *The Journal of Virtues and Leadership, 1*(1), 3-14.

Canales, A. D. (2006). Models for adolescent ministry: Exploring eight ecumenical examples. *Religious Education, 101*(2), 204-232.

Canales, A. D. (2014). Servant leadership: A model for youth ministry. *Journal of Youth & Theology, 13*(1), 42-62.

Coutu, D. L. (January 01, 2004). Putting leaders on the couch: A conversation with Manfred F. R. Kets de Vries. Harvard Business Review, 82, 64-73.

Dierendonck, D., (2011). Servant leadership: A review and synthesis. *Journal of Management, 37*(4), 1228-1261.

Ebener, D.R., & O'Connell, D. J. (2010). How might servant leadership work? *Nonprofit Management & Leadership, 20*(3), 315-335.

Goleman, D. (2000). Leadership that gets results. *Harvard Business Review, 78,* 78-90.

Greenleaf, R. K. (1977). *Servant leadership: A journey into the nature of legitimate power & greatness*. Mahway, NJ: Paulist Press.

Reed, L. L., Vidaver-Cohen, D., & Colwell, S. R. (2011). A new scale to measure executive servant leadership: Development, analysis, and implications for research. *Journal of Business Ethics, 101,* 415-434. DOI: 10.1007/s10551-010-0729-1

Spears, L. (2010). Character and servant leadership: Ten characteristics of effective, caring leaders. *The Journal of Virtues & Leadership, 1*(1), 25-30.

Spears, L. (2014). Robert K. Greenleaf and servant leadership. Retrieved from http://nyym.org/?q=Spark-January2014-Spears.

Tidball, D. (2012). Leaders as Servants: A resolution of the tension. *Evangelical Review of Theology, 36*(1), 31-47.

Wolff, S. B., Pescosolido, A. T., & Druskat, V. U. (2002). Emotional intelligence as the basis of leadership emergence in self-managing teams. *The Leadership Quarterly, 13,* 505-522.

SANBALLAT, SAPPHIRA, AND SYNTYCHE
Congregational Leadership and Difficult People

Mark Frost

When the congregation overwhelmingly affirmed him as a new elder, Brad was honored and humbled. Though he understood the seriousness of his responsibility, he was convicted that the Holy Spirit who had called him to this role had also given him a clear idea of the future direction his congregation should take. He was prepared to make significant sacrifices in order to be a godly leader. What he wasn't prepared for was the level of opposition he would encounter as an elder. People he considered close friends objected to almost every leadership initiative Brad proposed. Their criticism was unkind, mean-spirited and unending.

One Sunday after services, Brad's friend Charlie stormed up to him. In front of a dozen or more onlookers, he took Brad to task for a minor change in the order of worship the elders had recently approved. "Now you've done it," Charlie began. "You've wrecked the worship service. I hope you and your control-freak cronies are happy with the chaos you've created. I know twenty families that will be leaving the church because of what you've done. I'm not leaving. You can't drive me off that easily. But until you change your decision, you've seen the last of my contribution!"

Brad was wounded, confused, and disheartened. The joy and optimism he began his leadership role with were gone. He seriously considered resigning. At the next leadership meeting, all the elders reported receiving similar attacks and threats from angry members. Afraid of serious repercussions, they reversed the decision they had made.

No student of the Bible should be surprised when godly leaders encounter opposition. Every significant leader chronicled in Scripture had to deal with antagonists who sought to obstruct God's work. There is no progress apart from opposition.

Unfortunately, the fear of opposition and lack of skill in handling it keeps many churches paralyzed and stuck. I have observed church leaders whose prime objective was to maintain peace (at least on the surface) and prevent anyone from leaving the congregation. Unfortunately, this attitude effectively hands control of the church over to the hotheads

> *Unfortunately, the fear of opposition and lack of skill in handling it keeps many churches paralyzed and stuck.*

and malcontents among the flock. When these people threaten to make a stink or leave the church unless they get their way, ineffective leaders cave in to their demands and mischief prevails. True leaders will find ways to take back their rightful role by dealing forthrightly with these problematic people. Scripture relates at least three different kinds of opposition that may face church leaders, each represented by a character from the biblical story.

Sanballat: Open Hostility

The first is Sanballat, Nehemiah's nemesis. He represents people who openly oppose the vision of the leadership. One need not worry about where these antagonists stand. They array themselves in tireless, unyielding opposition to the official leadership and make no bones about it.

Nehemiah had a clear-cut mission, and he was unswervingly dedicated to it: rebuild the walls of Jerusalem. A clear mission like his calls forth like-minded people who unite behind it. But— and here's the downside we don't like to talk about—a crystal-clear mission can also arouse and animate those who oppose it. Consider what happened with Nehemiah: "When Sanballat the Horonite and Tobiah the Ammonite official heard about [Nehemiah's plan to rebuild the walls], they were very much disturbed that someone had come to promote the welfare of the Israelites" (Neh. 2:10). Note that in each succeeding mention of Sanballat, his group of supporters grows (Neh. 2:10, 18, 4:7). What was true in Nehemiah's day is still true today. Opponents like these seem to have a radar for finding each other. Then they band together, united in their opposition to the leadership. This presents a huge challenge for any leader.

Sanballat's primary reaction to Nehemiah's mission is anger (Neh. 4:1, 7). Anger is perhaps the most serious red flag leaders should be on the lookout for. When a well-thought-out and carefully-presented initiative is met with immediate and disproportionate fury, it is likely that you are dealing with more than just a garden-variety difference of opinion. You may have encountered a committed antagonist who bears little evidence of the fruit of the Spirit. A further red flag is evident when such people begin to behave aggressively (or in passive-aggressive ways).

The key tactic of Nehemiah's opponents was intimidation. Sanballat's aim was to strike enough fear into Nehemiah and his followers that they would shrink back and discontinue their mission. His intimidation took many forms. He used false accusations (2:19), ridicule (4:1-5), open letters intended to prejudice people who didn't know the whole story (6:5-9), plotting and pot-stirring (4:7-9), letter-writing campaigns (6:17-19), rumor-mongering (6:6), recruiting "concerned friends" (6:10-14), and repeatedly demanding to meet with the leadership (6:1-4). Any present-day leader who has faced opposition will recognize most of these tactics.

So how do we deal with this kind of open opposition? The most important — and perhaps the most difficult — advice from Nehemiah is simply, "Refuse to give in to fear!" He knows that fear is the enemy of faith. In fact, at one point he states that if he were to act out of fear, it would be sin (6:13). He is able to continue on his mission in the face of fear because he knows that "the God of heaven will give us success," (2:20) and "our God will fight for us." (4:20) Today's leaders would do well to remember the admonition of Prov. 29:25, "Fear of man will prove to be a snare, but whoever trusts in the Lord is kept safe."

Second, Nehemiah teaches us not to respond in kind to our critics. He responded honestly and straightforwardly, but never with anger, insult, unkindness, or threats. Even though he could have, he refused to offer a detailed defense to all the trumped-up charges levelled against him. He replied briefly to the charges, stating that they were untrue, but did not waste time on a point-by-point rebuttal.

Next, we learn from Nehemiah the importance of presenting a united front. He and his workers literally had each other's back (4:16-18). Antagonists frequently resort to "divide and conquer" techniques. When under attack, it is especially important for leaders to remain unified, especially in public communications to the church.

Another important lesson is to stay on task! Recognizing Sanballat's repeated demands for meetings as a diversion, he politely refused to attend (6:1-4). Leaders need to regularly remind themselves of the mission and avoid getting sucked into time-draining meetings and discussions where nothing is resolved and energy is wasted.

Of course, our most powerful weapon is prayer, and Nehemiah employed it frequently. Sometimes his prayers were short: "Now strengthen my hands" (6:9). At other times, he asked God to turn his opponents' insults and evil intentions back on themselves (4:4-5). The picture that emerges is that of a leader who is in constant conversation with God.

> *God's mission in the church is too important for it to be derailed by antagonists using fear and intimidation.*

God's mission in the church is too important for it to be derailed by antagonists using fear and intimidation. Contemporary leaders would do well to study Nehemiah's responses to Sanballat's attacks.

Sapphira: Satan's Secret Servants

The second example is Sapphira, who along with her husband Ananias, represents a class of opponents I call Satan's Secret Servants. These are people who appear to be faithful, active, and generous church members. But Satan is actively working through them to disrupt the church and undermine its witness.

The story of Ananias and Sapphira in Acts 5:1-11 is easily one of the most disturbing accounts in the New Testament, if not the entire Bible. Preachers avoid preaching on it and it is seldom included in the Sunday School curriculum for our children. But the incident recorded there has instructive value for those called to lead churches today. It forces them to face the troubling reality that spiritual warfare is real and the church is often the battle-ground.

In his war with the church, the Enemy employs undercover agents, a fact which is apparent when one includes the final verse of Acts 4 in the context of the account. There we learn that Barnabas sold a field and brought the proceeds to the apostles to be used for the relief of needy Christians. Chapter 5 begins by using identical terminology to describe Ananias and Sapphira's gift. To a casual observer they appeared to be as good, generous, and faithful as Barnabas. But in their case, selfishness, vainglory, hypocrisy, and deceit lurked beneath the surface.

It should not surprise us to learn that some who appear to be paragons of virtue might in fact be Satanic agents. Paul himself warned, "Satan himself masquerades as an angel of light. It is not surprising, then, if his servants also masquerade as servants of righteousness" (2 Cor. 11:14-15). The New Testament very clearly warns us to be on guard for those in the church who have intentions other than serving the Lord (see Rom. 16:17-18).

The account in Acts makes Peter's discernment of Ananias and Sapphira's duplicity sound easy and obvious. There is no doubt that this ability was given him by the Holy Spirit. But we have no idea how great a spiritual struggle it may have been for him to develop and employ that spiritual gift. What we do know is that attempting such discernment is difficult—and scary—for us.

However anxiety-provoking it may be, church leaders need to seek and pray for the ability to distinguish between healthy conflict and Satanic manipulation. The strategy for dealing with healthy conflict is vastly different from what is demanded by Satanic manipulation, and several bad things happen when we try to use tools that are appropriate for healthy conflict to deal with obstinate minions of the Enemy.

> *However anxiety-provoking it may be, church leaders need to seek and pray for the ability to distinguish between healthy conflict and Satanic manipulation.*

First, we waste valuable time and energy. It's like using a tack hammer to drive a railroad spike. The hammer will wear out long before the spike makes any real progress.

Second, we hang on to what M. Scott Peck calls "the (mostly) false hope for change." It is true that anyone can change, and God's Spirit makes that possible. But while we pray for even the most recalcitrant rebels to repent, we dare not adopt an unrealistically-rosy view of reality that shackles our better judgment to the expectation that they will.

Finally, when we do not correctly discern Satanic attack, we leave God's people vulnerable to devastation from within. Acts 20:28-30 makes it clear that these antagonists are as dangerous to a church as a wolf is to a flock of lambs.

So how do we identify "Satan's Secret Servants" among us? Scripture provides us with several important measuring sticks to use in discerning people's intentions. Galatians 5 draws a clear contrast between the acts of the flesh and the fruit of the Spirit. 1 Corinthians 13 beautifully describes a person who is acting out of love, not self-centeredness. And James 3:13-18 contrasts "wisdom" that is from the earth with true, heavenly wisdom. Surely these Scriptures were intended to help godly leaders distinguish those who build up the body from those who hasten its ruin. Certainly no one is perfect, and even the best among us will exhibit some of the negative qualities named in these passages from time to time, but that does not excuse leaders from examining a person's life *as a whole* and prayerfully drawing conclusions about the danger they may pose.

Another means of identifying these dangerous antagonists is offered by Kenneth Haugk. He identifies a number of "red flags" that help leaders discern those who would harm the church. Among these are a previous track record of stirring up dissension, appealing to "nameless others" to bolster one's arguments, offering gushing praise to a leader (while vilifying fellow leaders), and keeping file folders filled with "damning evidence" against the church leaders. (Haugk's book predates the World Wide Web, but I'm confident that if he were writing today, he would include among these red flags the censure of leaders via social media.) Again, on our worst days we all might be found to be in possession of one of these crimson banners. But when a person waves several of them at once (and consistently over time), leadership should sit up and take notice.

So how do we handle Satan's Secret Servants? Certainly, humbling ourselves before the Lord in ardent prayer is the obvious prerequisite. Beyond that, leaders must present a united front in dealing with such people. This is supremely important, since "divide and conquer" is a favorite ploy of antagonists. But the prime strategy for dealing with such people is isolation. Ray Fulenwider, long considered one of the most effective church leaders in our fellowship, suggested that elders write down the names of members who seem to never be happy with anything the leadership does. He maintained that even in large congregations the resulting list would number no more than twenty. He then counseled elders to lead the congregation with the needs of the remainder of the congregation in mind without striving to appease this small group of malcontents.

If that seems harsh and insensitive, consider Paul's counsel to the young evangelist Titus: "Warn a divisive person once, and then warn them a second time. After that, have nothing to do with them. You may be sure that such people are warped and sinful; they are self-condemned" (Titus 3:10-11). Isolation seems to be an eminently Scriptural strategy.

Finally, notice the twin results of the Lord's judgment against Ananias and Sapphira. First, "great fear seized the whole church" (Acts 5:11). But then, "More and more men and women believed in the Lord and were added to their number" (Acts 5:14). When leaders prayerfully identify and carefully isolate Satan's Secret Servants, they can expect some anxious reactions from church members. But they can be confident that their actions will promote a healthy, growing body.

Syntyche: Good People Who Can't Get Along

Finally, there is Syntyche, a lady the apostle Paul calls out along with Euodia in Philippians 4. These two are representative of good people who just can't seem to get along. These kinds of difficult people are involved in interpersonal conflicts in the body that seem to grow and expand until dozens of people are involved.

> *I plead with Euodia and I plead with Syntyche to be of the same mind in the Lord. Yes, and I ask you, my true companion, help these women since they have contended at my side in the cause of the gospel, along with Clement and the rest of my co-workers, whose names are in the book of life. Phil. 4:2–3*

Paul urges Syntyche and Euodia to settle their differences and he asks others to help them do so. A couple of quick observations are in order. First, this difficulty was happening in a good congregation. The church in Philippi was the one Paul had the closest, most loving relationship with. It was the model of a healthy, happy, growing church. And yet its peace and tranquility was marred by interpersonal

> *A healthy church is not one devoid of conflict. It is one where the inevitable conflict is handled in a godly way.*

conflict. Even healthy churches have problems. Church leaders who define congregational health as the absence of conflict will be regularly disappointed. A healthy church is not one devoid of conflict. It is one where the inevitable conflict is handled in a godly way.

Second, this disagreement was between good people. We are not surprised when conflict arises among members who are minimally involved and who apparently believe that criticism and complaint are their spiritual gifts. But this was different. Euodia and Syntyche were both hard workers who were highly esteemed by Paul. They had given of themselves sacrificially for the cause of the kingdom. And yet, they just couldn't seem to get along with each other.

Nor was this just a minor, fleeting spat. It had been reported to Paul, most likely by Epaphroditus, who had been sent by the Philippian church to care for Paul's needs in Rome. Paul felt the situation was serious enough to warrant a special mention in the letter to the Philippian church that he sent back with Epaphroditus. Apparently the Holy Spirit, whose inspiration Paul wrote by, concurred. We need to recognize that interpersonal conflicts like this can have repercussions well beyond the people immediately involved. Edwin Friedman correctly observed that a congregation is an extended family system, subject to all the dynamics that shape such systems. And one of the key tenets of family dynamics theory is that dysfunction in one part of the system can have far-reaching, negative effects on all other parts.

This is why Paul, even as he instructs Euodia and Syntyche to work out their differences, also urges other members of the church to be involved in the process. He specifically calls upon a respected leader in the Philippian church—a person he calls his true companion, or "yokefellow"—to help facilitate a reconciliation between these two beloved women. But he also mentions Clement and other unnamed co-workers, perhaps to enlist their help and support as well. While it is true that unhealthy conflict between individuals can make an entire family system sick, it is also true that a healthy response to conflict throughout the entire system can stimulate the healing of broken relationships. Simply stated, there are times when the whole church—and especially its leaders—will need to get involved to help restore strained relationships.

So how was the rift between Syntyche and Euodia to be bridged? And how can leaders today be constructively involved in restoring strained relationships? Earlier in Philippians, there is a great example of the kind of exhortation that could help these two to "agree in the Lord." At the beginning of chapter 2, Paul urges his readers to be like-minded, united in mind and spirit. He advises them to avoid selfish ambition and to value others above themselves. These are nuggets of practical wisdom, but they are much more than that. They are rooted in the deepest truths of the faith. Paul elaborates thus:

> *"In your relationships with one another, have the same mindset as Christ Jesus: Who, being in very nature God, did not consider equality with God something to be used to his own advantage; rather, he made himself nothing by taking the very nature of a servant, being made in human likeness. And being found in appearance as a man, he humbled himself by becoming obedient to death – even death on a cross!" (Phil. 2:5-8).*

The path to relational wholeness lies in every member of the body cultivating the sacrificial mindset of the Lord Jesus Christ. When good, sincere believers have trouble getting along, one of the best things a leader can do is to call them back to the sacrificial mindset of Jesus. It is also helpful to offer some concrete ways the individuals might do that.

Once I sat with a group of elders as they attempted to counsel a young husband who was on the verge of divorcing his wife. Wearing our best "counselor hats," we listened sympathetically as he recounted the actions of his wife that had upset him. Finally, one of the newer elders asked him, "John, where is Jesus in all of this?" The young man fell silent for a long time. Finally, he said weakly, "I don't suppose I know." The other elders then began to share challenging circumstances they had faced in their own marriages and how they had learned the value of sacrificing their own desires for the good of their wives. Without talking down to him, the elders were providing this young man with godly examples to guide him in imitating Jesus.

Disagreements will arise even between dedicated believers. But the sacrificial love of Jesus provides the motivation, the power, and the wisdom necessary to restore unity to the body. A church that encourages and nurtures His spirit of self-sacrifice is one that will promote healing and reconciliation between believers who are at odds with each other. Leaders who model this attitude before their flock will be true "yokefellows" in the reconciling work of Jesus.

> *A church that encourages and nurtures His spirit of self-sacrifice is one that will promote healing and reconciliation between believers who are at odds with each other.*

PLAYGROUND BULLIES
Courageous Strategies for Dealing with Bullies

Grady D. King

I like to be honest and encouraging, but this is one subject that needs to get out in the open. Too many congregations have a bully on the playground. No one likes a bully. It is safe to assume that everyone has a story about a bully. The mere mention of the word "bully" evokes memories of my elementary days on the playground. I can see his face to this day and re-member his name. He was a big boy—taller, heavier, and stronger than anyone in my third-grade class. He enjoyed ridiculing others, taking food from lunch boxes, tripping people in the hallway and on the playground, simply being mean. He was sneaky. His cronies always laughed at his antics and cov-ered for him. He went to the principal's office on a regular basis. Everyone knew that he was a bully. Hopefully, he grew out of such behavior, but there is no guarantee. Sometimes, bullies don't grow up in spite of discipline, and their behavior takes a toll—

One who is often reproved, yet remains stubborn, will suddenly be broken beyond healing. (Prov. 29:1)

There was a time, supposedly, when bullying or standing up to the bully was considered a rite of passage—simply part of growing up. For me, avoidance at all cost was my way through this rite of passage. It is no innocent rite of passage today.

- Almost one out of every four students 12-18 years of age report being bullied during the school year (2015).
- More than a person's identity, bullying is a behavior, and astoundingly, 64% of students 12-18 years old did not report being bullied.
- More than half of bullying situations (57%) stop when a peer intervenes on behalf of the student being bullied.[1] Peer intervention is essential.[2]

Being a bystander is not an option in stopping bullying. Some bullies never grow out of their behavior and the playgrounds change to the workplace, home, community groups, athletic fields, and yes, even down at church. I am not writing theoretically, or simply from one bad experience as a minister. I share from forty-plus years of ministry in six congrega-

> *I share from forty-plus years of ministry in six congregations: in rural, urban, and suburban contexts ranging from 150-1,200 members.*

[1]http://www.pacer.org/bullying/resources/stats.asp The Center of Disease Control reported in 2015 that among high school students, 15.5% are cyber-bullied and 20.2% are bullied on school property. Among middle school students, 24% are cyber-bullied and 45% are bullied on school property. The percentages of individuals who have experienced cyber bullying at some point in their lifetimes have nearly doubled (18% to 34%) from 2007-2016.

[2] As a behavior, bullying is generally defined as the use of use of force, threat, or coercion to abuse, intimidate, or aggressively dominate others. The behavior is often repeated and habitual.

tions: in rural, urban, and suburban contexts ranging from 150-1,200 members. In addition, co-leading HOPE Network has given me a front-row seat at many congregations and hours of conversation with church leaders. Yes, there has been a bully in almost every church and/or leadership. At times, there has been more than one bully who rallied others and they became a "mob" — in every sense of the word. Although "mob" is crude and inconsistent with Christian community, it is nonetheless a visceral reality and not foreign to the church of the first century.[3] I use the term "visceral" because emotion, not reason, drives a bully and a mob. Thom Rainer, author of *Autopsy of a Deceased Church*, describes an alliance of bullies as a "church cartel." It is strong language and vivid imagery. Rainer says,

> Churches that have cartels usually know they are present. They know who the bully is. They know who the bully followers are. They see them. They hear them. And they often fear them. Courageous leaders must confront and stop church cartels. If no one is willing, the church is already on a path toward decline and death.[4]

Before going any further it is helpful to define "bully." I was not in congregational ministry very long before hearing the phrase, "head elder." To say the least, it was not an endearing term. After an experience as a young preacher with one "head elder" I recalled a childhood experience with a bull in rural northwest Oklahoma. I had climbed over a fence to get to a creek to play. I knew the old bull was in the pasture but didn't see him. Just as I headed to the creek, there he was, standing between me and the

---

[3] See Acts 15:1; Gal. 1:6-8, 3; Eph. 4:14; 3 John 9; for individuals whose motives show up in their behavior impacting others (i.e., various characteristics that may be indicative of a "bully").

[4] Taken from blog and podcast — Rainer on Leadership: The Painful Reality of Church Bully Cartels. December 16, 2016.
(http://thomrainer.com/2016/12/painful-reality-church-bully-cartels/)

path to the creek. His beady brown eyes stared me down. I moved. He moved. I tried scare tactics with boyish hollering. It didn't work. Before I knew it, his head was down and he was running toward me. He won. I jumped back over the fence, ripped my pants, and he had his way. In a very real sense, I had been bullied.

Defining a Bully

You may be reading this with a bully in mind. How would you describe a bully? More importantly, have you experienced how church allows a bully to hold her hostage? In preparing for this chapter, I asked over twenty church people, some in leadership, most not, what comes to mind when hearing the phrase "church bully." The overwhelming response was, "someone who gets their way no matter what." Closely related was the word "power." My friend Julie, wife of an experienced minister, says it plainly – *"When a bully is allowed to satisfy his thirst for power, someone is abused. There is an opportunity cost. Saying yes to the bully means saying no to the flock."*

> *It is interesting how we tend to soften the harsh word or judgment of someone who is a bully. This raises the question, "Is being a bully an identity or behavior?"*

Almost everyone I asked about a church bully said a specific person came to mind, and immediately unsolicited stories began to flow. Nearly everyone who was asked qualified their comments with, *"He does good things, and isn't necessarily a bad person, just very controlling."* It is not unusual to hear certain refrains about a bully's behavior. *"He's a good man who gets things done. He means well. His personality is just stronger than others." "It doesn't matter what others think, she gets her way."* Or, there is a deep sense of resignation from years of interaction – *"I've known him a long time and he's not going to change."*

It is interesting how we tend to soften the harsh word or judgment of someone who is a bully. This raises the question, *"Is being a bully an identity or behavior?"* Being human is complex, and behaviors are loaded with layers of motivations and meaning. Certainly, those that bully would deny their behavior or characterization as a bully. Their behaviors have multiple triggers—how they see themselves in the system; their role and/or responsibility; what they deem necessary or even their own need for significance, security, or response to a threat. And when you factor in their good qualities—what they preserve, protect, or accomplish, some people consider it "unspiritual" to call them into question. There are, however, some questions to consider related to the bully or the group dynamic in question.

1. **Reputation**: When their name is mentioned, what is the response?
2. **Decisions**: Do all decisions depend on their approval?
3. **Conflict Avoidance**: Is there a pattern of postponing decisions to avoid conflict with the person?
4. **Language/Emotion:** What language and/or emotions does the person use when speaking? (i.e., fear, anger, extremes, over-generalizations, threats, "all or nothing," anxiety, etc.)
5. **Body Language:** What is the body language of those in the room when this person is speaking or expressing their position?
6. **Alliances:** Who does the person seek out for private conversations, emails, texts, to influence direction?
7. **Public/Private:** Is the person inconsistent in spirit and behavior in public and private?

These reflection questions help discern patterns over time calling for action. The goal is not to judge or label, but rather to identify the issues for growth and to assess how to move forward. To ignore such a consideration is what I have come to refer to as "sanctifying peculiarities" as *that's just the way it is.*" The cliché — "*It is what it is*" will inevitably lead to passivity, loss of energy, and polarization, stifling growth and enabling an unhealthy environment.

As leaders, our capacity to take responsibility for our own thoughts and feelings is a sign of healthy functioning. Learning to speak first person instead of "you" and "them" is a necessary component of healthy functioning as well. This is essential regardless of personality type, theological viewpoint, or doctrinal commitment. Healthy theology necessitates rigorous consideration of our behaviors with and for others.[5]

> *The cliché — "It is what it is" will inevitably lead to passivity, loss of energy, and polarization, stifling growth and enabling an unhealthy environment.*

"The Church Cartel"

What is true of individuals only multiplies when the bully rallies followers. A congregation allows herself to be taken hostage when a controlling person and/or group becomes dominant. Like all hostage situations, it is dangerous. Rainer has five very dangerous realities of what he calls "the church cartel."[6]

1. When a cartel is allowed power, the church is already unhealthy. The cartel is, by its definition, self-centered and power-driven. A church is already very sick if members remain silent and do not confront this evil directly.

---

[5] Consider: The Ten Commandments (Ex. 20, Deut. 5); The Sermon on the Mount (Matt. 5-7); Rom. 12; Gal. 5:19-22; 2 Peter 1:3-11. Also, Jesus' rebuke of the Pharisees, Matt. 23.
[6] Rainer on Leadership: (http://thomrainer.com/2016/12/painful-reality-church-bully-cartels/).

2. A church cartel leaves carnages of wounded and dying people. If you have any doubts about this danger, please see my post on "Autopsy of a Deceased Pastor." See the comments. See the pain and questions and defeat the cartel leaves behind.

3. Church cartels drive away healthy leaders. Some of these leaders are driven away by the cartel. Others leave on their own accord because they want to be in a joyous and healthy church. Their departure exacerbates the problems in these churches.

4. Church cartels cause church leaders to work from a posture of fear. Instead of moving forward in faith, church leaders often spend more time worrying about how their decisions will impact the cartel. These leaders know the cartel will come after them if they go contrary to the carnal group's wishes.

5. We are told in Scripture to manifest the fruit of the Spirit; the church cartel causes the church to do just the opposite. Gal. 5:22-23 is clear about the fruit of the Spirit: love, joy, peace, patience, kindness, goodness, faith, gentleness, and self-control. Church cartels bring hate, discord, anxiety, impatience, evil, fear, brutality, and chaos.

No Reasoning with Emotion

The impact of a "church cartel" is debilitating and the deeds of the flesh perpetuate chronic anxiety. Chronic anxiety has a spiraling effect on any system and one of the responses is bullying behavior.[7] The amygdala — that part of the brain that is

---

7 Peter Steinke. *Teaching Fish to Walk: Church Systems and Adaptive Challenge.* New Vision Press, Austin, Texas (2015), p. 35-36. He writes that there are a

responsible for the response and memory of emotions, particularly fear — dominates the bully or mob. You cannot reason with emotion.[8] When the bully is in full throttle mode, reasoning is futile. When it gets to the mob dynamic, emotional processes take over completely. Steinke draws on the work of Murray Bowen, one of the pioneers of family therapy and founders of systemic therapy for understanding anxiety and related behaviors.

Bowen defined emotional as whatever is instinctual, reflexive, reactive, and mindless in our interactive with another. The center of the emotional operation is where the central nervous system connects with the lower brain, sometimes called the lizard brain. Once triggered, the primitive brain sends off a cascade of somatic effects, such as the stiffening of muscles and the activity of the sweat glands. When anxiety grabs hold of the lower brain, it limits the range of possible responses. The brain's imaginative valve is shut off. At best, our thinking becomes narrow and fixed on threat."[9]

---

multitude of triggers for behaviors but there are common igniters. Disruptions: change, loss, separation, innovation, transitions; Feeling Trapped: hopelessness, helplessness, powerlessness, being unable to effect an outcome; Hostile Forces: real or imagined threats to one's well-being; Uncertainty: puzzling, contingent, ambiguous, unpredictable situations; and Differences: things that are peculiar, strange, bizarre.

[8] See Acts 21-22 for a case in point regarding some Jews' response to Paul's announcement about what God had done among the Gentiles through his ministry (21:19). First, they praised God, but some reported false things about what Paul was teaching the Gentiles (21:20-21). Paul responded by doing what they asked but it did not appease a group of Jews (21:22-30). Six times from chapters 21-26 the word "kill" is used in reference to the response of the Jews to Paul regardless of reason or the tribune's judgment.

[9] Peter Steinke. *Teaching Fish to Walk: Church Systems and Adaptive Challenge.* New Vision Press, Austin, Texas (2015), p. 33-34.

When it comes to church, we know "lizard brain," don't we? How is it that a group of people can allow one person or a small group of people to dominate? I have seen it happen way too often. Intelligent, talented, and strong people surrender to the bully to the detriment of the whole. Sometimes, it goes on for years with the hope that a new elder-selection process will break the cycle. More times than not, good men who are asked to serve and could make a difference find a way to bow out, knowing the reality, what they have heard through the years of their own dealings with the bully or the controlling group. Ministers can be bullies as well. This is why clear job descriptions with consistent growth reviews and accountability are indispensable to staff and church health. Whether a church member, elder, or minister, the cycle continues mainly because people choose to be a victim rather than stand up and endure the consequences. My friend Jon says it this way—"*We get what we put up with.*" If a bully or group is allowed to dominate, we allow it to happen—put up with it. So, who will stand up and refuse to be a victim? This is the question.

No Victims Here

Ministers

Why hasn't anyone stood up to the bully? It should be clear by now that a bully will continue to bully because people allow their behavior to go unchecked. In this sense, the church plays the victim. It is a posture of fear—of conflict, division, even retaliation. In the case of ministers, it is often about the risk of constant tension that is exhausting, or worse, the risk of losing a job.

> *It should be clear by now that a bully will continue to bully because people allow their behavior to go unchecked.*

A good friend and former executive in the banking industry reminded me that in the corporate world there are generally ways to appeal (procedures, policies, etc.). In other words, there is an outlet for at least your voice being heard. Of course, high-end executives, as he noted, have their ways that do fall into the category of bullying.

In the church, however, there are few structures, policies, and procedures beyond "be Christian" that give people an outlet to appeal. The reality is that as human beings we are very sophisticated at justifying our actions, assigning motives, building a case against someone for an intended result. Bullies can get away with almost anything in the name of religion. *No victims here* must be the guiding value for being healthy and moving forward.

Elders
In the case of the internal dynamic with elders, there are emotional dynamics, conflict avoidance, and at times, long-term friendships that sustain what has come to be normative—as unhealthy as it may be. It is called homeostasis—fixed patterns of behavior that no matter what is attempted, the system seeks for familiarity (homeostasis). Discomfort cannot be tolerated or to a greater extent, pain is seen as bad and quickly alleviated. The capacity to endure the discomfort of pain in self is directly proportionate to enduring the pain in others. Rescuing self or others from pain means bullying will continue while at the same time tolerated and resented. We must get over the idea that it is unspiritual to confront bullying behavior.

Congregation
When it comes to the congregation dealing with bullies, there is conflict avoidance and, more significantly, an unspoken value of being nice—as if, it is a fruit of the Spirit (Gal. 5:22). It is not.

Kindness is a fruit of the Spirit but we can be kind and direct in speaking truth.

- We have confused being nice with speaking the truth in love (Eph. 4:15). The entire context for "speaking the truth in love" is about Christian behavior and emotional growth — of growing up in Christ. Yes, we are called to bear with one another in love in humility, gentleness, and patience (Eph. 4:2), but this does not mean we ignore speaking truth.
- Making every effort to maintain the unity of the Spirit in the bond of peace is our calling (Eph. 4:3). When a bully is allowed to dominate, there can never be unity of the Spirit in the bond of peace. Peace is not being nice or even kind. It assumes the presence of conflict and working through it. If our peace with God came through the blood of His (Christ's) cross (Col. 1:20), then, how much more are we called to work through pain with others?
- Bullying left unchecked opens up the possibility of the presence of the forces of darkness. After all, our struggle is not against flesh and blood, but principalities and powers (Eph. 6:12).

Eugene Peterson's translation of Eph. 6:12 is even more vivid.

This is no afternoon athletic contest that we'll walk away from and forget about in a couple of hours. This is for keeps, a life-or-death fight to the finish against the Devil and all his angels."
(The Message)

Bullying is Sin

Controlling or abusing others is sin, and all sin separates us from God and each other. When it comes to a member of the   congregation confronting a bully elder, it is seldom done and most members will choose to remain silent or leave. There is, however, biblical guidance on how to treat an older brother and sister (1 Tim. 5:1) and more significantly, how to rebuke an elder who sins (1 Tim. 5:17-22).

> *Controlling or abusing others is sin, and all sin separates us from God and each other.*

Playing the Unspiritual Card

Finally, a word about playing the unspiritual card. For some who are peers of the bully, they will not confront him because they have surrendered to God and no longer choose to act according to the flesh as a carnal person. To confront, especially a fellow leader is in their minds to be unspiritual and risk allowing the carnal man to take up residence again. It is a more prevalent dynamic in leadership than one would expect. In the end, however, it further exacerbates the impact of the bully or controlling group.

What to do about a BULLY?

Pray without ceasing for wisdom and courage.
If you have been reading to this point and not jumped ahead, it goes without saying—dealing with a bully is not easy, but absolutely necessary. It is a spiritual issue with life and death consequences for leaders and congregations.

Enough is Enough
To ignore the bully thinking he will go away is absurd. If you are in a leadership capacity with other leaders dealing with a "mob" or "church cartel," appeasement strategies will not work. You have to get to the point where your stewardship of God's people and mission compels you to speak directly, "Enough is enough."

We have to realize that bullies are relentless. The longer they bully (which can take the form of pouting, manipulation, private meetings, threatening to leave, or saying others will leave if you don't _____). And of course, the "We will stop our giving" is the card often played. It is simply a power move—a threat. Instead of capitulating to a threat, avoiding conflict or worse, doing nothing, there are things that can be done. It will take courage and a willingness to live with some pain for a while. In essence, it will take nerve and an avoidance of a quick-fix approach.

Take a stand. Stay calm. Stay connected.
Edwin Friedman, in his work *A Failure of Nerve: Leadership in an Age of Quick Fix*, boils down nerve to three phrases: Take a stand. Stay calm. Stay connected. I know, it is easier said than done, but it can be done. Boxers have a phrase—"Lead with your chin." When you take a stand, intentionally, thoughtfully, without anger or retaliation and stay the course, you are leading with your chin. Yes, it is posture of vulnerability, of taking a risk, but it is what it means to be a leader. There is always a price to pay with any action and the system will always respond with initial anxiety. As a leader, you cannot be anxious. Like a duck on the water, you may be paddling hard underneath, but it cannot show on the surface.

Expect Sabotage
Once a stand is taken there will be sabotage. Sabotage's effect on leaders can be summed up in one word—blame. When a bully is challenged by other leaders who stand up, the blame game is routine. At this point, courage and calmness, not fear and reactivity, is the best response. Bullies have perfected the art of sabotage and in your most anxious moments, you must not give in or give up. Remain steadfast in humility and as a group, stay united in the same message and response with integrity. When

you don't, the bully or bullies control the system and regardless of your title as a leader, they lead.

If you don't write down anything else from this chapter, get a sticky note and write in big print—Anxious leaders are leaderless! Leading from a place of courage and resolve is hard work, but it is the way forward in breaking control and/or a stuck system. Can you live with discomfort, even pain, knowing that it is part of changing the system from unhealthy to healthy? Here are a few next steps in the process.

> *Anxious leaders are leaderless!*

Next Steps

1. Reflect on the bully or bullies and their impact on you, the church, and God's mission in your congregation. Write it out. Read it out loud. Submit it to God.
2. Take inventory of your own behavior in meetings and how you will change your response to the bully in the meeting.
3. Go to the bully and take a stand in the spirit of Matt. 18:15-17. For anyone who complains about the bully, encourage them to speak directly to the bully, document the conversation, and follow up with them for support, prayer, and discernment.
4. Share with other leaders the need to deal with bullying behavior.
5. Discuss with your leadership the need for ongoing training in self-awareness, pastoral dynamics, church as family system, and for a behavioral covenant among leaders.
6. Review addendum 1 and 2 for consideration and conversation about being proactive regarding expected congregational and leader behaviors.

Behavioral covenants are helpful for outlining expected behaviors and core values for healthy community life as leaders and with churches. They proactively cultivate what it means to lead with a community of leaders and to be a part of a church community. In a culture of individualism, entitlement, and consumerism, being clear about community-life expectations and process under the Lordship of Christ can go a long way in dealing with a bully on the playground.

Addendum 1 – A Membership Covenant

One congregation, with a history of division, made a commitment to be a healthier, covenant-keeping people. The rationale is that God is a covenant maker and keeper. Therefore, we will be as well.

On Placing Membership –

1. Prospective members place membership only on Sunday mornings by coming to the front after the sermon.

2. The minister introduces the one(s) placing membership by having them stand up in front with him facing the seated congregation.

3. Then he addresses the new members…

"Is it your intention in placing membership here today to become a member of this congregation; to submit to the authority of the elders God has called to shepherd/serve in this church; to shun divisiveness; to live your life, both publicly and privately, in faithfulness to Jesus Christ; and to work alongside all in this congregation to build up the body of Christ? Is that your intention today?

4. They respond simply by saying, "Yes."

5. The minister then asks the members of the congregation to stand and asks:

"Will you promise to welcome, love, and receive as fellow members the John Smith family, whom the Lord has accepted; to work alongside them, and encourage them in faith, hope, and love; and together build up the body of Christ in this place? If so, say "We will." Congregation responds, "We will."

6. Minister says to all: "May the Lord help us keep the promises we have made to each other today." This is also done with newly baptized on the Sunday they are baptized or the first Sunday after their baptism if they were baptized during the week.

Addendum 2 — A Shepherd's Covenant

A behavioral covenant among leaders is helpful for group functioning and accountability. Simply saying, "'Be Christian' is our covenant" is naive about human nature and what it means to be a community of leaders. Here are two actual examples as a beginning point of discussion. This is most effectively used in elder orientation prior to ordination of elders and to be shared with the congregation. It raises the bar for what it means to be a leader consistent with 1 Tim. 1:3-7; Titus 1:5-9; 1 Peter 5:1-5; and Acts 20:28 and John 10:11-18.

Example 1

Elders' Covenant

All shepherds have agreed to the following stipulations. Their purpose is to lay the ground rules for the interaction of the shepherds for the benefit of the congregation and the eldership. By signing this statement, I agree to abide by these policies.

1. Although I am a shepherd of the _____ (name of congregation), I am also part of the flock within the eldership and I will submit to the eldership as I expect every other member to have a submissive spirit. If I am asked to resign by the eldership, I will do so immediately without questioning their judgment.

2. Decisions made by the eldership are made by majority vote, not by minority rule.

3. If I am not present for a vote, I will not bring up any issue decided upon in my absence for the purpose of reversing that decision.

4. Once the eldership has decided an issue, I will support it even if I did not agree with the decision.

5. I will not make major decisions on my own, realizing that I have no authority as an individual elder. Authority resides in the eldership as a whole.

6. I will treat my fellow elders with respect and as an equal.

7. I will not engage in derogatory discussions about any elder or the eldership, any deacon, or any staff member. I will at all times speak positively about the leadership or I will not speak at all.

Having read this code of conduct, I pledge to abide by it and count it a privilege to serve as a shepherd at the _____(name of congregation).

Example 2

Elders' Covenant
I believe that the task of shepherding God's people is both a God-given privilege and a serious responsibility. I believe that such leadership requires a high degree of discipline and accountability. I believe that my growth in spiritual maturity will be a direct result of my relationship with God and that my ability to be an effective shepherd will ultimately be the result of consciously seeking the character of Christ.

Personal
- I will serve willingly and eagerly as a shepherd of God's flock at _____ (name of congregation)

with Christ as an example of a servant to the flock of God.

- I recognize my family to be my most precious earthly responsibility. I will make every effort to lovingly encourage and spiritually strengthen my spouse, children, and parents.
- I will seek to live in such a way that, by my conduct at home, at work, and in the community, those around me may detect Jesus in my life and be drawn to Him.

General

- I will treat my fellow elders with respect and as an equal. Even as I desire to be known and understood by you, I pledge to be sensitive to you and your needs to the best of my ability. I will try to hear you, see your point of view, understand your feelings, and draw you out of the spirit of possible discouragement or withdrawal.
- I submit to the oversight of my fellow elders and expect to be held accountable in the role of elder by them. I agree to resign as elder if asked to by the elder group.
- My wife and I agree to be partners in shepherding responsibilities, agreements, and activities.

Functional

- I will not engage in derogatory discussions about any member of the _____ Leadership Team. I will at all times speak positively about them, or I will not speak at all.
- I will follow the model portrayed in Matt. 18 concerning conflict management. Whenever possible, I will encourage the individual to privately address the matter with the appropriate person to resolve the conflict.
- I agree with the Elder Group Policies and recognize them as the resource for governance for_____

(name of congregation), for the Elder Group, and for the entire Leadership Team.

- _____   _____
  Elder signature   Date

I attest that I know of no scriptural reason my husband should not serve as a shepherd of God's people and affirm his personal spiritual qualities to be in compliance with this covenant. I will support and encourage him as I am able, that he might grow in his relationship with Christ and that he might effectively carry out his duties as an elder of _____ (name of congregation) Also, I will hold to the standards of this covenant as they pertain to my spiritual walk, actions, and growth.

Afterword

Philip Jacob Spener, a minister who followed in Luther's footsteps in the late 1600's, wrote: "Theology is a practical discipline; everything must be directed to the practice of faith and life." Spener was right, and today's church leaders are called to constantly pay attention to leadership that nourishes faith and partners with God to foster life.

This collection of essays serves that important work. Written by practitioners with long experience in congregations, this book provides keen insight to the practices of leadership. Whether you are an elder or a minister, whether you are in youth ministry or chair of a church committee, you will discover practical wisdom to aid you as you live out your calling. That wisdom is rooted in scripture, in proven practices, and in the learning that comes from the social sciences about the ways people behave. Consider these authors as wise friends who bring their experience alongside your work and experience. Take the time to read and reflect. Then test this wisdom as you seek to practice healthy leadership in your context.

We all need encouragement to do ministry well. These essays serve well to fuel your imagination and hope in the work of congregational leadership. May God bless you as you attend to the practices of faith and life in your congregation!

Carson E. Reed
Executive Director
Siburt Institute for Church Ministry
Abilene Christian University

319

Resources

Church Health Assessment

HOPE Network collaborates with the Siburt Institute for kingdom ministry and resources. Some of our partners, along with Harding School of Theology, Missions Resource Network, and various ministers and professors were part of the initial conversation shaping a standard assessment particular to Churches of Christ or those whose congregations are elder governed.

We met with statistical and social researchers Dr. Carley Dodd and Dr. Suzie Macaluso and they developed and beta tested a robust and statistically reliable instrument for assessing nine areas of congregational members' perceptions. A few of our HOPE Network people were trained as facilitators/coaches of the assessment.

For further information or to order this service, call (325) 674-3722 or email: **siburtinstitute@acu.edu.**

Grip Birkman Assessment

The Grip-Birkman is about stewardship of people — their gifts, personality and place in the body of Christ. It is a behavioral and spiritual gifts assessment looking at three primary questions: Where am I strong? Where am I weak? and Who do I need? This in-depth tool provides new insight into how their natural behavior interacts with the God's empowerment. The focus of this assessment is how one can powerfully play their God-designed role in the Body of Christ most effectively.

HOPE Network uses Grip Birkman for elder and minister team building as well as coaching individual leaders in spiritual identity and growth. It is fee based.

For further information go to RESOURCES — "Why HN Uses Grip Birkman" on our website — **www.hopenetworkminstries.org.**

Hope Network Ministries

Co-Leaders

Grady D. King, D.Min   Euless, TX

Jon Mullican   Sunnyvale, TX

Partners

Jimmy Adcox   Jonesboro, AR

Greg Anderson, Ed.D   College Station, TX

Jon Anderson   San Antonio, TX

Lynn Anderson, D.Min   San Antonio, TX

Mark Frost   Detroit, MI

Chris Goldman   Seattle, WA

Carlus Gupton, D.Min   Memphis, TN

Rhesa Higgins   Dallas, TX

Evertt Huffard, Ph.D   Memphis, TN

Jay Jarboe   Bedford, TX

Jim Martin, D.Min   Memphis, TN

Doug Peters, D.Min   Houston, TX

Jason Thompson, Ed.D   Nashville, TN

Phil Ware   Fort Worth, TX

Julie Woodroof   Nashville, TN

Tim Woodroof, Ph.D   Nashville, TN

Associates

Bruce Black   Forest Mill, SC

Randy Daugherty   Stephenville, TX

David Fleer, Ph.D   Nashville, TN

Rob McRay   Nashville, TN

Shannon Rains   Lubbock, TX

Rubel Shelly, Ph.D   Nashville, TN

John Siburt, D.Min   Richardson, TX

Bret Testerman   Orlando, FL

Operations Manager

Beth Hadley   Baton Rouge, LA

Administrative Assistant

Bridget Price   Dallas, TX

Financial Accountant

Sharon McIlory, CPA   Dallas, TX

HOPE Network Ministries is a 501(c)3 organization and all donations are tax deductible.

Contact Us

info@hopenetworkministries.org
(214) 586-0375
www.hopenetworkministries.org

Connecting for Assistance

Click on RESOURCES on our website to fill out a Church or Minister Intake form.

Follow Us on Facebook and Twitter (@hopenetworknow)

Made in the USA
Lexington, KY
08 May 2017